A Political Sociology of Public Aid to Industry

This is Volume 45 in the series of studies commissioned as part of the research program of the Royal Commission on the Economic Union and Development Prospects for Canada.

This volume reflects the views of its authors and does not imply endorsement by the Chairman or Commissioners.

A Political Sociology of Public Aid to Industry

André Blais
with Claude Desranleau
and Yves Vanier

Published by the University of Toronto Press in cooperation with the Royal Commission on the Economic Union and Development Prospects for Canada and the Canadian Government Publishing Centre, Supply and Services Canada

University of Toronto Press

Grateful acknowledgment is made to the following for permission to reprint previously published and unpublished material: Academic Press Canada; *Brookings Review*; Centre for the Study of Public Policy, University of Strathclyde; Chief Statistician of Canada; Organisation for Economic Co-operation and Development; Jacques Parizeau; Princeton University Press (*World Politics*); SEDES; University of Ottawa Press.

Printed in Canada
ISBN 0-8020-7290-9
ISSN 0829-2396
Cat. No. Z1-1983/1-41-45E

CANADIAN CATALOGUING IN PUBLICATION DATA

Main entry under title:
A Political sociology of public aid to industry

(*The Collected research studies / Royal Commission on the Economic Union and Development Prospects for Canada*,
ISSN 0829-2396 ; 45)
Includes bibliographical references.
ISBN 0-8020-7290-9

1. Industry and State — Canada. I. Blais, André. II. Royal Commission on the Economic Union and Development Prospects for Canada. III. Series: The Collected research studies (Royal Commission on the Economic Union and Development Prospects for Canada) ; 45.

HD3616.C33P65 1985   338.971   C85-099636-8

PUBLISHING COORDINATION: Ampersand Communications Services Inc.
COVER DESIGN: Will Rueter
INTERIOR DESIGN: Brant Cowie/Artplus Limited

CONTENTS

FOREWORD

When the members of the Rowell-Sirois Commission began their collective task in 1937, very little was known about the evolution of the Canadian economy. What was known, moreover, had not been extensively analyzed by the slender cadre of social scientists of the day.

When we set out upon our task nearly 50 years later, we enjoyed a substantial advantage over our predecessors; we had a wealth of information. We inherited the work of scholars at universities across Canada and we had the benefit of the work of experts from private research institutes and publicly sponsored organizations such as the Ontario Economic Council and the Economic Council of Canada. Although there were still important gaps, our problem was not a shortage of information; it was to interrelate and integrate — to synthesize — the results of much of the information we already had.

The mandate of this Commission is unusually broad. It encompasses many of the fundamental policy issues expected to confront the people of Canada and their governments for the next several decades. The nature of the mandate also identified, in advance, the subject matter for much of the research and suggested the scope of enquiry and the need for vigorous efforts to interrelate and integrate the research disciplines. The resulting research program, therefore, is particularly noteworthy in three respects: along with original research studies, it includes survey papers which synthesize work already done in specialized fields; it avoids duplication of work which, in the judgment of the Canadian research community, has already been well done; and, considered as a whole, it is the most thorough examination of the Canadian economic, political and legal systems ever undertaken by an independent agency.

The Commission's research program was carried out under the joint direction of three prominent and highly respected Canadian scholars: Dr. Ivan Bernier (*Law and Constitutional Issues*), Dr. Alan Cairns (*Politics and Institutions of Government*) and Dr. David C. Smith (*Economics*).

Dr. Ivan Bernier is Dean of the Faculty of Law at Laval University. Dr. Alan Cairns is former Head of the Department of Political Science at the University of British Columbia and, prior to joining the Commission, was William Lyon Mackenzie King Visiting Professor of Canadian Studies at Harvard University. Dr. David C. Smith, former Head of the Department of Economics at Queen's University in Kingston, is now Principal of that University. When Dr. Smith assumed his new responsibilities at Queen's in September 1984, he was succeeded by Dr. Kenneth Norrie of the University of Alberta and John Sargent of the federal Department of Finance, who together acted as Co-directors of Research for the concluding phase of the Economics research program.

I am confident that the efforts of the Research Directors, research coordinators and authors whose work appears in this and other volumes, have provided the community of Canadian scholars and policy makers with a series of publications that will continue to be of value for many years to come. And I hope that the value of the research program to Canadian scholarship will be enhanced by the fact that Commission research is being made available to interested readers in both English and French.

I extend my personal thanks, and that of my fellow Commissioners, to the Research Directors and those immediately associated with them in the Commission's research program. I also want to thank the members of the many research advisory groups whose counsel contributed so substantially to this undertaking.

DONALD S. MACDONALD

INTRODUCTION

At its most general level, the Royal Commission's research program has examined how the Canadian political economy can better adapt to change. As a basis of enquiry, this question reflects our belief that the future will always take us partly by surprise. Our political, legal and economic institutions should therefore be flexible enough to accommodate surprises and yet solid enough to ensure that they help us meet our future goals. This theme of an adaptive political economy led us to explore the interdependencies between political, legal and economic systems and drew our research efforts in an interdisciplinary direction.

The sheer magnitude of the research output (more than 280 separate studies in 70+ volumes) as well as its disciplinary and ideological diversity have, however, made complete integration impossible and, we have concluded, undesirable. The research output as a whole brings varying perspectives and methodologies to the study of common problems and we therefore urge readers to look beyond their particular field of interest and to explore topics across disciplines.

The three research areas, — *Law and Constitutional Issues*, under Ivan Bernier; *Politics and Institutions of Government*, under Alan Cairns; and *Economics*, under David C. Smith (co-directed with Kenneth Norrie and John Sargent for the concluding phase of the research program) — were further divided into 19 sections headed by research coordinators.

The area *Law and Constitutional Issues* has been organized into five major sections headed by the research coordinators identified below.

- Law, Society and the Economy — *Ivan Bernier and Andrée Lajoie*
- The International Legal Environment — *John J. Quinn*
- The Canadian Economic Union — *Mark Krasnick*

- Harmonization of Laws in Canada — *Ronald C.C. Cuming*
- Institutional and Constitutional Arrangements — *Clare F. Beckton and A. Wayne MacKay*

Since law in its numerous manifestations is the most fundamental means of implementing state policy, it was necessary to investigate how and when law could be mobilized most effectively to address the problems raised by the Commission's mandate. Adopting a broad perspective, researchers examined Canada's legal system from the standpoint of how law evolves as a result of social, economic and political changes and how, in turn, law brings about changes in our social, economic and political conduct.

Within *Politics and Institutions of Government*, research has been organized into seven major sections.

- Canada and the International Political Economy — *Denis Stairs and Gilbert Winham*
- State and Society in the Modern Era — *Keith Banting*
- Constitutionalism, Citizenship and Society — *Alan Cairns and Cynthia Williams*
- The Politics of Canadian Federalism — *Richard Simeon*
- Representative Institutions — *Peter Aucoin*
- The Politics of Economic Policy — *G. Bruce Doern*
- Industrial Policy — *André Blais*

This area examines a number of developments which have led Canadians to question their ability to govern themselves wisely and effectively. Many of these developments are not unique to Canada and a number of comparative studies canvass and assess how others have coped with similar problems. Within the context of the Canadian heritage of parliamentary government, federalism, a mixed economy, and a bilingual and multicultural society, the research also explores ways of rearranging the relationships of power and influence among institutions to restore and enhance the fundamental democratic principles of representativeness, responsiveness and accountability.

Economics research was organized into seven major sections.

- Macroeconomics — *John Sargent*
- Federalism and the Economic Union — *Kenneth Norrie*
- Industrial Structure — *Donald G. McFetridge*
- International Trade — *John Whalley*
- Income Distribution and Economic Security — *François Vaillancourt*
- Labour Markets and Labour Relations — *Craig Riddell*
- Economic Ideas and Social Issues — *David Laidler*

Economics research examines the allocation of Canada's human and other resources, the ways in which institutions and policies affect this allocation, and the distribution of the gains from their use. It also considers the nature of economic development, the forces that shape our regional and industrial structure, and our economic interdependence with other countries. The thrust of the research in economics is to increase our comprehension of what determines our economic potential and how instruments of economic policy may move us closer to our future goals.

One section from each of the three research areas — The Canadian Economic Union, The Politics of Canadian Federalism, and Federalism and the Economic Union — have been blended into one unified research effort. Consequently, the volumes on Federalism and the Economic Union as well as the volume on The North are the results of an interdisciplinary research effort.

We owe a special debt to the research coordinators. Not only did they organize, assemble and analyze the many research studies and combine their major findings in overviews, but they also made substantial contributions to the Final Report. We wish to thank them for their performance, often under heavy pressure.

Unfortunately, space does not permit us to thank all members of the Commission staff individually. However, we are particularly grateful to the Chairman, The Hon. Donald S. Macdonald; the Commission's Executive Director, J. Gerald Godsoe; and the Director of Policy, Alan Nymark, all of whom were closely involved with the Research Program and played key roles in the contribution of Research to the Final Report. We wish to express our appreciation to the Commission's Administrative Advisor, Harry Stewart, for his guidance and advice, and to the Director of Publishing, Ed Matheson, who managed the research publication process. A special thanks to Jamie Benidickson, Policy Coordinator and Special Assistant to the Chairman, who played a valuable liaison role between Research and the Chairman and Commissioners. We are also grateful to our office administrator, Donna Stebbing, and to our secretarial staff, Monique Carpentier, Barbara Cowtan, Tina DeLuca, Françoise Guilbault and Marilyn Sheldon.

Finally, a well deserved thank you to our closest assistants: Jacques J.M. Shore, *Law and Constitutional Issues*; Cynthia Williams and her successor Karen Jackson, *Politics and Institutions of Government*; and I. Lilla Connidis, *Economics*. We appreciate not only their individual contribution to each research area, but also their cooperative contribution to the research program and the Commission.

IVAN BERNIER
ALAN CAIRNS
DAVID C. SMITH

PREFACE

This study by André Blais is the most systematic ever written on government aid to industry. It deals with all the instruments used by governments to support industry, both in Canada and in the other advanced capitalist democracies, and it describes their evolution since the end of World War II.

The author bases his analysis on all the information which Canadian, American, and European literature has to offer on the subject, as well as on a large number of statistics. Not only is the perspective vast, but the grid is at the same time original and ambitious. On the one hand, André Blais studies the political motives which induce a government to intervene and to accord privileges and preferential treatment to some sectors of industry, or to refrain from doing so. On the other hand, he raises the difficult but crucial question of the agreement between the policy directions governing these measures and the preferences, opinions, and values shared by most citizens. According to him, government aid to industry responds, in the end, to the demands of the population.

At a time when it is considered good form to cast doubt on the good will of the state to act in the best interest of the majority, this conclusion will certainly not meet with the spontaneous approval of readers. However, all will agree that the arguments advanced by André Blais carry weight. They will also acknowledge the incontestable merit of this scholar, who not only possesses the rigorously critical mind that is needed to deal with a question methodically but who, at the same time, has the broad outlook of the political scientist who takes into account studies carried out in other disciplines and all over the world.

ALAN CAIRNS

ACKNOWLEDGMENTS

I would like to give my sincere thanks to the many people who supported me, in various ways, in preparing and carrying out this project, first among them being my assistants and collaborators, Claude Desranleau and Yves Vanier. They participated in every stage of research and wrote the preliminary versions of several sections. The numerous discussions we had regarding each page of text were highly stimulating. Their assistance has been invaluable.

I would also like to stress the contribution of the members of my advisory committee: Herman Bakver, David Cameron, Michael Jenkin and Robert Young. They were able to pinpoint the main weaknesses of the initial draft and made interesting suggestions for improvements. Marsha Chandler, Stéphane Dion, Robert Young, and two anonymous revisers read a first draft of the text. Their comments have been highly useful for the final formulation of the study.

It is to my director of research, Alan Cairns, that I owe the greatest debt of gratitude. In spite of his other great responsibilities, he supported me throughout the project and gave me valuable advice. His enormous intellectual curiosity was very stimulating and I sincerely thank him for it. His assistants Cynthia Williams and Karen Jackson did everything to make things easier for me in administrative matters. I was greatly impressed by their efficient work and am highly appreciative of their effort to leave no stone unturned to ensure that this work is of high quality. Finally, I would like to stress the cooperation of the other research coordinators, particularly Bruce Doern, Richard Simeon, Keith Banting, François Vaillancourt and Donald McFetridge. The formal and informal exchanges we had undoubtedly contributed to improving the final product.

ANDRÉ BLAIS

Introduction

In 1976, Corden and Fels published a book entitled *Public Assistance to Industry: Protection and Subsidies in Britain and Germany*. In the preface, the authors stress that "expressing protection, whether by tariff or non-tariff means (including subsidies) in terms of 'public assistance to industry,' serves to put the issues in an appropriately broad perspective." While we believe that this approach to the matter is fully justified in principle, as we hope to be able to demonstrate farther on, it is also in line with the reality of government intervention. In 1979, for instance, the Government of Canada published a document entitled *AIDE-Assistance et information pour le développement de l'entreprise*, which is an inventory of the programs, services and incentives designed for firms. This explicitly acknowledges the fact that there is indeed a set of measures that are covered by the term "industrial aid."

The main purpose of this study is to explain why governments aid industry and why they do it the way they do, rather than in some other way. Research is obviously a part of this field of study, which is generally called "policy analysis." Dye (1976) put it well, observing that policy analysis seeks to answer three main questions: What do governments do (government output)? What do governments change (impact of policies)? Why do they do what they do, and why do they not do what they do not do (causes of policies)? Our study will be focussed on this last question. However, it must be recognized that the causes of the policy cannot be analyzed in an isolated manner and that such analysis could be misleading if the policy is not sufficiently well defined. This is why we have stated elsewhere (Blais, 1980) that an accurate description of state intervention should be a prerequisite for any discussion of its causes or consequences (see also Simeon, 1976). In line with this methodological approach, the first chapter will summarize the main characteristics of aid to industry. Interpretation proper can only commence once these characteristics have been determined. On the other hand, the causes and consequences of a policy are often related (e.g., if such-and-such policy is adopted, it is partly because it is expected that it will have such-and-such an effect). Thus, an evaluation of the effects of a policy is to some extent a part of understanding its causes (Blais, 1980). Hence, throughout the study, we shall also discuss the impact of government intervention, inasmuch as this will contribute to explaining its origin. However, some clarifications are in order first.

Subject Outline

What is really meant by "aid to industry"? The literature in this respect is exceedingly threadbare. The work by Corden and Fels (1976), for instance, never did clearly state the measures included and excluded by the term. Some articles in that work (Hiemenz and Rabenau, 1976; Oulton, 1976) first review tariff protection, then some non-tariff barriers, without truly justifying the approach conceptually. Other works have titles as vague as "Subsidies and Other Industrial Aids" (Ohlin, 1978). The main difficulty is not to define the concept of aid, the meaning of which seems evident, but to construct a typology of forms (or instruments) of aid. More often than not, the list of the instruments considered remains implicit. When there is such a list, the logic governing its formulation is virtually never discussed.

The most common distinction is that between tariffs and non-tariff barriers. This dichotomy between a specific instrument and a makeshift category ("the rest") is, to say the least, lacking in elegance. The popularity of this oft-invoked distinction is due to the exceptional importance which tariffs have traditionally had, and to the fact that, since the end of World War II, they have been the primary object of international negotiations. Although this "special status" must be recognized, we do not believe that it therefore justifies being the sole criterion of conceptual design. It should also be added that the term "non-tariff barrier" is a particularly ill-chosen one, because it has a negative connotation[1] which might bias the analysis from the outset (i.e., the market is the standard, and anything that prevents the market from operating freely is a barrier, and therefore a bad thing). Moreover, if one uses this logic, any state intervention is a non-tariff barrier, except perhaps for legislation establishing the right of ownership, which is a prerequisite for the operation of the market (see Breton and Wintrobe, 1982; Zysman, 1983). For these reasons, we shall avoid this terminology as much as possible.

Another classification principle, used by Walter (1972a) and Pestieau (1972), consists of distinguishing between measures which are primarily designed to assist domestic production in facing international competition, and those which are not primarily designed to do so but are sometimes used for the purpose; and to distinguish the measures aimed at assisting domestic production from those which are absolutely not designed to do so but which may have an effect upon world trade. Within the first group, a distinction is also made between aid designed to protect against imports and aid designed to boost exports (Walter, 1972a).

This classification has several shortcomings. First of all, the basic criterion — the objective sought — is not without its problems. The observer is forced to ascribe motives to governments, and this is an extremely delicate task (Blais and Faucher, 1981). Worse still, the typology forces one to distinguish between "priority" and "secondary" objectives. Finally, the third category introduces a second dimension — the impact of intervention — which renders "operationalization" virtually impossible.

A more promising approach is to look at the locus and form of government aid. The simplest, most basic distinction, in our opinion, is that between "internal" aid, which applies specifically to domestic production, and "external" aid, i.e., protection at the border (see Grey, 1981, p. 5; Faucher et al., 1985), which is aimed at imports. By raising the cost of imports or by restricting their quantity, protection at the border promotes domestic production. This dichotomy is much clearer, because it is based on the locus of government intervention.

Internal aid and protection both consist of a number of concrete instruments that relate to the form of aid. Internal aid may be financial or technical. Financial aid may be direct (grants, loans, guarantees) or indirect, through the tax system (tax advantages) or through government purchases (public contracts). Although, in the case of protection, the principle selected could have been that distinguishing between measures which affect the price of imports and those which determine the quantity of imports (Pestieau, 1972, p. 57), we prefer another distinction, that between the more general measure of tariffs and the special measures which are subsequently added to the initial tariff under special circumstances. Special measures include retaliatory steps (offset and anti-dumping duties) and exceptional quantitative restraint measures. In addition to being politically more relevant (each government first sets its tariffs, then occasionally resorts to additional measures), this typology is more in line with the manner in which the data are usually collected.

The meaning of the term "industry" should also be specified. The term sometimes refers to the entire production and flow of wealth, sometimes to production activities only (primary and secondary sectors), and sometimes, still more restrictively, to the manufacturing sector alone. The literature is often vague on this point. For example, Corden and Fels (1976, p. 1) introduce their work as follows:

> The book presents six research studies containing basic information about the ways in which the governments of the Federal Republic of Germany and of the United Kingdom have assisted or protected their industries — principally their manufacturing industries.

In fact, most studies cover the manufacturing industry. Since our research attempts to provide an overall picture of aid to industry, we shall deal with overall economic activity. However, because of the availability of data, our study of measures involving the manufacturing sector will sometimes be more detailed.

Aid to industry is part of a broader framework, usually known as "industrial policy." This term is also ambiguous, and attempts to define it are beyond the scope of this study (see Blais, 1985a). Nevertheless, it should be stressed that one of the basic features of industrial policy is its selective nature. We shall only deal with aid to industry if it is selective, i.e., if it promotes some activities, industries, regions, or types of firm at the expense of others.

The Issues

The main issue that we shall deal with throughout this monograph pertains to the causes of aid to industry. This apparently simple issue can be subdivided into several sub-issues. First of all, since we operate within the framework of capitalist economies based on the principle of a free market, government intervention must be weighed against this principle. If governments intervene, it is because the political leadership believes (rightly or wrongly, it does not matter for the time being) that the market has shortcomings which government action is supposed to correct.[2] The field of intervention is thus defined by the relative roles assigned to the government and to the market. One's judgment of the role which the state should play is closely dependent upon the assessment made of the performance of the market and upon the definition of industrial "problems" which result therefrom, as well as upon the ability of the state to solve these problems. As emphasized by Zysman (1977, 1983), the logic of the market and that of the state are clearly different, and a basic choice must be made as to the place each one deserves.

A school of analysis predicated on the argument of the "economic rationality" of aid to industry (Breton, 1974; Binhammer, McDonough and Lepore, 1983; Ritchie, 1983; McFetridge, 1977) is based on such considerations. Its approach consists of defining

> the conditions under which the workings of the competitive private market should produce a level and composition of output which is socially optimal. The corollary is the identification of causes of deviation from the optimal output and of measures to correct or offset these distortions (Ritchie, 1983, pp. 38–39).

On this basis, the state should intervene when it is proven that the market does not lead to optimal resource allocation. If, for example, the gain derived by a firm, for its own private purposes, from its research and development (R&D) is less than the benefit to the community as a whole, the state could be justified in providing financial incentives for such activities. This type of analysis can provide some clues as to what governments should do if they want to maximize a particular objective, namely, optimal resource allocation.

However, this approach is far less useful in attempting to understand why governments do what they do, unless one assumes that this is the fundamental objective of governments and that they make their decisions only (or mainly) on the basis of their own "technical" assessment of the consequences of their interventions. In fact, this is obviously not the case. What is known about the political process would indicate that "political rationality" is very different. Studies on pressure groups have shown that some of them are better organized than others (Olson, 1965). It is perhaps not the welfare of the community that counts so much as the welfare of some powerful groups which governments cannot deflect. More generally, the "public choice" school of thought claims that the policy market has a logic of its own (Blais, 1982). It does not follow that studies on the economic rationality of aid to industry are useless when attempting to explain its political dynamics. On the contrary, we have already seen that the causes and consequences of a policy cannot be isolated from each other. Indeed, such studies have had an influence on the debate regarding industrial policy (Blais, 1985a); but the choice between market and state is basically a political one, and this is how we shall deal with it here.

Once the choice in favour of government intervention has been made, the target of such intervention must be selected. Since aid to industry is, by definition, selective, the reasons why the government favours certain types of industry, or certain types of firms, must be explained. More specifically, we shall attempt to determine to what extent and why governments are more interested in certain industrial sectors, in certain areas, in large or small firms, and in domestic rather than foreign firms. Along the same lines, we shall attempt to specify the aspects of economic activity that are the major objectives of government aid.

Finally, once the target industry has been selected for aid purposes, a last choice must be made regarding aid terms, namely the choice of the instrument of intervention. One could, no doubt, debate the economic or technical rationality of various instruments (see, for instance, Economic Council of Canada, 1982); but since governments often lack the freedom to choose the instrument which would technically be most effective (Trebilcock et al., 1982, p. 32), we believe that an approach based on more specifically political considerations would be preferable. It is such an approach that we shall attempt to formulate, based on a critical analysis of the literature in this field.

The most common strategy, when trying to discern the causes of a policy, is to examine the variations in that policy over time or space and to relate the variations to a number of independent variables which can account for them (Blais, 1980). We shall make frequent use of this strategy. We therefore attach great importance to the comparative approach, which can shed light on the specific nature of the Canadian case (which we shall study closely), including a historical overview, which can place the latest trends in their proper perspective. We shall ask ourselves why governments intervene or adopt a given stance in some countries but not in others, and why they do so at certain times. We shall see that the answers to these questions are far from simple, particularly since the information available is often fragmentary; but this is no reason to avoid these crucial issues. Moreover, we do not intend to examine the variations alone. As we have emphasized elsewhere (ibid.), there is the risk that a study of the variations might ignore the structural constants that are found in every country, with little change over time. These constants must also be interpreted, even though this is a more delicate task.

The frame of reference is that of the advanced capitalist democracies, i.e., the countries which

> have in common a parliamentary mode of decision-making within the limits of formal-liberal rule of law and a socio-economic system predominantly based on private ownership of the means of production and a consumption pattern that functions mainly via market procedures (Keman, 1984, p. 166).

and which have achieved a relatively high standard of living. This group of countries is fairly homogeneous as regards certain basic characteristics, and one can therefore isolate the specific effect of those variables in which the group is heterogeneous:

> The predominant view among social scientists seems to opt for the strategy of "concomitant variation." Such studies are based on the belief that systems as similar as possible with respect to as many features as possible constitute the optimal samples for comparative inquiry. . . . This type of design is a "maximum" strategy. It is anticipated that if some important differences are found among these otherwise similar countries, then the number of factors attributable to these differences will be sufficiently small to warrant explanation in terms of those differences alone (Przeworski and Teune, 1970, p. 32).

The merits of such an approach are increasingly recognized. As a result, most comparative political economy studies now confine themselves to the 20 or so countries of the Organisation for Economic Co-operation and Development (OECD) which have a democratic tradition and a relatively developed economy[3] (Keman, 1984; Paloheimo, 1984; Castles, 1982; McCallum and Blais, 1985; Cameron, 1982; Schmidt, 1984; McCallum, 1983). More specifically, this study will cover 18 OECD countries.[4] Countries which cannot be considered democratic throughout the period (Greece, Portugal, Spain, and Turkey) have been excluded, as have Iceland and Luxembourg, since they have a population of less than 500,000. It should be stated at the outset that in several cases the data are available for only some of the 18 countries; thus, of necessity, comparisons will be limited.

The period we have chosen is that following World War II, for it is long enough to permit analysis of the variations of government intervention over time. In addition, this period has been homogeneous enough for pertinent comparisons to be made. This is also the "most similar design" strategy which we believe to be the most valid. The period starts with the establishment in 1947 of the GATT (General Agreement on Tariffs and Trade), which triggered the trade liberalization process that had a crucial impact on the evolution of industrial policy (Blais and Faucher, 1981).

Some readers will have noted that while taking great pains to explain the issues dealt with, we have not specified in any way the type of answer we intend to give. The reason for this is that our intent is not to specify a given theoretical model and test it empirically. As will be explained later in this Introduction, we have instead adopted an approach based on a critical discussion of existing interpretations, with all the advantages and drawbacks this entails. Nevertheless, our thinking is guided by certain theoretical assumptions which we feel should be defined at this point.

The first assumption is that since society consists of a system of social controls (Bélanger, 1985), our analysis must be focussed on the nature and direction of these controls, and this makes it necessary to consider the power relationships. Although the study of power is fraught with considerable methodological problems, these difficulties are inherent to sociological analysis, and there is no point in attempting to avoid them (Blais, 1974). On the contrary, the issue of the balance of social forces and its impact on government policies should be met head on. Quite rightly, the radical American school and the Marxist school of thought have emphasized the fact that for analysis to be truly relevant, it must deal with this fundamental issue of the power of the various groups or classes, in order to determine which interests are being defended by the state (Blais, 1980).

Thus, it seems essential, if we are to give an adequate interpretation of industrial aid, that we should take into account the political power of industry, since it is the target clientele of the policy. Although business circles have enjoyed a privileged position in the political process (Marsh, 1985), one cannot gain a full understanding of the evolution of aid to industry without studying the position of the industrialists, the pressures they exert, and the threats they bring to bear. Similarly, one must discuss the power of the state and its ability both to resist the pressures to which it is subjected and to guide industrial development, which is sometimes known as "the relative autonomy of the state" (Poulantzas, 1974), while making a distinction between the relative influence of the bureaucratic apparatus and that of the political apparatus.

Secondly, this study will emphasize the political calculations which cause governments to adopt a given policy. We shall examine the very logic of government intervention, the reasons for which governments act, and their strategy. To do so, we shall make preferred use of what we have elsewhere called the "subjective" causes of government output (Blais, 1980). We believe that this choice is readily justified. Since the prevailing trend in the study of industrial aid is to examine its "economic rationale," the need for a study focussed on the "political rationale" seems obvious. However, this political rationale can only emerge once the very perspective of government decision makers has been examined closely. Although this may not be a sine qua non, it is nevertheless a necessary condition. (For a discussion of the concept of rationale and its epistemological implications, see Wilson, 1970.)

Based on the actors' strategy, this approach can and must incorporate an analysis of the "objective" causes of government output. These external factors act as a constraint upon decision making. For instance, if industry has considerable political power, politicians will take this into account and will propose programs that are not likely to elicit opposition to the point where they would be scuttled. This situation is due to what games theory calls the "interdependence of choices" (Lemieux, 1979). The balance of social forces thus shapes the government's entire strategy.

Any strategic analysis requires that the objectives of the parties involved be established first (Lemieux, 1979). One of the concerns of this monograph will therefore be to point out what the main objectives underlying aid to industry ought to be. To this end, we shall devote special attention to the respective roles of growth and efficiency, the classic economic objectives, because these criteria are often invoked in the debate regarding industrial policy; we shall also dwell on electoral considerations, since vote maximization (which, according to the theory of public choice, is the main motive of politicians) has the advantage of giving politicians unique functional dynamics (Blais, 1982).

The introduction of electoral considerations into the analysis logically raises the issue of the relationship between political elites and voters. As emphasized by Ippolito, Walker and Kolson (1976, p. 3), citizens can influence politicians in several ways:

> The types of influence available to the public are: (1) direct constituent influence upon representatives through the use of rewards and sanctions-votes, campaign assistance, various forms of pressure; (2) constituent influence upon representatives through membership in a support for mediating groups, such as interest groups or political parties . . . ; and (3) indirect constituent influence, which results when representatives act in accordance with constituent preferences because (a) they share such preferences or (b) they believe such preferences should prevail over their own judgments or preferences.

We shall therefore attempt to determine to what extent the orientation of aid to industry diverges from, or is in line with, the majority preferences, views, and values of citizens. Obviously, the existence of agreement would not necessarily imply that public opinion is a determinant, since the agreement might be misleading or might result from a government's manipulation of public opinion (Dye, 1978, chap. 3). This is nevertheless the necessary condition, inasmuch as the existence of a substantial discrepancy between government policies and majority preferences could justify rejecting this type of interpretation. Only if there is concordance and if other explanations for it can be rejected will one be able to conclude that the majority views and values of citizens directly or indirectly influence state policy in this field.

Lastly, we should add a few words about the title of this study. The presence of the word "political" should surprise no one, since this is the work of a political scientist. The reason why a political *sociology* perspective has been adopted is that we believe sociology to be the discipline which sheds the brightest light on social phenomena (Bélanger, 1985) and that it is particularly suited to the general nature of this study. Moreover, inasmuch as we wish to examine the politicians' calculations, and inasmuch as these calculations are linked to electoral concerns, we shall examine previous studies on electoral sociology as well as public opinion surveys.

The objectives of this study are very ambitious. The issues are many and complex. We must admit from the outset that it is impossible to answer all the questions involved in a complete, satisfactory manner. We hope, however, to be able to give some answers to the most fundamental questions raised by aid to industry. We shall now specify how we shall develop these answers.

The Approach

Firstly, this monograph concentrates on a critical review of the existing literature rather than on the production of new information. We chose this approach because we believe that a substantial number of studies already exist on the subject and that no attempt has been made to integrate them, or at least systematically discuss them. We believed that we could contribute more to the study of the subject by reassessing and reinterpreting the existing studies than by carrying out empirical research, which could have covered only some aspects of aid to industry.

This approach carries some important limitations. Regarding several issues, the data are fragmentary or even nonexistent. In other instances, although studies exist, the quality of their analysis is so poor that either the data are highly suspect or their interpretation is. On several points, the discussion will therefore have to be brief and speculative. The goal is to draw up a balance sheet of what is known or not known on a subject, and to point out the trends and explanations which seem plausible, given the current state of knowledge, even if such trends and explanations have not yet been rigorously demonstrated.

Although our discussion will primarily cover studies already carried out, we shall present new information where possible. Indeed, we found that the documentation on industrial policy was even poorer than we originally believed; we therefore thought it advisable to fill some gaps by presenting statistical data whenever suitable and even by undertaking occasional empirical "tests."

This monograph has four main chapters. The first is descriptive and is designed to give an overview of aid to industry. What is the relative magnitude of aid to industry and its various components? Which industries or activities are favoured? What are the major variations by country? What are the major aspects of evolution over time? Chapter 1 highlights the basic trends that will be reviewed and analyzed in subsequent chapters. This is a crucial chapter because it sets the tone for the rest of the study.

The next three chapters deal with the reasons for the trends noted in Chapter 1. Government output results from (explicit or implicit) political choices, and it seems to us that aid to industry raises three basic issues which governments address in some way. The first, which is the subject of Chapter 2, concerns the choice between state and market, between intervention and non-intervention. Why is aid to industry greater in some countries than in others, and why does it increase (or diminish) over time? Chapters 3 and 4 analyze the choices that must be made once the government has decided to intervene. First of all, the target must be chosen. Why does the state seek to favour some industries or activities at the expense of others? Next, the instrument of intervention must be selected. Once the government has decided to aid a given industry (or activity), why does it favour a given form of aid rather than some other?

Chapter 1

Trends and Orientations

This first chapter gives a general outline of government aid to industry. We shall examine each intervention instrument that is available to the state, and we shall attempt to determine its relative importance in order to distinguish the more significant instruments from the rather marginal ones. In each case, we shall also attempt to identify the countries where there is more (or less) marked government intervention, and to record the major changes since World War II. Finally, we shall attempt to determine the major orientations of aid to industry. Since industrial policy is characterized by its selectiveness, the sectors or types of firm that benefit the most and the least from government aid must be specified. In this respect, four dimensions of aid distribution will be assessed: sectorial distribution, spacial distribution, distribution by firm size (does the state favour big business or small business?), and distribution by ownership (does the state favour the domestic industry at the expense of foreign industry?).[5] Along the same lines, the industrial activities to which the government devotes the most (and the least) amount of interest will be noted.

In order to base the analysis on the most concrete data possible, we shall review each of the major instruments of intervention in order to highlight its salient features. The typology of the aid forms was presented in the Introduction. We shall make the distinction between the "domestic" and "external" components of aid, i.e., internal aid and protection. Internal aid may be financial or technical. In turn, financial aid is subdivided into direct aid (grants, loans, guarantees) and indirect aid, which is provided through the tax system (tax advantages) and through government purchases (public contracts). Protection assumes the form of tariffs or special measures, which include retaliatory measures (offset and anti-dumping duties) and quantitative restraints.

Protection

The external component of aid to industry, which corresponds to what is generally known as trade policy, comprises, on the one hand, the classical protection tool of tariffs, and, on the other hand, a number of special measures to which a government may resort in special circumstances. Let us look at tariffs, the most systematically studied instrument of protection.

Tariffs

Two questions arise here. Firstly, what is the average level of tariffs in a country? Secondly, what is the tariff structure or, to put it differently, which industries have a higher or lower tariff level? Two fundamental concepts must be defined at the outset: the nominal tariff protection and the effective tariff protection. The nominal tariff protection corresponds to the customs duty on imports, expressed as a proportion of the value of imports. The concept of effective protection was introduced because the nominal tariff is an inaccurate indicator of the effective protection, inasmuch as one must also take into account the tariffs on inputs, which increase production costs. The actual protection could thus be defined as "the net effect of the structure of nominal duties upon the price a manufacturer can ask foreign countries for his products, as compared with the prices he must pay for his intermediate inputs. This basically amounts to the effect upon his value added" (Melvin and Wilkinson, 1968, p. 3). Although in principle the effective protection rate (EPR) is considered more valid than the nominal protection rate (NPR), NPR data are much more abundant. Since we intend to make comparisons, we shall therefore use the latter indicator. Moreover, the average protection rate may be weighted or unweighted. Weighting is generally preferable in order to account for the relative value of each product in the trade figures. The usual weighting criterion is that of total imports, either of the country involved or of a certain number of countries, or of all countries together. According to Balassa (1965, p. 579) and Hawkins (1972, p. 43), the greater the level of aggregation, the smaller the bias. On the following pages, we shall attempt to compare the average rate of tariff protection in various countries and at various times, and to examine the tariff structure, i.e., the variation in protection rate by industry.

AVERAGE TARIFF LEVEL

In 1947, 23 countries created GATT to foster trade cooperation. Signatory countries pledged to reduce approximately 45,000 tariffs and to

TABLE 1-1 Evolution of the Average Nominal Protection Rate (NPR) in the Advanced Capitalist Democracies (percent)

	1967	1972	1979	1987
NPR	9.16	6.79	6.61	4.43

Source: Appendix A.

TABLE 1-2 Nominal Protection Rate of the Primary (including agriculture) and Secondary Sectors in Canada (percent)

	1961	1965	1970	1975	1978	1987
NPR[a]	10.99	10.23	9.09	8.45	7.72	4.79[b]

Source: Philippe Faucher, André Blais, Robert Young and Manuel De La Fuente, "Politique commerciale et politique industrielle du Canada," in *La nouvelle division internationale du travail et le Canada*, edited by Duncan Cameron and François Houle (Ottawa: Presses de l'Université d'Ottawa, 1985), table 2.

a. Unweighted average of the nominal protection rate of 27 industries in the primary and secondary sectors.

b. Estimate based on the reduction rate in nominal protection ascribable to the Tokyo Round agreements, which will be 38% for Canada (Hugh Corbet, "Importance of Being Earnest about Further GATT Negotiations," *World Economy* 2 (September 1979), table 1, p. 328).

adopt procedural rules and principles to govern international trade. The first round of negotiations in Geneva in 1947 substantially reduced the tariffs. The next four rounds, at Annecy (1948), Torquay (1951), and Geneva (1956 and 1960–1961), had a relatively limited impact, the reductions being in the order of 4 to 5 percent in each case (Lazar, 1981, p. 1; Economic Council of Canada, 1975, p. 95). In 1967, the average tariff was approximately 9 percent for the major industrial countries (Table 1-1), Canada ranking somewhat above the average with an average NPR of 10 percent (Table 1-2).[6]

There was a new push during the Kennedy Round negotiations, which lasted three years (1964–67). The principle of linear tariff reduction was adopted at the time as a substitute for negotiations involving each separate product. The objective was to reduce all tariffs by 50 percent. However, several exceptions were made. Agriculture, in particular, was given special treatment and the reductions in that field were generally lower (Dam, 1970, pp. 70–71, 265–66). For the 53 signatory states, customs duties were reduced on average by approximately 35 percent (Lazar, 1981, p. 3; Hawkins, 1972, p. 53) over a five-year period from 1967 to 1972. Japan was somewhat less affected, the overall rate being reduced by approximately 25 percent, probably because agriculture plays a relatively larger role in Japan. Four countries (Australia, New Zealand, South Africa, and Canada) were also exempted from the general procedure, the first three "because they would be unable to achieve reciprocity if they were forced to cut tariffs on industrial and consumer goods while receiving only whatever uncertain benefits might emerge from the agricultural negotiations" (Dam, 1970, p. 71). The exemption granted to Canada had a different explanation:

> Canada too argued that its heavy dependence on agricultural exports required its exclusion from the linear negotiations. It added (without any reasoned public explanation) that its proximity to, and extensive trade relations with the United States precluded its cutting tariffs as deeply as the United States cut U.S. tariffs (Dam, 1970, p. 72).

One can assume that the American "neighbour" argument was more convincing than that of agricultural exports, because the share of agriculture in Canadian farm exports in 1970 was less than 10 percent and was lower than that of countries such as Ireland, the United States, Denmark, and the Netherlands. The tariff cuts that were agreed to within the framework of the Kennedy Round were much lower in Canada than those implemented in most other countries (Economic Council of Canada, 1975, p. 94).

Immediately following the Kennedy Round, the average rate of nominal protection in the industrial countries was approximately 7 percent (Table 1-1). Obviously, the protection level varied from one country to the next. Table 1-3 shows the estimates of various studies; these estimates are not directly comparable.[7] However, for most countries, the results of the various studies are similar. Thus, tariffs were considerably higher in New Zealand, Australia, and Austria, and were considerably lower in Switzerland and the Scandinavian countries, while being "average" in the United States and the European Economic Community (EEC). In three studies out of four, Canada is ranked in the median category, which casts some doubt on the claim that "Canadian tariffs are high compared to those of most industrialized countries" (Economic Council of Canada, 1975, p. 12; see also Economic Council of Canada, 1983, p. 113). The case of Japan is more ambiguous. The estimates of Hawkins and the Economic Council differ substantially from those of Corbet and of Deardoff and Stern. The discrepancy is partly due to the fact that the first two studies cover the early 1970s, while the last two studies cover the late 1970s when Japan had effected unilateral reductions of the order of 20 percent (Corbet, 1979). Furthermore, only Hawkins's data include agriculture, which is strongly protected in Japan. All things considered, it would seem that tariffs were fairly high in Japan during the early 1970s and were average rather than high toward the end of that decade.

By the spring of 1970, two years ahead of initial expectations, Canada completed implementation of its commitments made during the Kennedy Round negotiations. In the early 1970s, the NPR was of the order of 9 percent. The nominal rate dropped by another percentage

TABLE 1-3 Estimates from Various Studies on the Tariff Protection of Some Industrial Countries for the Post–Kennedy Round Period (percent)

	Primary (including agriculture) and Secondary Sectors[a]		
	Unweighted Estimates	Estimates Weighted by the Country's Imports	Estimates Weighted by the Region's Imports
Austria	12.0	11.2	11.4
Canada	7.7		
Denmark	6.5	4.1	3.6
EEC	8.9	5.4	7.0
Japan	10.3	6.7	9.6
Norway	8.2	4.0	4.4
Sweden	5.5	4.8	3.2
United Kingdom	11.6	8.0	9.1
United States	10.6	5.6	6.0
Average	9.0	6.2	6.8

	Primary and Secondary Sectors (excluding agriculture)[b]		
	Unweighted Estimates	Estimates Weighted by the Country's Imports	Estimates Weighted by the Countries' Combined Imports
Canada	9.1	6.7	7.0
EEC	8.1	4.2	7.0
Japan	10.0	6.3	9.8
United States	11.2	7.1	7.5
Average	9.6	6.1	7.8

	Unweighted Estimates	Estimates Weighted by the Country's Imports
Austria	11.6	9.0
Canada	12.4	12.7
EEC	8.1	6.6
Finland	13.0	6.0
Japan	10.2	5.2
New Zealand	26.2	22.4
Norway	8.5	4.2
Sweden	5.9	5.2
Switzerland	3.8	3.2
United States	12.1	6.2
Average	11.2	8.1

point between 1970 and 1978 (Table 1-2). Canada was still in the median category. The negotiations of the Tokyo Round were held from 1973 to 1979. The standard selected for tariff reduction was a formula proposed by Switzerland to reduce the discrepancies by cutting the higher tariffs to a greater extent (Deardoff and Stern, 1979, p. 39). Overall, however,

TABLE 1-3 (cont'd)

	Secondary Sector (manufacturing)[c]	
	Estimates Weighted by the Country's Imports	Estimates Weighted by the World Imports
Australia	17.0	15.3
Austria	15.4	13.3
Canada	7.3	8.9
EEC	8.4	8.2
Finland	9.6	8.5
Japan	3.9	6.7
New Zealand	18.9	21.9
Norway	6.9	7.3
Sweden	6.4	5.7
Switzerland	3.9	3.8
United States	6.5	6.7
Average	9.5	9.7

Sources:

a. Robert G. Hawkins, "Tariffs and Tariff Structure: An International Comparison," in *The United States and International Markets*, edited by Robert G. Hawkins and Ingo Walter (Lexington, Mass.: D.C. Heath, 1972), table 3-1, p. 43, gives estimates for 1972 based on various weightings.

b. The Economic Council of Canada, *Looking Outward* (Ottawa: Minister of Supply and Services Canada, 1975), table 2-1, p. 13, gives estimates for 1973 based on various weightings; Hugh Corbet, "Importance of Being Earnest about Further GATT Negotiations," *World Economy* 2 (September 1979), table 1, p. 328, gives estimates for the pre–Tokyo Round period.

c. V. Allan Deardoff and Robert M. Stern, *An Economic Analysis of the Effects of the Tokyo Round of Multilateral Trade Negotiations on the United States and Other Major Industrialized Countries* (Washington, D.C.: U.S. Congress, Senate Finance Committee, June 1979), table 8, p. 41, table C-5, p. 151, give estimates for the post–Kennedy Round period.

Note: See Appendix B for the agreement between the various results.

the formula does not seem to have been applied systematically (ibid., p. 49). The average reduction was in the order of 33 percent (Lazar, 1981, p. 8; Corbet, 1979, p. 378).

Table 1-4 shows the estimates of Corbet (industrial sector) and Deardoff and Stern (manufacturing sector) regarding the reductions agreed to by a number of countries. Reductions were greatest in Japan and the United States. As a result, these two countries are now among those with low protection (Table 1-5).[8] In Canada, the tariff reduction due to the Tokyo Round was of the order of 38 percent, which is greater than the overall trend. When the adjustment period of the Tokyo Round agreements are completed (i.e., in 1987), the average nominal tariff will be of the order of 4 percent for the industrial countries as a whole (Table 1-1) and 5 percent for Canada (Table 1-2).

Since the Canadian economy is closely linked to the U.S. economy, special attention must be devoted to Canada–U.S. trade relations.

Table 1-4 Tariff Reductions Agreed to During the Tokyo Round (percent)

	Primary and Secondary Sectors (excluding agriculture)[a]	
	Unweighted Estimates	Estimates Weighted by the Country's Imports
Austria	30	13
Canada	42	38
EEC	31	27
Finland	14	20
Japan	41	49
New Zealand	24	21
Norway	23	23
Sweden	19	23
Switzerland	26	23
United States	42	30
Average	38	33

	Secondary sector[b]	
	Estimates Weighted by the Country's Imports	Estimates Weighted by the World Imports
Australia	2.8	3.0
Austria	21.5	22.6
Canada	29.1	28.1
EEC	27.1	26.8
Finland	25.2	24.7
Japan	25.3	28.4
New Zealand	11.8	8.0
Norway	24.8	26.0
Sweden	23.0	24.6
Switzerland	21.2	21.1
United States	34.1	35.8
Average	22.4	22.6

Sources:

a. Hugh Corbet, "Importance of Being Earnest about Further GATT Negotiations," *World Economy* 2 (September 1979), table 1, p. 328, gives estimates of the tariff reductions agreed to during the Tokyo Round.

b. V. Allan Deardoff and Robert M. Stern, *An Economic Analysis of the Effects of the Tokyo Round of Multilateral Trade Negotiations on the United States and Other Major Industrialized Countries* (Washington, D.C.: U.S. Congress, Senate Finance Committee, June 1979), table 10, p. 43, give estimates of the tariff reductions agreed to during the Tokyo Round.

Canada has signed two sectorial free trade agreements with the United States, the Canada–U.S. Defence Production Sharing Program in 1959 and the Autopact in 1965. Furthermore, the Tokyo Round agreements provide a reduction of nearly 40 percent in customs duties on industrial products shipped to the United States. In 1987, four-fifths of Canadian

TABLE 1-5 Estimates from Various Studies on the Tariff Protection of Several Countries for the Post–Tokyo Round Period (percent)

	Primary and Secondary Sectors (excluding agriculture)[a]	
	Unweighted Estimates	Estimates Weighted by the Country's Imports
Austria	8.1	7.8
Canada	7.2	7.9
EEC	5.6	4.8
Finland	11.2	4.8
Japan	6.0	2.6
New Zealand	20.0	17.6
Norway	6.5	3.2
Sweden	4.8	4.3
Switzerland	2.8	2.5
United States	7.0	4.4
Average	7.9	6.0

	Secondary sector[b]	
	Estimates Weighted by the Country's Imports	Estimates Weighted by the World Imports
Australia	16.5	14.8
Austria	12.1	10.3
Canada	5.2	6.4
Finland	7.1	6.4
EEC	6.1	6.0
Japan	2.9	4.8
New Zealand	16.7	20.1
Norway	5.2	5.4
Sweden	5.0	4.3
Switzerland	3.1	3.0
United States	5.0	4.3
Average	7.6	7.8

Sources:

a. Hugh Corbet, "Importance of Being Earnest about Further GATT Negotiations," *World Economy* 2 (September 1979), table 1, p. 328, gives estimates of the tariff reductions agreed to during the Tokyo Round.

b. V. Allan Deardoff and Robert M. Stern, *An Economic Analysis of the Effects of the Tokyo Round of Multilateral Trade Negotiations on the United States and Other Major Industrialized Countries* (Washington, D.C.: U.S. Congress, Senate Finance Committee, June 1979), table 9, p. 42 and table C-6, p. 152, give estimates for 1987, based on various weightings.

Note: See Appendix B for the agreement between the various results.

exports to the United States will enter duty-free and over nine-tenths will be subject to a tariff of less than 5 percent (Economic Council of Canada, 1983, p. 110); the average tariff will be in the order of 1 percent. Canada–U.S. trade relations have thus been greatly liberalized over the last 25 years.

Tariffs are undoubtedly an important instrument of industrial policy. Since the mid-1960s, however, tariffs have been reduced by half, and the nominal rate will be 4 percent by the end of the Tokyo Round. The magnitude of the reduction effort is very similar from one country to the next, except in Japan and the United States, where the cuts have been more substantial, and in countries such as New Zealand and Australia, which have been partially exempted because of the exceptional role played by agriculture in these countries. Tariff protection is particularly high in Austria, New Zealand and Australia, and particularly low in the Scandinavian countries, in Switzerland and, more recently, in Japan and the United States. Canada is in an intermediate position, together with the EEC.

The Tariff Structure

In most countries, it is the manufacturing industry that is the most protected; the primary and tertiary sectors have virtually no NPR (Hawkins, 1972, Table 3-2, p. 44, and Appendix, pp. 57–62; Faucher et al., 1985; Wilkinson and Norrie, 1975). However, this does not hold true in Japan and the EEC, where it is agriculture that has the highest protection rates. Otherwise, the tariff structures are very similar. In all countries, finished products are more protected than semi-finished products, the rate of the latter being approximately three-fifths that of the former (Hawkins, 1972, Table 3-2, p. 44).[9] More specifically, the clothing industry[10] has the highest rates, followed closely by the footwear industry. In general, the correlations between the tariff structures of the various countries are very high, as seen in Table 1-6.[11]

The tariff structure has remained stable since 1947. The reduction rate is fairly homogeneous from one industry to the next,[12] except for clothing, footwear, and agriculture, which have been spared, relatively speaking, so that the gap between these more protected sectors and the others has grown.[13]

There are very few studies on the regional dimension of tariff protection. The information available to us pertains to Canada only.[14] It is central Canada, where manufacturing is concentrated, that is the most protected. Moreover, within the manufacturing sector, it is the Quebec industry that enjoys the highest levels of protection (Pinchin, 1979, Table 2-1, p. 27). The main difference, however, is still that between industry in central Canada (i.e., Quebec and Ontario) and industry in the other provinces.

Several authors have attempted to explain the level and evolution of the tariff structure.[15] The results vary greatly from one study to the next, without such discrepancies being really reconciled.[16] One must therefore determine whether all studies are equally valid, or whether some of them are clearly more persuasive. In this respect, the research by Lavergne (1983) on the U.S. tariff structure seems to stand out. In

TABLE 1-6 Correlation Matrix of the Nominal Tariff Structure of the Advanced Capitalist Democracies, Post–Tokyo Round (manufacturing sector)

	Australia	Austria	EEC	Canada	Finland	Japan	New Zealand	Norway	Switzer-land	Sweden	United States
Australia	1.00	0.93	0.76	0.88	0.80	0.72	0.95	0.82	0.87	0.79	0.83
Austria		1.00	0.86	0.90	0.82	0.73	0.90	0.85	0.92	0.86	0.81
EEC			1.00	0.84	0.73	0.76	0.72	0.89	0.74	0.92	0.81
Canada				1.00	0.85	0.88	0.81	0.92	0.88	0.93	0.85
Finland					1.00	0.75	0.68	0.84	0.70	0.88	0.93
Japan						1.00	0.65	0.90	0.68	0.88	0.75
New Zealand							1.00	0.74	0.85	0.71	0.73
Norway								1.00	0.76	0.97	0.84
Switzerland									1.00	0.76	0.71
Sweden										1.00	0.81
United States											1.00

Source: V. Allan Deardoff and Robert M. Stern, *An Economic Analysis of the Effects of the Tokyo Round of Multilateral Trade Negotiations on the United States and Other Major Industrialized Countries* (Washington, D.C.: U.S. Congress, Senate Finance Committee, June 1979), table C-6, p. 152.

addition to reviewing the works on the subject systematically and examining the level of tariffs in 1964, 1972, and 1979, together with its evolution over time, Lavergne has included no less than 32 different independent variables, whose relevance is occasionally hinted at by the documentation. Among other things, the study accounts for historical continuity and makes it possible to neutralize its effect when measuring the impact of other variables. We believe that the results of this study are much more reliable than those of all the others, and it is on these results that our analysis is based.

Lavergne draws up equations that account for the level of the tariff (for different years) and for its evolution over time. The estimates regarding the change are far more relevant, for the reasons stated by Lavergne:

> Tariff changes may be more explicable than tariff levels. This is so, first of all, because some variables, such as measures of susceptibility to displacement costs or of the bargaining advantage to be gained, will affect changes directly and levels only cumulatively. It also arises because in the presence of important status quo privileges, pressure group variables may come to affect changes rather than levels. In such circumstances the successful exercise of pressure may be best measured not by how much protection an industry has but by how well it succeeds in keeping what it has (Lavergne, 1983, p. 47).

Moreover, we prefer the nominal tariff because "it is not unlikely that our results might prove to be better for nominal than for effective tariffs for reasons associated simply with the quality of the data" (Lavergne, 1983, p. 51).

Table 1-7 identifies the variables which seem to have affected the evolution of the U.S. tariff protection during the Kennedy Round and the Tokyo Round. It appears that tariffs have been lowered less in industries which have many employees, which face increased competition from foreign producers,[17] and which have a rural location. The industries that are already more protected than others are also spared. Finally, the specific tariffs are reduced less than ad valorem tariffs.

In summary, except for agriculture in a number of countries, it is the manufacturing industry that is the most protected. Within the manufacturing sector, the tariff structure hardly varies from one country to the next. The highest tariffs are found in clothing. The protection structure remains relatively stable over time. The industries which the liberalization process spares the most are those which have a large number of employees, which face foreign competition, and which operate in rural locations.

Special Measures

Although tariffs are the basic instrument of trade policy, they are not the only one. Governments may resort to a whole battery of supplementary

TABLE 1-7 Variables Having a Significant Impact on the Evolution of the U.S. Tariff Structure, According to the Estimates of Lavergne

	Change in the NPR at the Kennedy Round		Change in the NPR at the Tokyo Round	
	Beta	*t*	Beta	*t*
Total employment	−0.091	1.57	−0.077	1.17
Imports/sales	+0.084	1.08	+0.085	1.06
Change (imports/sales)	−0.076	1.01	−0.173	2.43
Proportion of specific tariffs	−0.220	3.84	−0.135	2.03
Proportion of tariffs in *ad valorem* equivalent below 5%	+0.363	6.42	+0.266	2.58
Rural residents' share in manpower	−0.063	0.99	−0.227	3.10
Tariff before cuts[a]	−0.178	1.06	−0.307	1.33

Source: Réal Lavergne, *The Political Economy of U.S. Tariffs: An Empirical Analysis* (Toronto: Academic Press, 1983), tables 7-1, 7-2, 7-3, 7-4, 7-5, 7-6 and 7.7.

a. We take into account only the equations involving the changes in the NPR (see text). The variables shown in the table are those that have a *t* greater than 1.00 (and an identical sign) in both equations. We deemed it advisable to make an exception for the rural environment variable, which has a *t* of 0.99.

measures with respect to imports. The two main features of these measures are that they are added to the initial tariff and that they only apply in specific circumstances. Thus, there are retaliatory measures, which are taken explicitly in response to the actions of foreign producers or governments, and there are exceptional measures for quantitative restraint. We shall attempt to assess the relative scope of these measures, their orientation, and their variations in time and space. We shall see that the data are, alas, often fragmentary, but we believe that, despite this, the major trends can be detected.

Retaliatory Measures

Retaliatory measures are designed to protect domestic production against competition that is deemed to be "unfair." The source of "unfairness" may be a foreign producer who sells his products in this country at a price below the sales price on his own domestic market; in this case, anti-dumping duties will be levied. The "unfairness" may also be due to a foreign government subsidizing one of its domestic productions, with the result that Canadian producers can no longer compete; in this case, offset duties will be levied to neutralize the effect of the foreign subsidies. In both cases, the government sets an additional tariff which is designed to protect domestic producers against "unfair" commercial practices.

As early as 1947, Article 6 of the GATT provided for the levying of additional customs duties, when dumping injured or threatened to injure the industry of a country, in order to cancel out the difference between the domestic price and the export price. At the Kennedy Round, a new anti-dumping code was adopted, "which strengthened the requirement of GATT Article 6 by describing more precisely the definition of degree of injury, quantity and quality of causation, and the meaning of injury and industry" (Lazar, 1981, p. 32). Another, less restrictive code was negotiated at the Tokyo Round, eliminating the requirement according to which "the dumped imports are demonstrably the principal cause of material injury" (GATT, Article 6: 3a, 1967; Article 6: 3-1, 1979).

What, though, is the concrete importance of the anti-dumping measures? Everything seems to indicate that they are quite marginal. In the United States, which is probably the country where this instrument is in greatest use, anti-dumping duties "were imposed in only 8 out of 194 investigations between 1958 and 1965" (Baldwin, 1970, p. 140). According to Ehrenhaft (1979, p. 1375), the complaints came almost exclusively from the chemical, textile, ferrous metals, rubber, and plastic industries, as well as from the automotive parts industry.[18] In Canada, the anti-dumping tribunal carried out 106 investigations between 1969 and 1980, and concluded that there was injury in 63 cases (Faucher et al., 1985, Table 9). However, in practice, anti-dumping duties are virtually never levied because "while a finding of injury is in effect, dumping from the sources covered by it tends to disappear" (Stegemann, 1982, pp. 574–75).

GATT's Article 6 also provides the possibility for a government to levy offset duties when foreign production subsidized by foreign governments causes severe injury to domestic production. It was not until the Tokyo Round that a code similar to the code governing anti-dumping duties was adopted, specifying the rules of procedure which the various governments had to follow. However, once again, everything seems to indicate that it is a seldom-used measure. In the United States, there were 47 cases between 1962 and 1977 (Balassa, 1978, p. 416), and the complaints were concentrated primarily in the food, textile, leather, and ferrous metals industries (Ehrenhaft, 1979, p. 1375).[19] In the other countries, such cases were virtually nonexistent. Thus, when in 1968 the French government set up a program to provide a 6 percent wage subsidy in exporting industries, the United States was the only country that adopted countervailing duties (Baldwin, 1970, p. 48).

In summary, the exceptional retaliatory measures do not have great scope. The U.S. government seems to resort to them the most often and has done so somewhat more often since the 1970s (Balassa, 1978, p. 416;

Herander and Schwartz, 1984, pp. 68 and 72).[20] From 1975 to 1979, only 2.2 percent of U.S. imports were affected by retaliatory measures (Finger, Hall and Nelson, 1982, p. 466), and it is mainly considerations linked to employment (ibid., Table 2, p. 460) or to its evolution (Herander and Schwartz, 1984, Table 2, p. 67) that increase the complainant's probability of winning his case.[21]

Obviously, one must consider the uncertainty effect that the mere existence of such measures can have (Lazar, 1981, p. 36; Baldwin, 1970, p. 140; Herander and Schwartz, 1984), but this effect must not be exaggerated, particularly if one takes into account the delays that inevitably occur between the time a complaint is filed, the time a decision is made on the justification of the complaint, and, finally, the time when a concrete step (additional tariff) is taken (Faucher et al., 1985).

Exceptional Measures: Quantitative Restraint

The creation of GATT could be interpreted as an attempt to end what to many is the worst protectionist catastrophe, namely the use of quotas:

> The quota became the embodiment of all that was evil in the pre-World War II international economic system. A major policy goal of the United States in its G.A.T.T. and I.T.O. initiatives was to eliminate the use of quotas as a protectionist device. The longest and most difficult part of the preparatory negotiations leading to G.A.T.T. was concerned with the drafting of the four articles relating to quota obligations and these articles are the longest, most detailed set of governing rules for any single subject contained in G.A.T.T. (Jackson, 1969, pp. 306 and 307).

GATT Article 10 clearly specifies that the abolition of all quantitative restrictions must be the norm. This norm, however, does not apply to agricultural products covered by government measures designed to restrict domestic production. Nor does it prevent the implementation of defensive measures in case of balance of payment difficulties (Article 12), of unforeseen import growth (Article 19), or of threats to national security (Article 21).

There are a great many quantitative restrictions on agricultural products. A 1962 GATT report noted that they "covered 87 percent of production for butter, 84 percent for wheat, 59 percent for cheese, and 52 percent for sugar. More than two-thirds of the countries applied quantitative restrictions on at least some of the products examined" (Dam, 1970, p. 258). The United States adopted quotas for meat and dairy products;[22] the tariff equivalent is estimated at 20 percent in the first case and 90 percent in the second (Cline et al., 1978, p. 179). These are important measures. Cline et al. note that the impact of quotas in agriculture is approximately two-and-a-half times that of tariffs, so that the agricultural sector is just as protected as the manufacturing sector, if not more so (ibid., Tables 3-16 and 5-12). The situation is similar in Canada, where the import of dairy products, poultry, and eggs is controlled. Moreover, there has been a tightening of such restrictions; for example, in the 1950s, only butter was subject to a quota (Faucher et al., 1985). In Japan, the quota system is even more widespread and strict, and its impact on imports is three times greater than that of tariffs (Cline et al., 1978), which themselves are higher than in the United States. However, it is in the EEC that restrictions are the most substantial. Technically, the EEC imposes no quotas, but the community levy formula it uses has exactly the same effect:

> The variable levy system . . . is thus similar to a quota scheme. The levy is simply the difference between the foreign price and a fixed price within the Common Market that insures the sale of all internal production. Consequently, if the international price drops, the levy merely increases in order to prevent foreign sellers from increasing their sales (Baldwin, 1979, p. 33).

For several products, the tariff equivalent exceeds 100 percent (Cline et al., 1978, Table 4-2), and its overall impact is more than ten times greater than that of the tariffs.

In agriculture, the protection provided by quotas is thus much greater than the tariff protection. This additional protection merely expands the discrepancies between countries. It is in the EEC, where tariffs are already fairly high, that quantitative restrictions have the greatest weight. Finally, it would seem that these restrictions have been rising during the period under study.[23]

In the manufacturing sector, quantitative restrictions are implemented within the framework of defensive measures. There are, first of all, the measures provided by GATT Article 12, in the case of balance-of-payment difficulties. This type of intervention is now inoperative for all practical purposes (Robertson, 1977, p. 15), which is a significant change compared to the 1950s. In 1955, for example, 22 of the 34 countries that were signatory to GATT imposed restrictions for balance-of-payment reasons (Jackson, 1969, p. 708). Secondly, there is the clause in Article 19 which may be invoked to protect an industry suffering a "severe" injury due to the increase in imports.[24] The threat of unilateral defensive action can cause an exporting country to negotiate a voluntary restraint agreement.

During GATT's first 30 years, Article 19 was resorted to 98 times, and the frequency increased with time, the annual average rising from two during the 1950s to four during the 1960s, and to seven from 1973 to 1977 (Robertson, 1977, pp. 23–24). The industries involved were primarily agriculture and textiles. The duration of such measures is highly variable, but the median is approximately three years. The countries targeted are seldom compensated and they rarely resort to retaliatory measures.

The U.S. government took unilateral defensive action nine times between 1971 and 1981, including seven times since 1976.[25] The additional protection thus provided was generally 10 to 20 percent, i.e., approximately double the initial tariff (Morici and Megna, 1983, p. 30). Most of these measures apply to products manufactured in Asia, particularly in Japan (ibid., p. 28). Takacs (1981) has studied, on the one hand, the relationship between the number of complaints filed each year by U.S. industry and the number of favourable decisions made by the administration; and, on the other hand, a number of economic variables over the 1949–79 period. These results are very clear as regards complaints, which increase when economic conditions are poor, though the likelihood of success (measured by the number of favourable decisions made the previous year) also plays an important role. However, the trend is much less pronounced as regards the decisions, so that "economic activity does not appear to have the expected impact on protectionism" (Takacs, 1981). Finally, a period variable related to the implementation of the 1974 *Trade Act* (which made recourse to the defence clause easier) is significant. From 1974 on,[26] nine additional complaints and two additional positive decisions per annum were noted on average (ibid., pp. 690–91).[27] These measures have thus acquired some importance, but it must nevertheless be kept in perspective, since their tariff equivalent in 1976 was less than 0.005 percent (Morici and Megna, 1983, Table 2-14, p. 48).

Recourse to unilateral defensive action seems even less frequent in the other countries. For the 1947–66 period, Jackson noted that "the heaviest users of this clause have been the United States and Australia" (Jackson, 1969, p. 566). It was not until 1971, for instance, that the Canadian government enacted legislation enabling it to impose quotas (Faucher et al., 1985). During the 1970s, there were about a dozen defensive measures in Australia, Canada, and the EEC, but in the case of Canada and the EEC one-half of the products involved were agricultural.

In summary, unilateral action remains rare, although it is more frequent than it was. The impact of such action upon the target product is considerable, but since the number of such products is limited, its overall scope is minimal.[28] It is in the United States that such measures are the most popular.

On the other hand, more often than not, a country will use the threat of unilateral action to negotiate a voluntary restraint agreement with an exporting country. The best-known case is that of textiles, which have been governed ever since 1961 by international agreements. The short-term agreement on cotton textiles, in effect from October 1, 1961 to September 30, 1962, was followed by a long-term agreement on international trade in cotton textiles, in force from October 1, 1962, to December 31, 1973[29], and finally by the arrangement concerning the international textile trade (commonly known as the Multi-fibre Arrangement), in force from January 1, 1974, to July 31, 1986.[30] These international agreements established general principles on the basis of which bilateral agreements could be signed. The renewal of Multi-fibre Arrangement in 1978 provides for the possibility of "reasonable departures" from the general standards:

> The departures were not limited to any specific features. Thus all features, e.g., base levels, growth rate and flexibility, could be subjected to such departures. Since the word "reasonable" was not further elaborated or specified, the extent of departures was not put under any limit (Das, 1983, p. 98).

Therefore, the agreements "are obviously more restrictive, either because they cover a larger number of products, or — more often — because the annual rate of growth of the quotas is below the 6 percent provided by the MFA" (OECD, 1983a, p. 183). The new 1982 agreement specifies the conditions that can justify such "reasonable departures" so that "MFA III is less restrictive than MFA II but certainly more than MFA I" (Das, 1983, p. 104).

Textiles are not the only sector subjected to voluntary restraint. In the automotive field, Canada, the United States, Belgium, West Germany, and the United Kingdom have negotiated a voluntary restraint agreement with Japan (Canada, Department of Industry, Trade and Commerce, 1983, Appendix 6). In the steel sector, the United States and the EEC negotiated agreements with the major exporting countries, between 1969 and 1974 and between 1976 and 1981 (Morici and Megna, 1983, pp. 20–22; Borrus, 1983; Curzon Price, 1981, p. 89; Wilks and Dyson, 1983, pp. 21–22). Similarly, the United States has resorted to this type of protection for footwear and television sets (Morici and Megna, 1983, Table 2-1, p. 15). The tariff equivalent of these agreements varies from one case to the next but is usually less than 5 percent (ibid., Table 2-1). This is therefore a new phenomenon, but one of fairly limited scope globally.

Some claim that "the new protectionism . . . is manifest in the quantitative export restraints" (Mahon and Mytelka, 1983). This claim is not without merit. Recourse to quantitative restraints has increased over the last few years, although it must also be pointed out that defensive measures connected with balance-of-payment difficulties, which were relatively frequent in the 1950s, have disappeared. The level of protection which these new measures represent must nevertheless be placed in the proper perspective. Within the manufacturing sector, they usually apply to products already protected by high tariffs, and the additional protection they provide is usually smaller. The industries involved are also limited. The tariff equivalent of all quantitative restraints in the United States, in 1976, was 0.4 percent (Morici and Megna, 1983, p. 48). Moreover, and this is the main point, the agreements are often sufficiently ambiguous and flexible to provide all kinds of escape clauses which exporting countries can readily use (Yoffie, 1983b). Thus, "the Multi-fibre Arrangement has not been as restrictive and harmful to the newly industrializing countries as many feared it would" (ibid., p. 164) and "modern protectionism can still be a 'paper tiger'" (ibid., p. 202).

All things considered, it is in agriculture that the greatest quantitative restraints are noted, and it is the EEC that is the heaviest user. Protectionism in the manufacturing sector seems strongest in the United States. The target industries are usually characterized by the fact that they are already protected by high tariffs, so existing trends are merely reinforced.

Internal Aid

While the external component of aid to industry takes the form of protection against imports, the internal component consists in supporting domestic production. This support may be financial or technical. Financial aid may be direct (grants, loans, guarantees) or indirect, through the tax system (tax advantages) or through government purchases (public contracts). In the sections below, we assess the relative roles of these various instruments, summarize their evolution over time and the major national variations, and identify the main industries and activities involved.

Direct Financial Aid

The "purest" form of financial aid is undoubtedly the grant, which involves paying a certain amount outright to a firm. However, the state may also participate in the financing of firms by granting them loans or by guaranteeing the loans granted by private financial institutions.[31] In the latter case, there is financial aid or "implicit subsidy" if financial establishments, due to the terms they offer their clients, are not able to recover all their costs, including their costs of money and their administrative costs (Economic Council of Canada, 1982, p. 137). Direct financial aid thus comprises grants, plus the subsidies incorporated in government loans and guarantees. We shall examine the Canadian case first, for which more data are available.

THE CANADIAN CASE

The National Accounts include an item entitled "operating grants," which are defined as follows:

> All current transfers from the administration to the market production units of the private sector and to public units, and transfers from public authorities to market production units managed by the administration in order to

offset their operating losses when such losses manifestly result from the policy of public authorities designed to maintain prices at a level below production costs (OECD, *National Accounts, 1964–1981*, 1983, vol. 2, p. 307).

This item is the most readily available index of the overall magnitude of direct state financial aid and the one usually quoted when a rough idea of this type of intervention is to be given (Blais and Faucher, 1981, p. 10; Mutti, 1982, p. 10; Davenport et al., 1982, p. 12). The main shortcoming of this index is that it does not account for the direct cost of government programs. In the case of loans and guarantees, the government's opportunity cost is not accounted for except where it translates into a financial loss. It is therefore advisable also to take into account state aid through credit.

In 1983, Canadian governments paid firms $8.6 billion in operating grants, which amounted to 2.2 percent of GDP and 5.5 percent of government expenditures (Table 1-8); two-thirds of this amount came from the federal government (Tables 1-8, 1-9 and 1-10). In 1980, the various governments collectively accounted for loans[32] and guarantees totalling $18 billion, including implicit subsidies in the order of $700 million,[33] approximately three-quarters of which were at the federal government level (Table 1-11). Altogether, in 1980, direct financial aid amounted to 2.6 percent of GDP and 7 percent of government expenditures, 90 percent being operating grants and more than three-quarters coming from the federal government. The amount of aid increased rapidly over the period at both levels of government, although there was a slight reduction in the relative share of the federal government.

These figures give only a very approximate picture of the facts, because they include some elements which do not necessarily correspond to an aid to industry.[34] A more careful study of aid programs to the manufacturing industry (Blais, Faucher and Young, 1983a; Faucher, Blais and Young, 1983) provides a more accurate overview of government aid in a given sector. During the fiscal year 1979–80, the federal government provided a total of $410 million in grants. The total flow of loans and guarantees was in the same order of magnitude; the implicit subsidy component was approximately $50 million. Altogether, financial aid amounted to approximately 1 percent of value-added in manufacturing and of federal government expenditures, and 4 percent of investments. The aid programs of the Government of Quebec were of similar magnitude (1 percent of the value-added), while the aid provided by the Government of Ontario was more limited. Once again, it appears that grants are much larger than credit programs and that the federal goverment plays a greater role than provincial governments.[35] Finally, from 1960 to the mid-1970s, there was a strong increase in payments for all three governments,[36] though they have levelled out since then and there has even been some reduction.

It is difficult to determine whether government aid is principally aimed

TABLE 1-8 Operating Grants of Public Administrations in Canada

	Amounts ($ millions)		Grants/Gross Domestic Product (percent)		Grants/Current Government Expenditures (percent)	
Year	O	N	O	N	O	N
1950	63	64	0.34	0.34	1.78	na
1951	128	129	0.67	0.59	2.82	na
1952	100	102	0.41	0.41	1.79	na
1953	110	113	0.43	0.44	1.84	na
1954	86	89	0.34	0.34	1.40	na
1955	82	86	0.30	0.30	1.27	na
1956	123	127	0.40	0.39	1.77	na
1957	116	120	0.36	0.35	1.56	na
1958	146	150	0.44	0.43	1.74	na
1959	205	250	0.58	0.67	2.30	na
1960	235	314	0.64	0.81	2.40	3.19
1961	251	321	0.66	0.80	2.36	3.06
1962	292	361	0.71	0.83	2.57	3.21
1963	311	401	0.70	0.86	2.61	3.38
1964	323	436	0.67	0.86	2.51	3.40
1965	326	457	0.61	0.82	2.33	3.26

1966	516	639	0.87	1.02	3.20	3.95
1967	522	637	0.83	0.95	2.84	3.40
1968	500	641	0.73	0.87	2.46	3.01
1969	na	701	na	0.87	na	2.92
1970	na	756	na	0.87	na	2.71
1971	na	772	na	0.81	na	2.47
1972	na	884	na	0.83	na	2.49
1973	na	1,008	na	0.87	na	2.69
1974	na	2,619	na	1.76	na	5.23
1975	na	3,858	na	2.31	na	6.29
1976	na	3,344	na	1.73	na	4.80
1977	na	3,320	na	1.57	na	4.22
1978	na	3,527	na	1.50	na	3.97
1979	na	4,805	na	1.83	na	4.90
1980	na	7,103	na	2.38	na	6.32
1981	na	8,272	na	2.42	na	6.32
1982	na	7,793	na	2.11	na	5.43
1983	na	8,627	na	2.21	na	5.53

Source: OECD, *National Accounts of OECD Countries* (Paris: OECD, various years); and Statistics Canada, *National Income and Expenditure Accounts*, 1969–83, cat. no. 13-201 (Ottawa, 1984).

O = Old OECD National Accounts system.

N = New OECD National Accounts system.

TABLE 1-9 Operating Grants of the Central Administration in Canada

Year	Amounts ($ millions) O	Amounts ($ millions) N	Grants/Gross Domestic Product (percent) O	Grants/Gross Domestic Product (percent) N	Grants/Current Government Expenditures (percent) O	Grants/Current Government Expenditures (percent) N
1950	60	na	0.32	na	1.69	na
1951	124	na	0.58	na	2.73	na
1952	96	na	0.40	na	1.72	na
1953	106	na	0.42	na	1.78	na
1954	84	na	0.33	na	1.37	na
1955	75	na	0.27	na	1.16	na
1956	118	na	0.38	na	1.70	na
1957	108	na	0.33	na	1.45	na
1958	131	na	0.39	na	1.56	na
1959	189	na	0.53	na	2.12	na
1960	209	283	0.57	0.73	2.26	2.88
1961	221	285	0.58	0.71	2.07	2.72
1962	260	322	0.63	0.74	2.29	2.87
1963	275	355	0.62	0.76	2.31	3.00
1964	277	379	0.58	0.74	2.15	2.96
1965	259	372	0.49	0.66	1.85	2.66
1966	375	500	0.64	0.80	2.33	3.09
1967	390	519	0.62	0.77	2.12	2.77
1968	375	522	0.55	0.71	1.84	2.45
1969	na	555	na	0.69	na	2.31
1970	na	589	na	0.68	na	2.12
1971	na	513	na	0.54	na	1.64
1972	na	596	na	0.56	na	1.68
1973	na	738	na	0.59	na	1.83
1974	na	2,060	na	1.38	na	4.12
1975	na	3,183	na	1.91	na	5.19
1976	na	2,398	na	1.24	na	3.44
1977	na	2,222	na	1.05	na	2.82
1978	na	2,301	na	0.98	na	2.59
1979	na	3,225	na	1.21	na	3.29
1980	na	5,523	na	1.85	na	4.91
1981	na	6,494	na	1.91	na	4.96
1982	na	5,638	na	1.52	na	3.93
1983	na	5,683	na	1.46	na	3.64

Source: See Table 1-8.
O = Old OECD National Accounts system.
N = New OECD National Accounts system.

at primary, secondary, or tertiary industry, because, among the various grants mentioned in the National Accounts (Statistics Canada, *National Income and Expenditure Accounts*, cat. no. 13-201, Table 51), the largest[37] pertain to programs where the government grants aid in order to offset price regulation. Consequently, the beneficiaries of the grants are not their recipients; they are the industries which consume the

TABLE 1-10 Operating Grants of the Local Administrations in Canada

Year	Amounts ($ millions)		Grants/Gross Domestic Product (percent)		Grants/Current Government Expenditures (percent)	
	O	N	O	N	O	N
1950	3	na	0.02	na	0.09	na
1951	4	na	0.09	na	0.09	na
1952	4	na	0.01	na	0.07	na
1953	4	na	0.01	na	0.06	na
1954	2	na	0.01	na	0.03	na
1955	7	na	0.03	na	0.09	na
1956	5	na	0.02	na	0.07	na
1957	8	na	0.03	na	0.11	na
1958	15	na	0.05	na	0.18	na
1959	16	na	0.05	na	0.18	na
1960	26	31	0.07	0.08	0.14	0.31
1961	30	36	0.08	0.09	0.29	0.34
1962	32	39	0.08	0.09	0.28	0.34
1963	36	46	0.08	0.10	0.30	0.38
1964	46	57	0.09	0.12	0.36	0.44
1965	67	85	0.12	0.14	0.48	0.60
1966	141	139	0.23	0.22	0.87	0.86
1967	132	118	0.21	0.18	0.72	0.63
1968	125	119	0.18	0.16	0.62	0.56
1969	na	146	na	0.18	na	0.61
1970	na	167	na	0.19	na	0.59
1971	na	259	na	0.27	na	0.83
1972	na	288	na	0.27	na	0.81
1973	na	350	na	0.28	na	0.86
1974	na	559	na	0.38	na	1.11
1975	na	675	na	0.40	na	1.10
1976	na	946	na	0.49	na	1.36
1977	na	1,098	na	0.52	na	1.40
1978	na	1,226	na	0.52	na	1.38
1979	na	1,580	na	0.62	na	1.61
1980	na	1,580	na	0.53	na	1.41
1981	na	1,778	na	0.51	na	1.36
1982	na	2,155	na	0.59	na	1.50
1983	na	2,944	na	0.75	na	1.89

Source: See Table 1-8.
O = Old OECD National Accounts system.
N = New OECD National Accounts system.

product or service. If these programs are excluded, it appears that agriculture is particularly sheltered (Watson, 1983, p. 54).

On the other hand, more precise figures are available from the breakdown of aid within the manufacturing sector (Blais, Faucher and Young, 1983a; Faucher, Blais and Young, 1983). At the federal level, three industries are clear favourites: shipbuilding, the electronics industry,

TABLE 1-11 Direct Government Financial Aid in Canada

	Grants/Gross Domestic Product			Credits/Gross Domestic Product[a]			Financial Aid/Gross Domestic Product		
	($ millions)		Current Government Expenditures (percent)	($ millions)		Current Government Expenditures (percent)	($ millions)		Current Government Expenditures (percent)
1950									
Total	63	0.34	1.78	25	0.13	0.71	88	0.47	2.49
Federal	60	0.32	1.70	13	0.07	0.37	73	0.39	2.07
Provincial[b]	3	0.02	0.08	12	0.06	0.34	15	0.08	0.42
1960									
Total	314	0.81	3.19	43	0.11	0.44	357	0.92	3.63
Federal	283	0.73	2.88	36	0.09	0.37	319	0.82	3.25
Provincial[b]	31	0.08	0.31	7	0.02	0.07	38	0.10	0.38
1970									
Total	756	0.87	2.71	169	0.19	0.61	925	1.06	3.32
Federal	589	0.68	2.11	135	0.15	0.49	724	0.83	2.60
Provincial[b]	167	0.19	0.60	34	0.04	0.12	201	0.23	0.72
1980									
Total	7,103	2.38	6.32	746	0.25	0.66	7,849	2.63	6.98
Federal	5,523	1.85	4.91	568	0.19	0.51	6,091	2.04	5.42
Provincial[b]	1,580	0.53	1.41	178	0.06	0.15	1,758	0.59	1.56

Source: For grants, see Table 1-8.
For credits, estimates based on the data of the Economic Council of Canada, *Intervention and Efficiency: A Study of Government Credits and Credit Guarantees to the Private Sector* (Ottawa: Minister of Supply and Services Canada, 1982) (Tables A-1, 1-2, 1-3, 1-4, 1-5, 1-6, 3-1, B-6, B-7 and B-8).

a. This is the implicit subsidy included in loans granted by the government.

b. For grants, the data refer to the local administration, i.e., the provincial and municipal governments. However, everything seems to indicate that the share of the latter is minimal.

and the aeronautics industry. In general, declining industries seem to receive somewhat more aid than expanding ones. Firms in Quebec and the Atlantic provinces are favoured (inasmuch as their share of aid exceeds their share of Canadian value-added) at the expense of Ontario firms.[38] Big business is also favoured, but the bias has been reducing over time. Lastly, the domestic industry does not seem to receive favoured treatment. The aid programs of provincial governments are far less selective: no sector is clearly privileged, but small business is favoured somewhat. The sole effect of provincial government intervention would thus seem to be a slight attenuation of the main thrusts of federal programs.

In summary, direct financial aid in Canada mainly takes the form of grants, is primarily the federal government's domain, and has been growing throughout the period, having levelled out in the mid-1970s. It is targeted primarily on agriculture and on some manufacturing industries such as shipbuilding and the electronics and aeronautics industries. On the whole, the industrial centre[39] is disfavoured. Within the manufacturing sector, big business is favoured, but it should be emphasized that agriculture, which is still the stronghold of small business (Leanos, 1984), is highly subsidized.

The International Context

Overall, subsidies to firms in 1980 amounted to 3 percent of GDP and to 7 percent of government expenditures (Tables 1-12 and 1-13). After a decline in the early 1950s, they had been growing, the fastest growth being in the early 1970s. A distinction can be made between three groups of countries for the entire 1960–80 period: first, Ireland and Norway, where grants amounted on average to 5 percent of GDP; then 14 countries where the percentage was between 1 and 3 percent; and finally, Australia and the United States, where grants amounted to less than 1 percent of GDP. The five non-European countries were all below the average and the median. National variations were quite marked,[40] although they tended to diminish with time, particularly during the 1950s. It was in Canada and Sweden that grants grew fastest between 1960 and 1980.

In virtually every country, the bulk of grants comes from the central administration. Even in federal states, the central government has a clear primacy (Table 1-14). Centralization was strongest in the United States and weakest in Switzerland, with Canada being in the middle. Overall, there was a slight reduction trend in the relative share of the central government over the period studied.

We have seen that in Canada grants account for 90 percent of direct financial aid. As regards other countries, the few data available would indicate that the proportions are similar. In this respect, the trends in the

TABLE 1-12 Operating Grants Relative to Gross Domestic Product in Various Industrial Countries

		1950	1955	1960	1965	1970	1975	1980	Average 1960–80
					(percent)				
Australia	O	na	na	na	na	na	na	na	na
	N	1.28	0.38	0.52	0.71	0.72	0.49	0.77	0.68
Austria	O	1.80	1.39	1.58	1.92	na	na	na	na
	N	na	na	na	2.25	1.73	2.89	3.01	2.47
Belgium	O	na	0.91	1.27	1.15	1.33	1.19	1.51	na
	N	na	na	1.93	2.28	2.88	3.38	4.06	2.91
Canada	O	0.34	0.30	0.64	0.61	na	na	na	na
	N	0.34	0.30	0.81	0.82	0.87	2.31	2.38	1.44
Denmark	O	0.71	0.27	0.31	0.83	na	na	na	na
	N	na	na	na	na	2.69	2.78	3.18	2.88
Finland	O	2.06	3.36	2.77	3.27	na	na	na	na
	N	na	na	2.87	3.22	3.01	4.06	4.07	3.45
France	O	1.07	1.76	1.50	2.02	na	na	na	na
	N	na	na	1.62	2.17	1.97	2.44	2.51	2.14
West Germany	O	0.50	0.20	0.79	0.85	na	na	na	na
	N	na	na	0.83	1.25	1.74	1.99	2.02	1.57
Ireland	O	5.27	3.47	3.22	4.00	na	na	na	na
	N	na	na	3.28	3.95	4.88	6.88	8.38	5.47
Italy	O	na	1.07	1.51	1.37	na	na	na	na
	N	na	na	1.36	1.28	1.49	2.66	3.01	1.96
Japan	O	na	0.24	0.34	0.58	na	na	na	na
	N	na	na	na	0.71	1.10	1.49	1.47	1.19

flow of loans and guarantees are revealing. In Canada, the annual flows of loans and guarantees are in the same order of magnitude as the amounts pertaining to grants, at least within the manufacturing sector (Blais, Faucher and Young, 1983a, Table 2, p. 108). The same holds true for the United States, according to the data of Morici and Megna (1983, Table 4-3, p. 81 and Table 3-1, p. 56), and for Sweden, according to the data of Hamilton (1983, Table 1, p. 4). In France, the figures of Le Pors (1977, p. 44) show that loan flows are much smaller than the grant totals. If the amounts of loans and grants are identical and the rate of implicit subsidy of the loans is in the order of 10 percent, the loans are indeed ten times smaller. This is the situation that seems to prevail in the countries for which data are available. One would therefore be justified in believing that the data on operating grants give a good approximation of overall financial aid, of its evolution over time, and of the major national variations. (See Tables 1-13 and 1-14.)

TABLE 1-12 (cont'd)

		1950	1955	1960	1965	1970	1975	1980	Average 1960–80
Netherlands	O	1.35	0.91	1.26	0.73	na	na	na	na
	N	na	na	1.21	0.70	1.26	1.78	2.68	1.52
New Zealand	O	na	1.26	1.15	1.01	0.92	na	na	na
	N	na	na	1.14	0.97	1.01	3.40	1.43	1.59
Norway	O	na	4.24	4.34	4.61	na	na	na	na
	N	na	4.95	4.45	4.50	5.15	6.23	6.88	5.44
Sweden	O	1.70	0.98	1.42	1.45	na	na	na	na
	N	1.31	0.76	0.97	1.43	1.67	3.07	4.35	2.30
Switzerland	O	0.66	0.86	0.98	0.93	0.84	1.20	1.32	1.05
	N	na	na	na	na	na	na	na	na
United Kingdom	O	3.67	1.82	1.91	1.60	na	na	na	na
	N	na	1.84	1.93	1.61	1.74	3.53	2.35	2.23
United States	O	0.09	−0.02	0.05	0.02	na	na	na	na
	N	0.13	0.12	0.24	0.45	0.50	0.32	0.41	0.38
Average	O	1.60	1.41	1.47	1.59	na	na	na	na
	N	na	na	1.65	1.77	2.04	2.92	3.12	2.26
Standard deviation	O	1.45	1.24	1.07	1.22	na	na	na	na
	N	na	na	1.65	1.77	2.04	2.92	3.12	2.26
Variation factor	O	0.91	0.88	0.73	0.77	na	na	na	na
	N	na	na	0.68	0.67	0.63	0.57	0.63	0.61

Source: OECD, *National Accounts of OECD Countries* (Paris: OECD, various years).
O = Old OECD National Accounts system.
N = New OECD National Accounts system.

Everything seems to indicate that it is the primary sector, and particularly agriculture, that is the major beneficiary of financial aid.[41] Within the manufacturing sector, the most favoured subsectors are shipbuilding, aeronautics, the electronics/computer industry, the steel industry, and, more recently, the automotive industry.[42] Four out of the five are declining industries.[43] Denton (1976, p. 93) further notes a strong correlation in the United Kingdom between the rate of subsidy given to an industry and the rate of unemployment in that industry. Küster (1974, p. 74) notes that two-thirds of West-Germany's federal government grants are devoted to declining industries.[44] High technology, particularly that connected with national defence, is also favoured.

A substantial portion of financial aid is also earmarked for regional development. Although this is not the largest budget item,[45] it is far from negligible, and one must also take into account the fact that several highly subsidized industries (shipbuilding, the iron and steel industry, the automotive industry) are concentrated in outlying areas (Denton, 1976; Carmoy, 1978). It was basically during the 1960s that regional

TABLE 1-13 Operating Grants as a Percentage of Government Current Expenditures in Various Industrial Countries

		1950	1955	1960	1965	1970	1975	1980
				(percent)				
Australia	O	na	na	na	na	na	na	na
	N	na	na	2.72	3.36	3.91	1.58	2.53
Austria	O	8.47	6.02	6.29	6.68	na	na	na
	N	na	na	na	7.16	5.26	7.50	7.04
Belgium	O	na	3.79	4.49	3.88	4.01	2.89	3.14
	N	na	na	na	na	na	na	na
Canada	O	1.78	1.27	2.40	2.33	na	na	na
	N	na	na	3.19	3.26	2.71	6.29	6.32
Denmark	O	3.97	1.24	1.41	3.19	na	na	na
	N	na	na	na	na	na	6.39	6.08
Finland	O	10.48	16.24	12.66	12.68	na	na	na
	N	na	na	12.65	12.46	10.03	12.63	11.87
France	O	4.02	5.90	4.97	6.12	na	na	na
	N	na	na	na	6.43	5.68	6.23	5.83
West Germany	O	1.77	0.76	2.47	2.81	na	na	na
	N	na	na	2.93	4.07	5.35	4.57	4.71
Ireland	O	21.73	14.15	13.43	14.50	na	na	na
	N	na	na	na	na	14.23	16.40	17.34
Italy	O	na	4.36	5.69	4.42	na	na	na
	N	na	na	5.21	4.17	4.95	6.96	7.27
Japan	O	na	1.57	2.51	3.99	na	na	na
	N	na	na	na	5.00	7.84	7.14	5.77

development aid grew. Yuill, Allen and Hull describe that period as follows:

> In sum, the second phase of policy — what could be termed the "heyday" of regional policy — saw the introduction of increasingly valuable incentives and of a wider range of incentive types. It was, moreover, a period of great innovation and experimentation, reflected not only in the constant chopping and changing found in many countries, but also in attempts to target policy in a very specific manner through highly discriminatory schemes (Yuill, Allen and Hull, 1980, p. 219).

Subsequently, grants tended to level out:

> Whereas previously incentive expenditure had risen rapidly in most countries, in the year after 1973 it tended to level out, at least in real terms. Whereas previously the range of incentive types had widened considerably, the post-1973 period saw the main regional incentives remaining very much as they were (Yuill, Allen and Hull, 1980, p. 221).

TABLE 1-13 (cont'd)

		1950	1955	1960	1965	1970	1975	1980
Netherlands	O	5.67	3.57	4.50	2.21	na	na	na
	N	na	na	na	na	3.30	3.68	4.95
New Zealand	O	na	na	na	na	na	na	na
	N	na	na	na	na	na	na	na
Norway	O	na	17.43	15.50	14.48	na	na	na
	N	na	na	na	14.86	14.12	14.90	15.26
Sweden	O	7.21	3.78	4.95	4.56	na	na	na
	N	na	na	3.60	4.73	4.49	6.85	7.62
Switzerland	O	3.42	4.72	5.69	4.72	3.94	4.17	4.51
	N	na	na	na	na	na	na	na
United Kingdom	O	12.16	6.31	6.53	5.24	na	na	na
	N	na	na	6.47	5.19	5.23	8.61	5.57
United States	O	0.43	−0.07	0.19	0.74	na	na	na
	N	na	na	0.96	1.77	1.64	0.99	1.23
Average	O	6.76	5.69	5.85	5.78	na	na	na
	N	na	na	na	6.04	6.41	7.38	7.29
Standard deviation	O	5.68	5.30	4.25	4.16	na	na	na
	N	na	na	na	3.70	3.84	4.22	4.22
Variation factor	O	0.84	0.93	0.73	0.72	na	na	na
	N	na	na	na	0.61	0.60	0.57	0.58

Source: See Table 1-12.
O = Old OECD National Accounts system.
N = New OECD National Accounts system.

Since, moreover, the other types of aid were growing, the relative magnitude of regional incentives diminished (ibid., p. 223).

The priority of regional aid is investment (McAllister, 1982, p. 53). For the last few years, however, there has been a tendency to add hiring subsidies (McKerrie and Sengen Berger, 1983, p. 99). The proportion of the population living in the designated areas is approximately 35 percent (Yuill, Allen and Hull, 1980, p. 215). The grant rate was typically 25 percent and could reach 50 percent in some countries.

The dominant perception is that big business receives the bulk of government financial aid. According to Mikdashi (1974, p. 192), in Western Europe "there was a general tendency for governments to favor big business." Similarly, Hager (1982, p. 244) states that "there is a systematic bias toward large firms." The data confirming or denying these perceptions are scarce. It would appear that the innovation incentive programs do indeed favour big business (OECD, 1978, p. 9; Rothwell and Zegveld, 1984, p. 441). Moreover, the defence industry, which is among the main beneficiaries, is highly concentrated. Denton, however, noted only a slight (non-significant) correlation between the rate of subsidy to

TABLE 1-14 The Share of the Central Administration in the Operating Grants of the Public Administration of Federative States, 1950–81

	Australia		Canada		Germany		Switzerland		United States	
	O	N	O	N	O	N	O	N	O	N
					(percent)					
1950	na	na	95.23	na	83.67	na	na	na	na	na
1951	na	na	96.87	na	77.11	na	na	na	na	na
1952	na	na	96.00	na	58.43	na	na	na	na	na
1953	na	na	96.36	na	60.53	na	na	na	na	na
1954	na	na	97.67	na	47.83	na	na	na	na	na
1955	na	na	91.46	na	59.46	na	na	na	na	na
1956	na	na	95.93	na	77.88	na	41.18	na	na	na
1957	na	na	93.10	na	60.37	na	60.78	na	na	na
1958	na	na	89.72	na	54.27	na	68.18	na	na	na
1959	na	na	92.20	na	47.68	na	78.87	na	na	na
1960	na	88.00	88.94	90.13	52.66	58.13	76.39	na	na	100.00
1961	na	90.28	88.05	88.79	49.00	45.83	76.54	na	na	100.00
1962	na	80.61	89.04	89.20	44.07	40.56	72.62	na	na	100.00
1963	na	77.67	88.42	88.53	42.38	43.18	74.47	na	na	99.48
1964	na	81.60	85.76	86.93	47.09	49.27	75.96	na	na	99.64
1965	na	83.22	79.45	81.40	48.45	60.21	71.19	na	na	99.41
1966	na	85.08	72.67	78.25	48.51	60.97	72.95	na	na	99.41
1967	na	86.47	74.71	81.48	65.17	62.99	74.24	na	na	99.33
1968	na	88.09	75.00	81.44	60.08	61.15	79.52	na	na	99.37
1969	na	88.28	na	79.17	na	74.65	74.23	na	na	99.46
1970	na	90.66	na	77.91	na	74.35	70.39	na	na	99.51
1971	na	91.79	na	66.45	na	72.53	71.73	na	na	99.29
1972	na	91.05	na	67.42	na	74.86	67.97	na	na	99.22
1973	na	89.68	na	67.83	na	79.33	71.72	na	na	98.52
1974	na	87.38	na	78.66	na	75.06	61.82	na	na	96.73
1975	na	85.20	na	82.53	na	69.38	59.82	na	na	96.89
1976	na	81.09	na	71.71	na	69.56	59.78	na	na	96.74
1977	na	82.65	na	66.93	na	69.43	56.85	na	na	97.28
1978	na	83.89	na	65.24	na	71.74	65.22	na	na	97.49
1979	na	85.71	na	67.12	na	70.93	67.27	na	na	96.57
1980	na	85.56	na	77.76	na	69.43	66.67	na	na	96.70
1981	na	83.73	na	78.51	na	69.24	63.25	na	na	96.81

Source: See Table 1-12.

an industry and its concentration level in the United Kingdom (Denton, 1976, Table 10, p. 88). It should also be pointed out that agriculture, the most decentralized industry, is also the most subsidized sector.

During the 1960s, several European governments actively encouraged corporate mergers (Blais and Faucher, 1981; Vernon, 1974). Unfortunately, the amount of funds invested in such operations is not known. Finally, there are the salvage operations, where big business is much more likely to be involved than small business. As stressed by Hager (1982, p. 244), while big firms are being favoured, these are primarily the "worst performers among them." Overall, it would thus appear that there is some favouritism toward big business, but its extent should nevertheless not be exaggerated.

Finally, it is difficult to determine whether the domestic industry is favoured at the expense of foreign industry. The support given by governments to the "national champions" has been mentioned often (Vernon, 1974, p. 3; Black, Blank and Hanson, 1974, p. 32; Green, 1983, p. 165); but Hodges believes that even a government like the Labour government "did not seek to differentiate between foreign owned and domestic business enterprises in the formulation and execution of economic policies" (Hodges, 1974, p. 285). In Belgium, foreign firms received approximately one-half of the funds granted within the framework of incentive programs for new start-ups (OECD, 1983a, p. 108). The bias in favour of domestic industry would thus appear to be limited and to involve only some specific sectors (Blais and Faucher, 1981).

Direct financial aid to industry has been far from negligible. It amounted to approximately 3 percent of GDP and increased, particularly in the early 1970s. Grants were much larger than the subsidies incorporated into credit. This type of intervention was greatest in Europe. The main beneficiaries of aid were agriculture, declining manufacturing industries, peripheral regions, and big business. Finally, financial aid was earmarked primarily for investment. The trends were stable over time (except for regional development) and did not vary from one country to another.

Tax Advantages

A second means by which governments can assist industry consists of reducing the taxes industry must pay. The two main types of tax[46] levied upon firms are the corporate income tax and manpower taxes, the latter being mainly social security contributions to be borne by the employer, but also, in some countries, specific taxes such as the selective employment tax (1966–72) in the United Kingdom and the payroll tax (1969–79) in Sweden. Tables 1-15 to 1-18 indicate the GDP and public administration tax revenue shares of these two types of tax. In 1980, the income tax amounted to 2.7 percent of GDP and 7.5 percent of tax revenue, while the proportions for manpower taxes were 5.8 percent and 14.7 percent, respectively. Altogether, the two types of taxes amounted to 8.4 percent of GDP and 22.1 percent of government tax revenue.

As regards the evolution over time, the GDP share of earnings tax has tended to be relatively stable since 1960, whereas its tax revenue share dropped, until 1975, to a level that now seems to be stable. Manpower taxes increased continually (although they hit a plateau in 1975 relative to tax revenue). Together, the two taxes grew from 5.2 percent to 8.4 percent of GDP during the period. They accounted for 20 percent of govern-

TABLE 1-15 Corporate Income Tax as a Percentage of the Gross Domestic Product of Various Industrial Countries for Various Years

	1955	1960	1965	1970	1975	1980	Average
				(percent)			
Australia	3.59	3.95	3.93	4.23	3.57	3.68	3.28
Austria	1.80	1.81	1.87	1.57	1.68	1.43	1.69
Belgium	1.04	1.14	1.93	2.45	3.02	2.55	2.02
Canada	3.82	4.22	3.93	3.60	4.50	3.80	3.98
Denmark	1.37	1.18	1.36	1.07	1.29	1.46	1.29
Finland	2.98	2.48	2.48	1.76	1.52	1.56	2.13
France	na	na	1.84	2.24	1.98	2.09	2.04
West Germany	3.02	2.93	2.47	1.86	1.59	2.07	2.32
Ireland	1.67	1.43	2.36	2.75	1.55	1.66	1.90
Italy	1.68	2.36	1.88	1.83	1.82	2.69	2.04
Japan	2.47	4.03	3.17	3.97	3.38	4.47	3.58
Netherlands	3.53	3.21	2.85	2.66	3.54	3.03	3.14
New Zealand	4.05	4.58	5.07	4.74	3.54	2.44	2.07
Norway	3.78	1.54	1.27	1.29	1.28	6.25	2.57
Sweden	3.51	2.39	2.19	1.79	1.91	1.22	2.17
Switzerland	1.23	1.50	1.47	1.80	2.29	1.78	1.68
United Kingdom	5.06	2.75	2.15	3.44	2.23	2.79	3.07
United States	4.79	4.56	4.19	3.83	3.26	3.11	3.96
Average	2.91	2.71	2.58	2.60	2.44	2.67	2.64
Standard deviation	1.22	1.17	1.05	1.07	0.95	1.24	0.89
Variation factor	0.42	0.43	0.41	0.41	0.39	0.46	0.34

Source: OECD, *Public Revenue Statistics of OECD Member Countries* (Paris: OECD, various years).

ment tax revenue between 1955 and 1965, rose to 22 percent from 1965 to 1975, and have remained stable since then.

Differences between countries[47] are more marked in the case of manpower taxes (which were in decline during the period) than in the case of corporate income taxes. In the case of the former the dispersion is similar to that of operating grants, whereas for the latter it was closer to that of tariff protection. When the two taxes are taken together, the variations seem limited and stable over time.

Corporate income tax[48] was particularly important in the anglophone, non-European countries. Manpower taxes added up to substantial amounts in France, Italy, Belgium, and Austria and, more recently, in Sweden, but they were virtually nonexistent in New Zealand and Denmark. The two types of tax tended to be complementary, as the correlation between the two was moderately negative.[49] Altogether, corporate taxes were particularly high in France and Italy (and in Sweden for the last few years) and were particularly low in Denmark.

TABLE 1-16 Corporate Income Tax as a Percentage of Government Tax Revenue in Various Industrial Countries

	1955	1960	1965	1970	1975	1980
			(percent)			
Australia	15.87	16.81	16.08	16.66	12.27	11.98
Austria	6.03	5.97	5.40	4.40	4.35	3.48
Belgium	4.35	4.30	6.18	6.81	7.23	5.68
Canada	17.64	17.47	15.14	11.26	13.66	11.64
Denmark	5.85	4.64	4.54	2.64	3.12	3.23
Finland	11.12	8.95	8.24	5.47	4.22	4.45
France	na	na	5.27	6.30	5.39	4.91
West Germany	9.81	9.35	7.83	5.67	4.43	5.49
Ireland	7.39	6.46	9.06	8.80	4.83	4.55
Italy	5.50	6.86	6.89	6.55	6.31	8.18
Japan	14.43	22.15	17.84	20.13	16.09	17.26
Netherlands	13.44	10.66	8.03	6.67	7.72	6.61
New Zealand	14.97	14.27	20.66	17.85	11.78	7.76
Norway	13.34	4.92	3.81	3.28	2.85	13.28
Sweden	13.76	8.80	6.14	4.40	4.35	2.46
Switzerland	6.42	7.08	7.08	7.55	7.73	5.79
United Kingdom	17.01	9.66	6.97	9.17	6.20	7.75
United States	20.29	17.17	15.81	12.71	10.79	10.17
Average	11.60	10.32	9.50	8.68	7.40	7.48
Standard deviation	4.80	5.18	4.99	4.96	3.80	3.87
Variation factor	0.41	0.50	0.53	0.57	0.51	0.52

Source: See Table 1-15.

The tax advantages granted to industry are the last item deserving a closer look. In this respect, manpower taxes are of no interest, since they are generally not used for discriminatory purposes[50] and do not constitute an industrial policy instrument as such. We can therefore safely limit the rest of our discussion to corporate income tax. We have already seen the share of GDP and government tax revenue accounted for by this tax. It would also be advisable to place it relative to its base, i.e., with respect to earnings. We have collected the pertinent data for Canada and the United States in Table 1-19. In Canada, the effective tax rate was around 38 percent throughout the period, without any particularly clear trend, except for a substantial decrease between 1975 and 1979, followed by an equally substantial increase since then. The GDP share of corporate income tax was relatively stable (Table 1-15). In the United States, the tax rate tended to be higher, particularly in the 1950s, when it was in the order of 50 percent. The greatest changes occurred during the 1960s; the rate diminished by nearly 10 percent during the first half of that decade but returned to approximately 45 percent toward the

TABLE 1-17 Manpower Tax as a Percentage of the Gross Domestic Product in Various Industrial Countries

	1955	1960	1965	1970	1975	1980	Average
				(percent)			
Australia	0.90	0.90	0.82	0.77	1.67	1.50	1.10
Austria	5.92	6.09	6.92	7.16	8.51	9.54	7.36
Belgium	4.03[a]	4.62[a]	6.41	7.01	8.56	8.77	6.57
Canada	0.45[a]	0.70[a]	0.92	1.54[a]	2.03	2.14	1.29
Denmark	0.06	0.11	0.50	0.40	0.29	0.34	0.28
Finland	2.11	1.88	2.48	2.89	3.89	2.97	2.70
France	na	na	10.46	9.81	11.78	13.25	11.32
West Germany	4.61	4.87	4.90	5.64	6.88	7.02	5.66
Ireland	0.55	0.57	0.85	1.40	2.63	3.51	1.59
Italy	7.84[a]	9.04[a]	7.44[a]	8.43[a]	10.68	7.64	8.52
Japan	1.11	1.26	1.75	2.28	3.18	3.85	2.24
Netherlands	4.22	3.50	4.46	6.57	8.09	8.18	5.83
New Zealand	0.80	0.86	0.00	0.35	0.00	0.00	0.33
Norway	1.28	2.76	3.39	5.42	8.28	7.13	4.71
Sweden	0.54	0.46	3.19	5.21	9.98	15.02	5.73
Switzerland	1.48[a]	1.66	1.70	1.89	2.93	3.21	2.14
United Kingdom	1.45	1.67	2.34	4.32	3.70	5.02	3.09
United States	1.45	1.49	2.52	3.17	4.17	4.72	2.92
Average	2.28	2.50	3.39	4.13	5.44	5.77	4.08
Standard deviation	2.16	2.34	2.78	2.83	3.60	4.06	2.99
Variation factor	0.95	0.94	0.82	0.69	0.67	0.70	0.73

Source: See Table 1-15.

a. The available data give only the total social security premiums. In order to estimate the employers' share, we used data from subsequent years. We assumed that the employers' share was 50% in Canada, 65% in Belgium, 80% in Italy, and 35% in Switzerland.

end of the decade. The tax rate remained at that level throughout the 1970s, and the decline in the GDP share of income tax (Table 1-15) must therefore be ascribed to a gradual drop in profits (Bosworth, 1982). Overall, stability had the upper hand both in the United States and in Canada; over a period of 35 years, the corporate tax burden did not change at all in Canada and it diminished by 5 percent in the United States. The discrepancy between the two countries thus became somewhat smaller. In both countries, the 1960s saw the most changes, since the rates dropped during the first half of the decade (when the concern was to boost the economy after the recession in the late 1950s) and increased again subsequently, when inflation became the greater concern.

The obvious drawback to these data is that they do not take into account distortions due to inflation, which inevitably influence the effective rate of return and the effective rate of tax.[51] The studies which have included such adjustments, however, yield similar results. In Canada, the data of Tarasofsky, Roseman and Waslander (1981, Table 4-2, p. 22)

TABLE 1-18 Manpower Tax as a Percentage of Government Tax Revenue in Various Industrial Countries

	1955	1960	1965	1970	1975	1980
			(percent)			
Australia	4.00	3.83	3.37	3.05	5.74	4.88
Austria	19.82	19.96	19.76	20.08	22.05	23.16
Belgium	16.84[a]	17.55[a]	20.55	19.51	20.47	19.54
Canada	2.10[a]	2.85[a]	3.57	4.82[a]	6.15	6.55
Denmark	0.30	0.40	1.67	1.00	0.71	0.75
Finland	7.85	6.80	8.22	8.98	10.77	8.46
France	na	na	29.92	27.58	31.48	31.05
West Germany	14.98	15.57	15.05	17.21	19.14	18.59
Ireland	2.41	2.57	3.28	4.48	8.21	9.61
Italy	25.68[a]	26.26[a]	27.33[a]	30.22[a]	36.85	23.23
Japan	6.49	6.91	9.85	11.57	15.12	14.84
Netherlands	16.05	11.63	12.56	16.48	17.66	17.84
New Zealand	2.97	2.69	0.00	1.31	0.00	0.00
Norway	4.53	8.84	10.22	13.83	18.48	15.16
Sweden	2.13	1.70	8.95	12.79	22.71	30.30
Switzerland	10.75[a]	10.80[a]	8.23	7.96	9.89	10.44
United Kingdom	4.89	5.86	7.59	11.51	10.29	14.07
United States	6.15	8.23	9.51	11.42	13.80	15.43
Average	8.70	8.96	11.09	12.43	14.97	14.66
Standard deviation	7.16	7.00	8.26	8.14	9.52	8.70
Variation factor	0.82	0.78	0.74	0.65	0.64	0.59

Source: See Table 1-15.

a. The available data give only the total social security premiums. In order to estimate the employers' share, we used data from subsequent years. We assumed that the employers' share was 50% in Canada, 65% in Belgium, 80% in Italy, and 35% in Switzerland.

on the effective tax rate of non-farming and non-financial corporations show that this rate was approximately 45 percent throughout the 1947–76 period. In the United States, the data of Holland (see Grady, 1980, Table 5-4, p. 34) on the effective tax rate revealed a 10 percent drop (from approximately 50 to 40 percent) between 1947 and 1979. The U.S. tax rate dropped further following the 1981 *Economy Recovery Tax Act* which provided, among other things, a reduction in the tax rate for small businesses and tax credits for investment and for research and development (King and Fullerton, 1984, p. 251). However, everything seems to indicate that the American case is exceptional[52] and that the Canadian case is more representative. In Sweden, for example, "the effective corporate tax rate . . . was 37 percent in 1960, 41 percent in 1970 and 35 percent in 1980" (ibid., p. 142). Moreover, the GDP share of corporate income tax was fairly stable in most countries (Table 1-15), much as it was in Canada.

What matters most, though, is not the tax rate proper but the special

TABLE 1-19 Corporate Income Tax as a Percentage of Profits in the United States and Canada, 1947–83

Year	United States[a]	Canada[b]
1947	50.7	37.9
1948	42.2	33.7
1949	37.6	36.0
1950	52.8	38.1
1951	58.4	45.5
1952	53.7	45.5
1953	55.9	41.4
1954	50.0	40.2
1955	48.3	37.3
1956	50.3	36.5
1957	49.4	38.5
1958	49.3	36.4
1959	47.6	40.4
1960	47.7	40.5
1961	46.9	40.1
1962	42.4	38.9
1963	42.2	38.0
1964	40.5	35.7
1965	38.6	34.3
1966	39.6	34.9
1967	39.4	34.9
1968	44.0	36.6
1969	46.4	38.6
1970	47.9	39.7
1971	45.1	38.4
1972	43.0	36.1
1973	45.2	32.9
1974	54.4	35.2
1975	45.8	38.0
1976	46.2	35.4
1977	43.4	34.4
1978	43.2	31.8
1979	45.0	29.3
1980	46.6	31.7
1981	42.6	37.7
1982	35.9	54.2
1983	33.5[c]	39.2

Sources:

a. United States, *Economic Report of the President*, 1983, 1984 (Washington, D.C.: Government Printing Office, 1983, 1984),

b. Statistics Canada, *National Income and Expenditure Accounts*, catalogue no. 13-201 (Ottawa, 1969 to 1983), and *National Imcome and Expenditure Accounts*, vol. 1, *Annual Estimates*, catalogue no. 13-531, special issue, tables 1 and 45, 1976.

c. Preliminary.

arrangements that allow firms to deduct certain amounts from otherwise taxable income, under certain conditions. These advantages are sometimes known as "tax expenditures" (OECD, 1984a). In Canada, two studies have attempted to quantify all the tax expenditures linked to corporate income tax. Perry (1976) estimated that such expenditures totalled $1.8 billion in 1971, $2.3 billion in 1972, and $3.2 billion in 1973. Smith (1979) gave estimates of $4.9 billion in 1974 and $4.8 billion in 1975. These figures are equivalent to approximately 2 percent of GDP in the early 1970s and 3 percent in the mid-1970s. These are considerable amounts, somewhat greater than the amount of grants. However, two reservations must be made. First of all, these calculations do not take into account the effect of inflationary distortions on corporate accounting, particularly capital depreciation. For the year 1974, for instance, the inclusion of inflation in the depreciation estimate would reduce the total tax expenditures from $4.9 billion to $3.7 billion.[53] The tax expenditures would then amount to 2 percent of GDP and would be the same order of magnitude as the grants. Secondly, as we shall see farther on, tax advantages are less selective than grants, so it could be misleading to take into account only overall figures.

Blais, Faucher and Young (1983a) also studied the tax advantages granted by the federal goverment to the Canadian manufacturing industry over the 1960–80 period. By the end of that period, the advantages amounted to approximately 2 percent of manufacturing value-added, which is in fairly good agreement with the estimates of Perry and Smith. In this case, the accounting depreciation was adjusted for inflation and only the federal government was considered, which explains why the percentage is somewhat lower. Nevertheless, this study provides a better understanding of the evolution of tax measures over time. It appears that such measures were virtually nonexistent before the 1960s, that they grew at a remarkable pace during the first half of the 1960s (the peak of the tax advantage/value-added ratio was reached in 1966; it was never equalled subsequently, not even in the late 1970s); and that they have increased slightly since then. All of these corroborate fairly well the observed model, as regards the effective tax rate (Table 1-19).

The data for the other countries are very fragmentary. For the United States, Surrey (1973, pp. 78–79) estimated that the tax advantages were in the order of $15 billion in 1965, i.e., 2 percent of GDP. However, less than one-half of the amounts involved pertained to selective measures. In West Germany, the tax advantages granted by the federal government were equivalent, throughout the 1970s, to 8 or 9 percent of tax revenue and 1 percent of GDP (OECD, 1984a, Table 3-11, pp. 66–67). For the other countries, we have few direct data. We have good reasons to believe, though, that national variations were not very pronounced. On the one hand, the GDP share of corporate income tax was relatively similar from one country to another (Table 1-15). On the other hand, in the three countries for which data are available, the GDP share ranged from 1 to 2 percent.

In almost all countries, and even in federal states, corporate taxation is primarily within the jurisdiction of the central government. In Canada, 70 percent of corporate income tax revenue accrues to the federal gov-

TABLE 1-20 The Federal Government's Share of Corporate Tax Revenue in Canada

Year	Percentage
1954	95.61
1955	95.25
1956	95.56
1957	85.80
1958	82.63
1959	83.21
1960	83.68
1961	82.95
1962	76.65
1963	76.93
1964	78.58
1965	77.06
1966	75.53
1967	75.33
1968	77.02
1969	76.72
1970	76.08
1971	75.30
1972	74.91
1973	75.49
1974	71.92
1975	73.32
1976	71.14
1977	73.44
1978	71.09
1979	69.61

Source: Statistics Canada, *Consolidated Government Finance*, catalogue no. 68-202 (Ottawa, 1982).

ernment (Table 1-20). Although the share of the provincial governments increased during the period studied, the share of the federal government remained paramount. Moreover, in seven provinces, the tax system was determined by the federal government, with the provincial governments setting only the tax rate. As to the tax acts of Quebec, Ontario, and Alberta, for all intents and purposes they are copies of the federal act (Thirsk, 1983; Kellough and McQuillan, 1983). The share of the central government is also dominant in Australia and the United States, but "local" governments have a considerable share in West Germany and Switzerland (Table 1-21).

The breakdown of tax advantages is perhaps more important than their overall amount. Table 1-22 shows the effective tax rate (without adjustment for inflation) for Canada's major sectors of economic activity. The mining industry is by far the most favoured,[54] basically because of the generous provisions of the *Income Tax Act* regarding exploration and development expenses. By contrast, the tertiary sec-

TABLE 1-21 The Federal Government's Share of Corporate Income Tax Revenue in Federative States

Year	Australia	Canada	West Germany	Switzerland	United States
			(percent)		
1955	100.00	95.24	42.64	17.49	95.97
1960	100.00	83.68	26.23	26.19	94.80
1973	100.00	75.50	40.54	21.06	na
1982	100.00	67.83	38.90	26.26	76.74

Source: OECD, *Public Revenue Statistics of OECD Member Countries* (Paris: OECD, various years).

tor[55] is heavily taxed, mainly because, unlike the other sectors, it does not have the advantage of accelerated write-offs. The manufacturing industry is near the average, but it was somewhat disfavoured at the beginning of the decade. The data of Tarasofsky, Roseman and Waslander (1981, Table 4-2, p. 22) confirm this. The (non-adjusted) tax rate of the manufacturing sector was similar to that of all the other sectors taken as a whole, except during the 1965–71 period. However, the adjusted rates (taking inflation into account) varied to a greater degree: the rate of the manufacturing industry was substantially lower from 1947 to 1955, it matched the rate of the rest of industry between 1956 and 1964, and exceeded it from 1965 to 1971; the gap has diminished since. This is due to the fact that the manufacturing sector seems more affected by inflation (Tarasofsky, in Grady, 1980, p. 29). Overall, the manufacturing sector is neither highly favoured nor highly disadvantaged by the Canadian tax system.

One could also look at the finer variations within the various industrial subsectors. A number of observations can be made, based on a study now underway[56] on the tax rate in the 20 Canadian manufacturing industries from 1965 to 1980. Firstly, there is no structure that was constant over time, particularly after 1974: the correlation between the tax structure of different years is very low (some correlations are even negative). There is therefore no basic trend, and any study based on one single time could be misleading. Secondly, two industries are clearly taxed less than the others throughout the period: the oil industry and the primary metals industry. Since both are in the natural resources sector, they were allowed generous exploration deductions. The differences were small between the other 18 industries, the mean deviation of the average tax rate (over 15 years) being in the order of 2 percent. Consequently, the regressions that linked the tax rate to a number of economic variables gave disappointing results.

The picture that emerges for Canada as a whole is therefore that of a complex tax structure, comprising a great number of special provisions

TABLE 1-22 Corporate Income Tax as a Percentage of Pre-tax Profit in Canada, by Activity Sector, 1965–81

Sector	1965	1966	1967	1968	1969	1970	1971	1972	1973	1974	1975	1976	1977	1978	1979	1980	1981	Average
Agriculture, forestry and fisheries	29.0	30.8	31.7	35.2	31.3	46.8	72.3	37.0	24.3	38.6	176.7	54.5	52.6	29.5	26.4	22.5	18.9	44.6
Mining	12.0	11.2	13.6	12.0	11.9	17.1	14.8	19.7	15.4	26.2	34.3	30.6	30.6	24.1	20.5	20.7	23.9	19.9
Manufacturing	34.2	32.1	35.1	39.6	40.0	47.3	43.9	39.0	32.6	32.5	35.7	35.4	31.3	28.7	27.3	28.1	25.4	32.7
Construction	27.7	26.3	33.4	36.3	36.2	43.3	41.4	40.2	35.4	32.5	35.0	35.0	39.9	41.9	32.7	23.4	24.6	34.4
Transportation, communication and utilities	38.3	39.6	32.6	32.4	32.8	25.1	29.2	27.9	28.5	29.6	32.1	28.6	29.2	28.3	25.0	21.5	24.0	30.3
Wholesale	38.8	39.5	37.5	40.9	39.1	49.3	47.1	45.7	42.8	43.6	48.2	43.1	40.5	37.4	34.6	33.0	34.0	40.9
Retail	39.2	37.3	36.6	31.3	41.2	44.2	46.5	42.4	39.0	39.6	40.7	44.4	37.5	33.2	30.3	27.4	28.5	37.6
Finance	19.7	21.0	19.4	20.8	26.1	50.4	50.9	47.1	46.1	45.7	45.2	46.9	44.2	47.9	92.1	34.0	36.1	40.8
Services	33.4	30.6	35.1	32.2	35.4	47.0	45.6	53.5	44.8	42.6	46.4	50.6	41.9	39.7	35.5	28.6	28.6	39.5
Total	30.1	28.7	29.4	31.5	32.6	41.6	41.0	39.6	33.3	34.8	38.7	37.6	34.7	31.8	29.3	26.7	27.2	33.4

Source: Statistics Canada, *Corporation Taxation Statistics*, cat. 61-208 (Ottawa, 1982).

which do not, however, have a coherent sectorial scope and which only provide a clear benefit to the mining industry and to the primary processing of natural resources. Is this situation peculiar to Canada? In the United States, at least, the trends seem similar. The manufacturing industry tax rate seems to be "average" (Holland, 1980, Table 5-4, p. 34; Canada, Department of Finance, 1978, Table 13, p. 48). The mining sector is lightly taxed. Indeed, the four industries with the lowest effective tax rate in Siegfried's (1974) study on the primary and secondary sectors are all mining industries. Finally, the services sector has, as in Canada, a fairly high tax rate (Canada, Department of Finance, 1978, Table 13, p. 48). In a more detailed analysis of 110 mining and manufacturing industries, Salamon and Siegfried (1977) examined the relationship between the effective tax in 1963 and a number of economic variables; three of the five variables selected (median firm size, degree of concentration, and earnings ratio) were found to be statistically significant, which seems to contradict the remarks regarding the "incoherence" of the Canadian tax structure. However, this result is vulnerable because the data of Salamon and Siegfried only cover one year, and because there are good reasons to believe that the tax structure is not stable.[57] We therefore believe that we can maintain the claim of incoherence.

One should also look at whether the tax structure penalizes big business or small business to a greater extent. In 1981, the taxes paid by firms with assets below $1 million amounted to 29.1 percent of their earnings before tax; those with assets of between $1 million and $25 million paid 33.9 percent, and those with assets in excess of $25 million paid 19.9 percent (Statistics Canada, *Corporation Taxation Statistics*, cat. no. 61-208). It therefore appears that, as with grants, big business is favoured. A more detailed analysis of the manufacturing sectors over the 1974–79 period, taking into account, among other things, the losses of previous years and the inflationary bias in calculating depreciation, nevertheless indicates that the effective tax rate of small and large firms is similar, while that of medium-sized firms is slightly higher.[58] A study by McFetridge (1982b) reveals that, among tax-paying firms, small businesses are privileged.

Data are even scarcer on the tax treatment of domestic and foreign firms. It must, however, be emphasized that there are in Canada two "supplementary" taxes applicable to "foreigners": taxes on foreign firms' earnings that are not reinvested, and taxes on dividends paid out to non-residents. These two taxes totalled over $1 billion in 1981, i.e., over 12 percent of the basic tax (Statistics Canada, *Federal Government Finance*, cat. no. 68-211). Canadian firms are therefore favoured. Finally, there is no real regional dimension. In Canada, only investment and employment credits have rates which vary according to the region, and their weight in the overall tax structure is minimal.

As regards the focus of taxation, investment is clearly the primary target for incentives. In Canada, accelerated write-offs and investment credits are the most important measures within the manufacturing sector (Blais et al., 1983). In the mining sector, the most generous provisions cover exploration costs. The tax system has also provided considerable incentive to research and development activities, particularly over the last few years, and the Canadian tax system is particularly generous in this respect (McFetridge and Warda, 1983). However, it does not follow that high technology industries are automatically favoured, because "the asset mix of high technology industries gives more weight to intangible assets and . . . intangible assets are taxed at a high marginal effective rate" (Hulten and Robertson, 1984, p. 334).

All things considered, the tax advantages granted to industry are far from negligible. They amount to 1 to 2 percent of GDP, which is nevertheless below the level of direct financial aid. Their magnitude does not seem to vary at all over time or by country. The various measures adopted often tend to cancel out mutually, so that in practice there are no "winners" and "losers" other than the fact that the mining industry is favoured and the services industry is disfavoured. Domestic industry is also somewhat favoured. Finally, tax measures are aimed preferentially toward investment and R&D.

Public Contracts

While governments assist domestic production on a priority basis by giving it grants or tax advantages, they can also favour it through their purchases. As noted by Ponssard and Pouvourville:

> Although the original purpose of public contracts is to meet the procurement requirements of governments, . . . their monetary mass is often used in attempts to achieve overall or selective economic policy objectives (Ponssard and Pouvourville, 1982, p. 5; translation).

The amounts involved are no doubt considerable. In Canada, the public sector purchased $43.5 billion worth of goods and services in 1979, which amounted to 18 percent of GDP (Science Council, 1984, p. 21). One must determine the extent to which government practice differs from official competition doctrine when it is attempting to favour domestic production in general or, more specifically, some particular sectors or types of business.

The first element of selection is that between domestic production and foreign production. The Tokyo Round negotiations led to a code pertaining to public contracts, which in turn was to lead to a reduction in the preferential treatment of domestic production. Since this code only became effective in 1981, its real scope is still largely unknown. We shall therefore describe first the situation which prevailed in the 1970s, a period for which the data are more reliable.

Canada and the United States apply a premium of 10 and 6 percent, respectively, in favour of domestic production (Stegemann, 1973, p. 41; Morici and Megna, 1983, p. 39). These are the only countries where a premium has been formally established (OECD, 1976). Officially, at least, foreign producers are treated on the same basis as domestic producers. Still officially, however, three countries seem to be more nationalistic: Finland, where "the requirements of encouraging domestic production and employment as well as domestic manpower must be duly taken into account in government contracts" (ibid., p. 62), France, where, "for industrial contracts, the manufacturer must have French nationality" (ibid., p. 68), and Italy, where "state agencies in principle do not do business with foreign firms or suppliers" (ibid., p. 86).

In practice, things are obviously more complex. In Canada, it would seem that the 10 percent premium "is regarded as having little practical effect" (Peat, Marwick and Associates, 1981, 3:3). Other regulations are more important. Thus, the list of suppliers contacted often comprises only Canadian producers (Stegemann, 1973, p. 54).[59] When there are at least three Canadian suppliers, the government usually does not contact foreign suppliers (Peat, Marwick and Associates, 1981, 3:3). In negotiated contracts, "one of the subjects of negotiation is the Canadian content of the supplies or equipment to be procured" (ibid., p. 57). Altogether, approximately 20 percent of public contracts are "open" to foreign producers (de Mestral, 1982, p. 180; Science Council, 1984, p. 21). It might also be useful to examine provincial government policies. According to Jenkin's data (1983, Table 5-1, pp. 102–103) only the Government of Ontario has aligned itself with the federal policy. The other governments tend to apply a similar premium for "provincial" suppliers.

On the other hand, the preference shown to domestic production must not be exaggerated. For instance, the selection exercised by Crown corporations was limited. Stegemann has noted that "it seems to be a rare occurrence that the government directs the procurement of commercial Crown corporations towards domestic sources" (Stegemann, 1973, p. 44). Similarly, the preference shown by the provincial hydroelectric corporations seems fairly limited, and imports of electrical equipment remain relatively high (ibid., p. 65).

It is difficult to measure the real magnitude of the preference shown to domestic production. In some specific sectors, the purchasing policy could possibly play a crucial role. Thus, for the defence industry in general, for aeronautics, shipbuilding, and electronics, government purchases are considerable and the contracts are almost all awarded in Canada (Stegemann, 1973, p. 39; and Table 5, p. 59).

We have seen that in the United States the federal government premium favouring domestic production was somewhat less, i.e., 6 percent. On the other hand, U.S. government purchases, particularly those pertaining to defence, are much larger. Morici and Megna attempted to quantify the impact of these preferential purchases. They estimated that in 1976 such purchases amounted overall to a subsidy of 0.36 percent, which is 14 times less than the average tariff but is equal to the entirety of defensive measures (Morici and Megna, 1983, Table 2-13, p. 47). This is also much less than direct financial aid. In fact, preferential purchasing only appears to play an important role in the defence sector: "Foreign suppliers are excluded from federal procurement more for national security reasons and practical constraints than because of the Buy American legislation" (ibid., p. 40). The only other clearly favoured industry would appear to be steel for road construction work or public transportation purchases (ibid.).

What is the situation in the other capitalist democracies? We mentioned earlier the official policies, which appear to be "neutral" as regards foreign production. We noted that France, Italy, and Finland appear officially to be more protectionist than others. It can also be assumed that, as in Canada and the United States, discrimination is exercised primarily in the industries linked to defence, such as aeronautics. Even civil aeronautics is protected, for instance in the case of the Airbus aircraft in Europe (Kingdon, 1984).

Another industry directly affected by public contracts is that of computers. In this respect, the data of Mutti (1982) are particularly interesting. They show that among the five sectors examined (textiles, steel, automotive, pharmaceuticals, computers), government aid through public contracts is significant only in the case of computers. Government purchases are reserved almost exclusively for the domestic industry in Japan, France, and Great Britain. No data are provided for West Germany, where the government seems to intervene to a lesser degree.

In most countries, there is therefore a preference in favour of domestic production, but the preference is limited mainly to the defence and computer industries. For the other sectors, this instrument of industrial policy is not really important. Moreover, national variations do not seem very substantial; a country such as the United States, which is otherwise not very interventionist, resorts to preferential purchasing just as much as most European countries. Finally, everything seems to indicate that up to 1981, the use of government purchases as an industrial policy instrument did not undergo major changes.

The new public contracts code adopted within the framework of the Tokyo Round became effective on January 1, 1981. For all intents and purposes, the code prohibits the selective policies of central governments.[60] In Canada, according to de Mestral (1982, p. 186), the portion of the public market that is accessible to foreign suppliers should increase by $1 billion (taking 1978–79 as the base year); this will represent a relative increase of approximately 10 percent. In the United States, "in terms of 1979 procurement levels, the agreement freed up to about $12.5 billion in federal purchases" (Morici and Megna, 1983, p. 41). Thus, the effects of the agreement appear to be modest, but they have a liberalizing impact.

Public contracts may also have objectives other than the protection of domestic production. Indeed, they can be used for regional development or can be designed to promote big or small business. However, this seems to be rarely the case. There is, of course, Italy, where 30 percent of government purchases must be from suppliers in the south (OECD, 1976, p. 87). Similarly, the United States has set up a 12 percent (rather than 6 percent) premium for small businesses and for those located in surplus manpower areas. West Germany grants "a six percent margin in the case of tenders of up to 5,000 DM submitted by persons or firms in peripheral regions along the borders with the German Democratic Republic and around West Berlin" (ibid., p. 12). Finally, the United Kingdom "has taken administrative measures in order to grant some preference to firms located in areas to be developed and in Northern Ireland . . . a 25 percent share of contracts is reserved for suppliers residing in those areas" (ibid., p. 126).

Everything seems to indicate, though, that these are isolated cases. In Canada, "Ottawa does not appear to have consistently employed purchasing policy as a regional development tool" (Tupper, 1982, p. 20). In Quebec, the Department of Public Works has opposed the Department of Industry and Commerce, which demanded a "vigorous" purchasing policy (Bernier, 1984). Moreover, as Bernier points out (ibid., p. 86), "Les institutions relevant des ministères de l'Éducation et des Affaires municipales, en particulier, semblent avoir utilisé leur autonomie juridique pour résister à l'application intégrale de la politique" ("Institutions reporting to the Departments of Education and Municipal Affairs, in particular, seem to have used their legal autonomy to resist full implementation of the policy").

In summary, although public contracts are not negligible, they are clearly less important than financial aid or tax advantages. Their use seems stable over time, with a slight decline since 1981, and national variations are not marked. This is a type of aid that involves primarily the defence-related high technology industries.

Technical Aid

Finally, one must look at government technical assistance to industry. This involves the information, training, and advisory services which governments make available to businesses (see, in particular, OECD, 1975, chap. 6). These services round out the direct and indirect financial aid which government provides to industry.

The export promotion efforts made by all governments should be mentioned first. Thus, it would appear that the United Kingdom, Italy, France, Japan, and the United States spent between US$50 million and US$100 million in 1976 on promotional activities, while the Netherlands, West Germany, and Canada spent approximately US$15 million each (Wescott, 1983, p. 138).

Data on training and advisory services are even more fragmentary. In Canada, the Federal Business Development Bank offers the Counselling Assistance to Small Enterprises (CASE) program, which makes available to small business the expertise of retired businessmen, as well as offering them management seminars, courses, and workshops. In 1984, over 13,000 firms used CASE, and over 68,000 people took advantage of the management training programs (Federal Business Development Bank, *1984 Annual Report*). The total cost of these services amounted to almost $12 million in 1984. The National Research Council has also set up technical information services (National Research Council of Canada, *1982–1983 Annual Report*). The provincial governments provide management consulting services on a smaller scale. In Quebec, the Department of Industry, Commerce and Tourism makes management consultants available to small and medium-sized firms, in addition to organizing seminars on specific subjects. In 1982–83, nearly 900 firms used the consulting services (Department of Industry, Commerce and Tourism, *1982–1983 Annual Report*). Nevertheless, from a financial viewpoint, this type of aid is clearly less important than the other instruments already studied. However, this activity is increasing rapidly; the clientele of the CASE program, for instance, has been growing steadily (Federal Business Development Bank, *Annual Reports*). Finally, the role of the federal government seems greater than that of the provincial governments.

The data of other countries are even more incomplete. The U.S. government is probably the most active in this respect (Bénoun and Sénécourt, 1980, p. 431). The Small Business Administration organizes training courses, conferences, and workshops, in addition to making available to businesses its SCORE network (Service Corps of Retired Executives), a program that was picked up by the Canadian government in the early 1970s (Bénoun and Sénécourt, 1980, p. 83; *The United States Government Manual*, 1984–85, p. 613). The state governments also provide similar services (Bénoun and Sénécourt, 1980, p. 48). In Europe, it was only during the 1970s that governments set up technical assistance programs (ibid., p. 431). Only the West German government appears to have set up programs similar to those in the United States and Canada (OECD, 1978, p. 169).

In summary, technical assistance is a relatively small but growing type of aid targeted on small business. It plays a greater role in North America than in Europe.

Conclusion

We have examined a whole range of instruments used by governments to aid industry. Three of these are particularly important: tariffs, which on average will be 4 percent in 1987, followed by direct financial aid and by tax advantages, which constitute 3 percent and 1 to 2 percent of GDP, respectively.[61] These are in turn followed by quantitative restrictions and public contracts, such implicit aid being approximately 0.5 percent of GDP. Technical assistance and retaliatory measures play a marginal role, everything considered. Of all the instruments, tariffs have the greatest overall scope. It is fashionable today to call tariffs "obsolete" because they have been greatly diminished. Our data show that this type of aid remains substantial.

The most significant changes occurred, basically, in the mid-1960s. In 20 years, the average tariff dropped by somewhat more than one-half, from 9 to 4 percent (Table 1-1). On the other hand, quantitative restrictions greatly increased in number, and direct financial aid grew from 1.8 to 3.1 percent of GDP (Table 1-12). The role of tax breaks and public contracts remained more or less stable, while technical assistance made clear strides.

The fact that the reduction in tariff protection was accompanied by contrary trends, linked to an increase in some non-tariff barriers, has given rise to a whole school of thought which claims that a new protectionism is emerging:

> The preceding section examined the emergence of the "new protectionism" in the developed countries. . . . It has been noted that the new protectionism is characterized by the employment of non-tariff restrictions on trade, the granting of government aids to domestic industries, with further attempts made at organizing world trade (Balassa, 1978, p. 422; see also Mahon and Mytelka, 1983; Lazar, 1981).

This hypothesis is both right and wrong. Although it is true that some types of intervention have grown, especially quantitative restrictions and financial aid, one must place things in their proper perspective. In spite of some trends to the contrary, the trade liberalization process has continued. Over the period as a whole, tariffs diminished by nearly 5 percent, while financial aids increased by 1.5 percent. Since 1975, quantitative restrictions have added a supplementary protection which contains, however, several escape clauses. Nevertheless, this did no more than somewhat attenuate the 2 percent reduction in tariffs. The trend has been clear cut, as confirmed by the data on world trade (Tables 1-23 and 1-24). Between 1965 and 1970, and between 1970 and 1975, the total GDP share of imports and exports increased on average by 5.5 percent. Between 1975 and 1980, the increase was even faster: 8.3 percent. Growth was slower from 1980 to 1982 (0.8 percent), but trade continued to grow. We believe that all statements regarding the "new protectionism" are somewhat shortsighted, because they ignore the main trend.

A theme that is found systematically in industrial policy studies is that of the growing role of the state (Warnecke, 1975, p. 1; Young and Lowe, 1975, p. 7; Le Pors, 1977, p. 8; Curzon Price, 1981, p. 19). There is a major

TABLE 1-23 Value of Exports as a Percentage of the Gross Domestic Product in Various Industrial Countries

		1950	1955	1960	1965	1970	1975	1976	1977	1978	1979	1980	1981	1982
								(percent)						
Australia	O	na	na	na	na	na	na	na	na	na	na	na	na	na
	N	30.81	16.68	14.82	15.03	14.92	15.11	15.88	15.47	16.15	16.81	16.82	15.32	15.26
Austria	O	15.25	21.09	24.03	25.76	na	na	na	na	na	na	na	na	na
	N	na	na	na	25.65	32.43	33.67	34.66	34.47	35.04	36.90	38.78	41.33	41.40
Belgium	O	na	34.17	35.41	38.68	na	na	na	na	na	na	na	na	na
	N	na	na	38.40	42.65	51.86	53.72	57.02	55.87	53.94	59.46	62.81	68.67	73.18
Canada	O	22.65	20.89	18.96	21.14	na	na	na	na	na	na	na	na	na
	N	21.49	19.38	17.50	19.17	23.34	23.28	22.78	23.97	25.82	27.81	29.03	27.79	26.23
Denmark	O	27.24	33.10	33.16	30.20	na	na	na	na	na	na	na	na	na
	N	na	na	na	na	27.91	30.08	28.84	28.81	27.79	29.24	32.71	36.18	35.58
Finland	O	22.02	21.84	23.64	21.43	na	na	na	na	na	na	na	na	na
	N	na	na	22.70	20.56	26.18	24.26	25.77	29.18	30.80	32.51	34.15	34.71	31.89
France	O	16.29	15.78	15.57	14.33	na	na	na	na	na	na	na	na	na
	N	na	na	14.99	13.77	16.34	19.54	20.16	21.33	21.26	21.93	22.28	23.80	22.20

West Germany	O	11.56	20.25	21.21	20.14	na	na	na	na	na	na	na	na	na
	N	na	na	18.99	18.05	21.18	25.04	26.30	26.07	25.50	25.73	27.14	29.88	31.07
Ireland	O	37.13	35.61	37.58	37.63	na	na	na	na	na	na	na	na	na
	N	na	na	31.87	34.81	36.96	43.43	46.98	51.19	52.53	52.82	52.25	51.90	51.03
Italy	O	na	11.28	15.42	18.03	na	na	na	na	na	na	na	na	na
	N	na	na	14.05	16.07	17.77	22.75	24.65	26.27	26.79	27.88	25.08	26.68	26.69
Japan	O	na	11.38	11.43	11.17	na	na	na	na	na	na	na	na	na
	N	na	na	na	10.53	10.81	12.82	13.62	13.18	11.22	11.72	13.94	15.08	15.28
Netherlands	O	43.38	50.53	53.36	48.37	na	na	na	na	na	na	na	na	na
	N	na	na	48.06	43.20	44.89	49.71	50.86	47.55	44.89	49.08	52.51	57.85	57.46
New Zealand	O	na	28.45	23.37	na	na	na	na	na	na	na	na	na	na
	N	na	na	22.32	21.52	22.22	23.44	27.73	27.58	27.30	28.86	29.02	28.94	28.97
Norway	O	na	41.21	41.85	40.69	na	na	na	na	na	na	na	na	na
	N	38.10	41.40	41.29	40.68	41.82	41.82	41.11	39.82	40.93	44.16	47.29	47.56	45.67
Sweden	O	24.21	24.84	25.31	23.61	na	na	na	na	na	na	na	na	na
	N	22.13	22.43	22.94	21.96	24.10	28.15	27.65	27.39	28.22	30.41	29.81	30.43	32.53
Switzerland	O	25.18	27.57	29.31	28.74	32.77	31.42	33.60	36.66	35.09	35.33	36.74	37.40	35.41
	N	na	na	na	na	na	na	na	na	na	na	na	na	na

TABLE 1-23 (cont'd)

		1950	1955	1960	1965	1970	1975	1976	1977	1978	1979	1980	1981	1982
United Kingdom	O	27.71	24.87	23.29	21.85	na	na	na	na	na	na	na	na	na
	N	na	22.94	21.12	19.48	23.45	26.40	28.81	30.63	29.11	28.77	28.20	27.45	26.97
United States	O	4.81	4.91	5.35	5.66	na	na	na	na	na	na	na	na	na
	N	4.41	5.89	5.10	5.10	5.70	8.54	8.30	7.90	8.22	9.11	10.20	9.68	8.61
Average	O	22.95	25.40	25.78	25.46	na	na	na	na	na	na	na	na	na
	N	na	na	23.87	23.01	25.99	28.34	29.48	29.80	29.74	31.48	32.47	33.72	33.59
Standard deviation	O	10.15	11.21	11.48	11.09	na	na	na	na	na	na	na	na	na
	N	na	na	11.49	11.14	11.94	12.22	12.73	12.56	12.38	13.20	13.92	15.20	15.78
Variation factor	O	0.44	0.44	0.45	0.44	na	na	na	na	na	na	na	na	na
	N	na	na	0.48	0.48	0.46	0.43	0.43	0.42	0.42	0.42	0.43	0.45	0.47
Weighted average	O	10.45	11.17	12.18	12.62	na	na	na	na	na	na	na	na	na
	N	na	na	12.40	12.56	14.42	17.44	18.08	18.09	17.79	18.68	19.48	19.96	19.89

Sources: OECD, *National Accounts of OECD Countries*, vol. 1, main aggregates, 1953, 1982 (Paris: OECD, 1984).
OECD, *National Accounts Statistics*, 1950–1968 (Paris: OECD).

O = Old OECD National Accounts system.
N = New OECD National Accounts system.

exception to this trend, since the gradual reduction in tariffs marks a withdrawal of the state in favour of the market (Blais and Faucher, 1981, p. 21). The role of the state has shrunk somewhat, and this phenomenon has been the object of little study. On the other hand, in a more specifically political perspective, the scope of the various instruments of intervention is not strictly comparable. Financial aid could be a more flexible instrument that would be more likely to maximize the influence of government in its negotiations with industry. Although state intervention is quantitatively smaller, one cannot be sure that it has lost ground in the field of industrial development.

This chapter also attempted to identify the countries that are the most and the least interventionist. Protective barriers against imports are particularly high in New Zealand, Australia, and Austria, and particularly low in the Scandinavian countries, in Switzerland, and in the United States. As regards internal aid, direct financial aid is the most appropriate criterion, because national variations are less marked than those of other instruments of intervention. Subsidies seem considerable in Ireland and Norway, and they seem to be used to a limited extent in Australia and the United States; generally speaking, they tend to be higher in Europe. Differences between countries were fairly marked but have diminished somewhat over time. In all countries, aid to industry is the responsibility mainly of the central government, although the role of local governments has grown somewhat.

Who are the major beneficiaries of government programs? A number of studies have examined the breakdown of the overall tariff and non-tariff protection that is granted to various sectors of industry (Baldwin, 1970; Cheh, 1976; Oulton, 1976; Ray, 1981a, 1981b; Caves and Jones, 1977). However, these studies are not very persuasive in view of the incomplete nature of the measures considered. Thus, Baldwin's data, which are the most commonly used for the United States, do not include direct financial aid (except road construction grants) or public contracts. In other cases (Walter, 1972b), the data specify the frequency of non-tariff barriers, but not their magnitude, and are therefore not comparable. On the other hand, the analysis of Morici and Megna (1983) is more interesting because it obviously includes many more factors, but it only deals with the U.S. situation. We therefore believe that it would be preferable to take a more quantitative approach by doing a synthesis of the trends already noted.

First of all, it is clear that agriculture, textiles, and clothing are the most favoured industries. A second group, comprising mining, shipbuilding, aeronautics, the steel industry and the computer industry, is also given fairly substantial aid. By contrast, the tertiary sector is systematically neglected. Generally speaking, declining industries are among the major beneficiaries.

Secondly, big business receives somewhat more aid from the state

TABLE 1-24 Value of Imports as a Percentage of the Gross Domestic Product in Various Industrial Countries

		1950	1955	1960	1965	1970	1975	1976	1977	1978	1979	1980	1981	1982
Australia	O	na	na	na	na	na	na	na	na	na	na	na	na	na
	N	25.48	18.79	17.81	17.41	15.09	14.87	16.58	16.61	17.41	18.23	18.92	19.30	17.39
Austria	O	19.48	22.48	25.37	26.80	na	na	na	na	na	na	na	na	na
	N	na	na	na	26.23	31.45	33.03	36.18	37.17	35.01	37.65	40.71	42.31	39.11
Belgium	O	na	32.17	35.16	37.72	na	na	na	na	na	na	na	na	na
	N	na	na	39.28	42.86	49.42	53.32	56.72	56.65	54.86	61.20	65.53	70.86	74.27
Canada	O	24.57	23.33	21.97	23.30	na	na	na	na	na	na	na	na	na
	N	21.01	20.27	18.58	19.42	20.64	24.77	23.27	23.96	25.32	27.09	27.11	26.56	22.23
Denmark	O	31.09	32.38	34.07	31.64	na	na	na	na	na	na	na	na	na
	N	na	na	na	na	30.90	31.02	33.49	32.46	29.95	32.07	33.76	35.57	35.22
Finland	O	19.28	20.39	24.53	23.85	na	na	na	na	na	na	na	na	na
	N	na	na	23.41	22.28	27.44	30.45	27.88	27.53	26.91	31.01	34.94	33.05	31.41
France	O	15.57	14.23	13.71	13.31	na	na	na	na	na	na	na	na	na
	N	na	na	12.88	12.88	15.83	18.84	21.31	21.61	20.28	21.79	24.04	25.29	25.50
West Germany	O	12.86	17.96	18.79	20.28	na	na	na	na	na	na	na	na	na
	N	na	na	16.47	17.77	19.14	22.36	24.01	23.68	22.96	25.13	27.65	29.05	28.61
Ireland	O	47.98	44.47	39.70	43.38	na	na	na	na	na	na	na	na	na
	N	na	na	37.26	43.85	44.96	48.66	53.85	59.18	61.40	68.76	65.42	66.19	58.33
Italy	O	na	12.26	15.36	14.85	na	na	na	na	na	na	na	na	na
	N	na	na	14.26	13.44	17.24	22.74	25.90	24.99	24.20	26.54	27.97	28.58	27.65
Japan	O	na	10.51	11.04	10.02	na	na	na	na	na	na	na	na	na
	N	na	na	na	9.13	9.53	12.78	12.81	11.53	9.46	12.64	14.85	14.27	14.28

Netherlands	O	49.91	47.91	50.36	47.96	na	na	na	na	na	na	na	na	na
	N	na	na	46.22	43.87	46.62	46.36	47.48	46.34	44.86	49.59	53.04	54.30	53.76
New Zealand	O	na	30.62	25.64	na	na	na	na	na	na	na	na	na	na
	N	na	na	24.56	23.73	24.97	30.36	30.80	29.36	26.48	30.57	30.19	32.15	32.27
Norway	O	na	44.78	44.61	42.22	na	na	na	na	na	na	na	na	na
	N	43.64	44.37	43.11	41.58	43.11	48.51	50.62	50.52	41.82	41.54	41.18	39.48	40.05
Sweden	O	23.55	25.51	25.80	24.61	na	na	na	na	na	na	na	na	na
	N	21.48	23.26	23.52	22.83	24.66	28.35	29.33	29.05	27.20	31.41	31.71	30.66	33.41
Switzerland	O	26.25	26.87	29.60	29.58	34.47	28.56	30.30	34.08	32.65	35.84	40.27	38.39	35.03
	N	na	na	na	na	na	na	na	na	na	na	na	na	na
United Kingdom	O	25.30	25.59	23.77	21.22	na	na	na	na	na	na	na	na	na
	N	na	24.31	22.47	20.17	22.43	27.99	29.80	29.75	27.61	28.35	25.69	24.46	24.71
United States	O	4.19	4.57	4.56	4.67	na	na	na	na	na	na	na	na	na
	N	4.03	4.29	4.39	4.44	5.49	7.78	8.69	9.33	9.64	10.32	10.99	10.46	9.57
Average	O	25.00	25.65	26.12	25.96	na	na	na	na	na	na	na	na	na
	N	na	na	24.59	23.87	26.41	29.54	31.10	31.16	29.72	32.58	33.75	34.27	33.42
Standard deviation	O	12.66	11.92	11.66	11.98	na	na	na	na	na	na	na	na	na
	N	na	na	11.93	12.30	12.74	12.83	13.62	14.17	13.77	15.12	15.10	16.01	15.90
Variation factor	O	0.51	0.46	0.45	0.44	na	na	na	na	na	na	na	na	na
	N	na	na	0.49	0.52	0.48	0.43	0.44	0.45	0.46	0.46	0.45	0.47	0.48
Weighted average	O	10.14	10.91	11.61	12.02	na	na	na	na	na	na	na	na	na
	N	na	na	11.81	12.26	13.91	17.24	18.48	18.53	17.70	19.32	20.70	20.69	20.46

Sources: See Table 1-23.
O = Old OECD National Accounts system.
N = New OECD National Accounts system.

than small business. This orientation is manifest primarily with respect to financial aid. It should be emphasized, however, that technical aid is aimed at small business and that the other instruments of intervention are fairly neutral in this respect. The favoured treatment of big business is therefore limited.

Thirdly, although the state appears to have a "favourable prejudice" toward domestic capital, it does not appear that the latter is systematically favoured at the expense of foreign capital, except in the sectors related to national security or those that have a substantial technological component, in which case public contracts play a crucial role.

Finally, aid to regional development has been considerable in virtually every country, and it developed mainly during the 1960s. In Canada, financial aid is earmarked more for peripheral regions which are, however, handicapped by the tariff protection structure. We do not have at our disposal similar data on other countries, but it can be assumed that, overall, industry located in peripheral regions is favoured.

To conclude, the extremely high stability of the distribution of government aid should be stressed. This distribution is basically similar in all the countries studied and has changed very little in the course of time. While the intensity of government intervention varied greatly from one country to the next and changed considerably during the periods studied, its overall orientation remained constant in space and time.

Chapter 2

The Choice Between State and Market

This chapter begins the more analytical portion of our study. Its basic purpose is to interpret the major trends that were noted earlier. We shall first examine the decision to aid or not to aid industry, or, more specifically, the level of government intervention in this field. Why is intervention greater in some countries, and why does it change over time? Viewed domestically, the question concerns the relative magnitude of all internal aid; viewed externally, it involves the choice between protectionism and the liberalization of trade. The discussion will primarily cover the factors that cause governments to intervene or not to intervene, either domestically or externally. In both cases, we shall begin by examining the impact of government intervention, because the actual or perceived impact will necessarily influence the policy spectrum.

Free Trade or Protectionism?

The period studied was marked by a continuing process of trade liberalization. Trade liberalization reached its peak in the 1960s, and it continues to this day, although with less momentum. We shall look closely at this basic trend, because we believe that its political, sociological, and economic impact is substantial. We shall also attempt to gain some understanding of why certain countries enthusiastically went along with this movement, while others were rather reluctant to do so. Finally, we shall look at the Canadian case, and this will lead to a discussion of the current proposals for free trade with the United States. However, the main effects of free trade must be considered first, and the extent to which these effects can influence governments' strategy must be determined.

The Impact of Free Trade

The impact most commonly ascribed to free trade is the boosting of economic growth. The issue of the gains linked to trade liberalization is a controversial one. The estimates are usually made by using complex models, and the results are highly sensitive to the underlying assumptions of these models (Whalley, 1983). Until very recently, most studies noted a very small effect, usually less than 1 percent of GDP. However, doubt has been cast on these results by Harris (1985), who uses a more sophisticated methodology, comprising certain gains (increase in competition, economies of scale, product diversity) which are not included in the usual models. Harris's estimates for Canada are in the order of 10 percent. These estimates are extremely dependent on the initial assumptions, which seem to be plausible, by and large (Markusen, 1985); but it should be pointed out that there are several such assumptions and that if one of them is invalid, the effect would be smaller.

Another way of assessing the impact of free trade is to compare the economic growth of EEC countries with that of the other countries. McCallum and Blais (1985) studied the growth rate of OECD countries during three periods (1960–67, 1967–73, and 1973–79). Among other things, they measured the impact of participation in the EEC. This impact did not turn out to be statistically significant.

It could be argued that the analysis is unsatisfactory because other countries were also exposed to free trade — those within the European Free Trade Association (EFTA). This has led us to formulate other variables in order to account for this situation. The factor to be measured was the exposure to free trade, whether within the EEC or the EFTA. Two problems arose in this respect. The first pertained to the duration of the effects. The elimination of domestic tariffs was implemented by 1966 within the EFTA and by 1968 within the EEC, but there may be some time lag before the full impact of liberalization is felt. We therefore carried out two measurements, one predicated on the assumption that the impact occurred only between 1960 and 1967, and the other on the assumption that it also occurred between 1967 and 1973. The second problem concerned the three countries (Denmark, Ireland, and the United Kingdom) which joined the EEC in 1973. In the case of Denmark and the United Kingdom, there was a switchover from a free trade area to a customs union. For these two countries, we therefore did two different measurements, one based on exposure to free trade and the other on the lack of such exposure.

We thus ended up with four measurements of the "free trade experience" variable. In all instances, all EEC or EFTA member countries had the value of "one" for the 1960–67 period, as did Ireland for the 1973–79 period. The first measurement was limited to this. The second measurement assumed that the impact of liberalization could be spread over time, and thus EEC or EFTA member countries also had the value of "one" for the 1967–73 period. The third and fourth measurements cover the case of Denmark and the United Kingdom for the period 1973–79, the third being based on the assumption that the impact of the EEC on the first member states was limited to the 1960–67 period, and the fourth assuming that the impact was felt up to 1973.

We thus had to determine whether this variable, in any of its formulations, had a significant impact on economic growth. To this end, we took as our starting point one of the equations of the McCallum and Blais study on the economic growth of 16 countries during three periods (which provided 48 observation units).[62] We then added to that equation each of the four measurements of the "free trade experience" variable. The results are shown in Table 2-1. In every case, the coefficient had the predicted result, but it was not statistically significant. These data suggest that the impact of free trade is not as substantial as some economists would like us to believe. According to these estimates, average annual growth was 0.2 percent higher in the countries exposed to free trade, for an overall gain of approximately 3 percent over a 14-year period.

Free trade also has its costs, the main ones being those that affect employment. Harris and Cox (1984) estimate that approximately 6 percent of workers should switch to another industry, and this would undoubtedly cause short-term adjustment problems. Some may wonder whether trade liberalization causes increased production instability. This does not seem to be the case. On the one hand, Henry, Koffman and Charette (1984) reported that annual changes in the sectorial distribution of production and employment have not increased in Canada and the United States since the Kennedy Round agreements became effective. On the other hand, Buzelay (1983) concluded that the opening of markets among EEC member states cannot account for the increase in their economic difficulties. Although free trade does not necessarily increase instability, it is nevertheless a source of uncertainty. It increases the collective wealth of the countries involved, but it emphasizes the competition between national outputs. All countries do not have an equal share of growth, and it may even happen that the impact of free trade for a specific country will be negative. Therefore "protection will increase welfare for a society which is strongly risk-aversive and threatened by external uncertainty" (Cable, 1983, p. 149).

It is therefore important to determine who benefits from free trade. The question can be asked from a variety of viewpoints. Internationally, one could assume that the smaller countries are favoured: the classical argument is that "the smaller country is likely to have more to gain in terms of economies of scale, since its market increases more as a result of free trade" (Wonnacott and Wonnacott, 1982, p. 422). If this is so, one should be able to observe a negative correlation between the size of a country and its economic growth over the 1960–80 period, which was marked by substantial trade liberalization.

According to another interpretation, however, economic integration,

TABLE 2-1 Free Trade Experience and Economic Growth in OECD Countries

	Impact Measured Over the 1960–67 Period (without Denmark and the U.K. for the 1973–79 period)	Impact Measured Over the 1960–73 Period (without Denmark and the U.K. for the 1973–79 period)	Impact Measured Over the 1960–67 Period (with Denmark and the U.K. for the 1973–79 period)	Impact Measured Over the 1960–73 Period (with Denmark and the U.K. for the 1973–79 period)
Convergence effect	−0.97 (1.82)[a]	−0.99 (1.89)	−0.96 (1.79)	−0.96 (8.83)
Change in total employment	0.61 (5.11)	0.64 (5.18)	0.61 (5.06)	0.64 (5.15)
Social security transfers	0.09 (3.33)	0.09 (3.12)	0.09 (3.37)	0.09 (3.25)
Institutional sclerosis	−0.03 (3.75)	−0.03 (3.82)	−0.03 (3.73)	−0.03 (3.87)
Period effect (1973–79)	−2.17 (6.65)	−2.17 (6.67)	−2.18 (7.86)	−2.12 (7.73)
Impact of free trade	0.07 (0.25)	0.19 (0.75)	0.06 (0.23)	0.16 (0.69)
Constant	4.40 (5.69)	4.32 (5.77)	4.43 (5.93)	4.39 (5.98)
n	48	48	48	48
R^2	0.823	0.828	0.822	0.827

a. Student t test.

TABLE 2-2 **Correlation Between Economic Growth, the Size and the Wealth of the Country, for EEC or EFTA Member Countries, 1960–67**

	Simple Correlation	Partial Correlation
Size	−0.24 (*Pr* = 0.24)	−0.20 (*Pr* = 0.29)
Wealth	−0.56 (*Pr* = 0.04)	−0.55 (*Pr* = 0.05)

Note: We have grouped together Belgium, the Netherlands and Luxembourg, which already constituted a free trade zone prior to the creation of the EEC; this yielded 11 observation units.

which usually presumes the creation of new political institutions, has the main result of weakening those pressure groups, in a given country, which tend to block changes that favour efficiency and growth, in order to protect their narrower interests (Olson, 1982). Since institutional sclerosis affects all countries, regardless of size, economic integration would have equally beneficial effects in large and small countries.

Within the same perspective, the development level of a country can determine the benefits it will receive from free trade. Free trade can increase the probability of a convergence phenomenon (Abramovitz, 1983), thus favouring the less developed countries. On the other hand, Bairoch (1976, p. 294) noted that in the 19th century, "pour la quasi-totalité des pays de l'Europe, la phase libérale s'est traduite par une évolution défavorable, entraînant un élargissement de l'écart qui les sépare du pays le plus développé" ("in almost all European countries, the liberal phase was reflected by an unfavourable evolution that increased the gap between them and the most developed country").

The McCallum and Blais (1985) study on the economic growth of OECD countries during the 1960–80 period showed, firstly, that the size of a country does not appear to be a significant variable, contrary to what the classical thesis predicts. The same trend emerges when one considers only those countries that have been exposed to free trade within the framework of the EEC or EFTA. Among these countries, the correlation between size and economic growth, from 1960 to 1967, was very low (Table 2-2). This would indicate that the effects of free trade are altogether different from what classic economic theory predicts and it would rather tend to confirm Olson's interpretation.

Moreover, it does indeed appear that the least developed countries benefit most from free trade. On the one hand, the McCallum and Blais study (1985) confirms that there has been a convergence phenomenon since 1960. On the other hand, Table 2-2 shows a high negative correlation between economic growth during the period 1960–67, and the wealth of a country in 1960, among EEC and EFTA member countries.

The impact of trade liberalization on social economic disparities must also be discussed. The usual argument is that protectionism is regressive because "the incidence of federal import duties tends to fall relatively more heavily on low income groups" (Daly and Globerman, 1976, p. 20). This conclusion must largely be qualified. The theory according to which consumption tax is regressive rests "on evidence from cross-section data which shows that in any particular year, low-income families will on the average consume a higher fraction of their income, than will high-income families" (Musgrave and Musgrave, 1980, p. 453). In fact, income fluctuates substantially from one year to the next (Lilla, 1984), and this undoubtedly obscures the results:

> Households in any given income bracket, will include those whose income is permanently in that bracket as well as others who occupy it only temporarily. In the low brackets, these temporary groups will typically consist of units whose income is normally higher. If such households tend to maintain past consumption patterns, they will consume more than do households with permanently low income. . . . As a result, use of such cross-section data overstates the decline in the average propensity to consume when moving up the income scale. . . . Indeed if all income were consumed over a person's lifetime the consumption tax would be proportional in relation to lifetime income (Musgrave and Musgrave, 1980, pp. 453–54).

In summary, like consumption tax, tariffs are only slightly regressive.

One might also wonder whether trade liberalization is more beneficial to certain types of firm. For instance, it might favour big business. Indeed, big business is more export-oriented (Galbraith, 1984, Table 1) and is therefore in a better position to take advantage of the opening up of foreign markets. However, the main parties involved seem to have a different view. Bauer, De Sola Pool and Dexter (1972, Table 9-1, p. 131) report that in the United States small business is not greatly in favour of protectionism. A survey of the Canadian Manufacturers' Association (CMA press release, December 9, 1980) indicated that small firms believe, more so than large firms, that they would be in a position to profit from a free trade zone with the United States. The same conclusion applies when comparing multinationals with national firms. Indeed, according to the CMA survey, Canadian firms are more optimistic than foreign firms as regards the impact of a free trade zone with the United States. Evidently, more detailed studies are required. However, we believe that the assumption that free trade is more favourable to big business is quite plausible. The main effect of free trade is to promote economic growth. However, that growth is, unfortunately, accompanied by some adjustment costs in the field of employment and by increased uncertainty. In the recent past, the least developed countries have benefited the most from it. Domestically, large firms appear to be in the best position to benefit.

The Political Dynamics

We are now ready to deal with our central issue regarding the causes of free trade and of its opposite, namely, protectionism. We should first determine, statically, to what extent the macroeconomic impact of free trade renders this option politically attractive, thus providing a potential explanation for the liberalization movement noted since the end of World War II. We shall then take a more dynamic look at the link between the economic situation and trade policy. Thirdly, we shall look at the differences between states: Why are some countries more protectionist than others? Finally, we believe it is important to look at the internal political dynamics in order to determine the role of the major social groups, particularly business and unions. Although we have concluded that tariffs are not very regressive, it would be useful to see how the groups involved define their interests and to assess their degree of influence.

Economic Performance and Political Calculation

The main argument of free trade advocates is that governments should promote trade liberalization because it makes greater economic growth possible. Indeed, governments are interested in growth because numerous studies have shown that their popularity is greatly affected by macroeconomic conditions, and particularly by income growth (Winn, 1985; Johnston, 1985). However, there is no guarantee whatever that governments try to maximize growth, since they probably aim at moderate, stable growth. Indeed, prosperity favours governments proportionately less than a recession penalizes them (Bloom and Price, 1975). Politicians therefore "are more likely to maximize their support by establishing a stable pattern of earnings even if over the full course of the business cycle an unstable pattern would give private groups higher total incomes" (Krasner, 1978, p. 40).

Reiterating the thesis of Mosley (1976, p. 60):

> Government decision-makers . . . have not thought in terms of optima but rather in terms of values of targets which are satisfactory or unsatisfactory, i.e., they have considered that unemployment, say, or the rate of growth, did or did not need something to be done about it.

Although the economic consequences of free trade are still favourable overall from the politician's viewpoint, they are perhaps not as substantial as they would first seem and they are certainly not sufficient to determine trade policy by themselves. One might assume that, as regards this criterion, governments have a "favourable prejudice" but that other considerations could easily tip the scales the other way. Moreover, governments would only engage in free trade experiments with great care, since they are very concerned by the potential imbalances which may result. Ruggie (1983) noted that this is the thrust of the international arrangements that were concluded immediately after the war: the compromise, which he calls "embedded liberalism," consists of a greater opening up of the world economy, offset by government intervention designed to minimize its costs:

> Governments . . . would seek to encourage an international division of labor which, while multilateral in form and reflecting some notion of comparative advantage (and therefore gains from trade), also promised to minimize socially disruptive domestic adjustment costs as well as any national economic and political vulnerabilities that might accrue from international functional differentiation (Ruggie, 1983, p. 215).

In summary, although the economic advantages of free trade are not to be ignored, this is only one of government's trade policy criteria. As emphasized by Baldwin (1979, p. 233), "the belief that trade liberalization was an essential part of U.S. foreign policy accounts in considerable part for the strong liberalization trend in the administration of these presidents." Along the same lines, Kreinin (1980, p. 704) stated:

> During the 1940s and 1950s, the main thrust of the legislation was designed to forge a strong and coherent western alliance. . . . Absent from the legislative motives in those years was a desire to improve the efficiency of the economy.

This was also the case in the 19th century:

> Political rather than commercial or philosophical considerations motivated Britain's shift in its commercial practices. Both Britain and France looked to a commercial agreement as a basis for improving their relations (Stern, 1984, p. 364).

The Economic Situation

From a more dynamic viewpoint, a different argument states that protectionist and anti-protectionist trends are strongly influenced by the economic situation, with the liberalization process occurring during periods of prosperity and with protectionism arising during recessions. The data of McKeown (1984) and Gallarotti (1985), regarding the United States, Germany, and Great Britain during the 19th century, corroborate this hypothesis. Indeed, the 1945–85 period was one of unprecedented growth, and this economic background was highly favourable to the trend toward lower tariffs. According to the same logic, the fact that growth was slower during the 1970s could explain why the liberalization process, although it was maintained, was less vigorous. As regards Canada, Protheroe (1980, p. 76) noted that "in periods of greater unemployment, Finance has been more accepting of protective measures."

It remains to be explained why the economic situation so influences policy choices. One could imagine the opposite, namely that only when the economy is in dire straits will governments feel forced to avoid protectionism in order to boost output. In this respect, McKeown formulated an interesting hypothesis:

> If governments desire lower tariffs but are constrained from adopting them by the political strength of domestic protectionist forces, then governments will risk implementing tariff reduction only when they are already enjoying a large "surplus" of popularity. . . . If governments are more popular during prosperity than during depression, then tariff reductions will tend to occur during the peaks of business cycles (McKeown, 1983, pp. 87–89).

This argument is based on three assumptions. First, it assumes that, socially, the protectionist camp is stronger than the free trade advocates. We shall see later that this assertion is possible as regards interest groups only. In a subsequent article, McKeown also explained why protectionist pressure is greater during a recession:

> Since rates of entry into a sector tend to be positively related to that sector's rate of demand growth, we would expect entry rates to be smaller during a depression than during a period of prosperity. This implies that for a given level of protection the producers' surplus created by protective measures will be bid away by new entrants more slowly during the trough of a business cycle than during the peak. . . . Moreover, since during the trough the expected utility of exit into a more remunerative line of business is lower than at the peak, firms are more likely to resort to "voice" (i.e., political action) at such a time (McKeown, 1984, p. 219).

Secondly, governments are presented as preferring free trade and attempting to resist protectionist pressures. This view is probably correct for the period under study, since politicians and bureaucrats[63] naturally subscribe to the standard of the most open possible world economy (regarding the importance of norms, see Krasner, 1983). The study by Takacs (1981), moreover, tends to corroborate this hypothesis. Takacs demonstrated first of all that the requests for defensive steps increase substantially in the United States whenever the economic situation is poor. However, the trend is much less clear as regards decisions made by the administration, and this suggests that the government does indeed try to resist protectionist demands. These results indicate that "although the pressure for protection increases in times of economic stress, the government does not necessarily respond to it, perhaps in an attempt to avoid duplicating the counterproductive beggar-thy-neighbor policies of the 1930s" (Takacs, 1981, p. 691).

Finally, McKeown believes that only when governments are enjoying exceptional popularity do they take the risk of reducing tariffs. This last statement is more doubtful. Indeed, everything seems to indicate that politicians rarely feel that they are excessively popular.[64] In fact, though, this assertion is not really necessary. As pointed out by McKeown himself, during prosperous times, firms probably have no precise stand regarding tariff policy, and this leaves the government a great deal of elbow room:

> Officials will time their proposals to fall within periods of prosperity because of the previously noted relationship between prosperity and the attractiveness to firms of exiting from economically or politically disadvantaged sectors. If exiting is easy, firms opposed to reduction will be much less likely to resist them strenuously or to seek to remove officials who propose them (McKeown, 1984, p. 220).

The economic situation thus has a substantial impact on trade policy. From this viewpoint, it seems extremely significant that the liberalization movement continued during the 1970s and even the 1980s, despite a large decline in economic growth. The economic situation is not inoperative, as it undermines that movement, but it is not sufficient to reverse the trend.

Comparative Advantages

The economic situation can account, at least in part, for the evolution of tariffs over time. We must also look at the variation in protection by country. The most important theory in this respect is that of hegemonic stability, which assumes that "the existence of a state possessing clear superiority over its nearest rivals — the United Kingdom in much of the 19th century and the United States in much of the 20th — is a necessary and sufficient condition for an open system to emerge" (McKeown, 1983, p. 73).

This theory has the advantage of simultaneously explaining changes in time and changes in space. The hegemonic country is less protectionist than others, and it is in a hegemonic system that trade liberalization is most likely to occur, since the hegemonic country manages to impose the momentum. Systematic discussion of this hypothesis would require a whole chapter (or even a book). We shall limit ourselves here to a number of comments. Firstly, although the concept of hegemony is ambiguous (McKeown, 1983), there is no doubt that Great Britain, for most of the 19th century, and the United States, for most of the 20th century, were dominant powers. We should begin, then, by determining their level of protection. According to Conybeare (1983, Table 1), Great Britain was the only country where tariff protection (within the manufacturing sector) was nonexistent at the beginning of the century, which tends to corroborate the hegemonic thesis. The case of the United States is more complex. U.S. tariffs, although lower than average, are not the lowest. On the other hand, as we saw in Chapter 1, the United States is probably the country where tariff reductions since World War II have been the most substantial. The hypothesis therefore retains some plausibility.

However, it is less certain that the existence of a hegemonic system is a prerequisite for the establishment of a liberalization movement. Of course, this argument seems valid as regards the recent past:

> The G.A.T.T.'s origins are to be found in Washington; its early elaboration came in talks between the Americans and the British. The U.S. also set the pace and limits of tariff reductions within the G.A.T.T. Multilateral negotiations have always followed the President's authorization by Congress to begin such talks, and the terms of congressional authorization have always established the limits of multilateral trade liberalization (Lipson, 1983, p. 235).

On the other hand, it should be stressed that the Kennedy Round and the Tokyo Round occurred at times when American power was in relative decline (Krasner, 1976). As regards the 19th century, McKeown concluded that Britain's efforts to bring down the tariffs of the other countries were quite limited: "British efforts simply were not successful in inducing major changes in other states' tariffs; when tariff liberalization occurred, it was in the absence of British pressure" (McKeown, 1983, p. 88). In summary, although it seems that a hegemonic power generally tends to adopt a more open trade policy, this hypothesis sheds no light on "the motivations and capabilities of the nonhegemonic states that are most likely to rival the hegemonic power" (ibid., p. 76) and it cannot account for changes over time (see also Lawson, 1983; Stern, 1984).

Yet why would the hegemonic powers be more favourably inclined toward free trade? Krasner makes the clearest statement in this respect:

> The hegemonic state will have a preference for an open structure. Such a structure increases its aggregate national income. It also increases its rate of growth during its ascendency — that is, when its relative size and technological lead are increasing. Further, an open structure increases its political power, since the opportunity costs of closure are least for a large and developed state (Krasner, 1976, p. 322).

This last point is particularly important. Free trade creates an interdependence situation which emphasizes the vulnerability of small countries. With their more open economy, they would be affected to a greater extent than large states by an eventual return to protectionism. On the other hand, in the short term, liberalization affords greater benefits to the least developed countries, and it is by no means a foregone conclusion that the hegemonic power will be more of a "winner" than the other states. As emphasized by Stern, "Great Britain and the United States accepted a system for which they bore higher costs than did others" (Stern, 1984, p. 383).

The explanation might have to be provided by socialization rather than by "rational" calculation, whether economic or political. Perhaps the political leaders of hegemonic powers, because of their very function, have more of a "world" outlook and are therefore more sympathetic to free trade. It should be recalled that according to Bauer,

De Sola Pool and Dexter (1972, p. 168), travel has a considerable impact on the attitudes of American businessmen:

> The political effect of travel on tariff attitudes was to counteract the force of self-interest. It made a man see the trade issue in national terms rather than in the parochial terms of his own industry.

This interpretation is rendered particularly plausible by the fact that the political leaders of a declining power do not appear to alter their perspective in any way:

> Great Britain was, in the 1920s, in the peculiar and ambiguous position that confronts all imperial powers during their decline. National interests might best have been served by abandoning the principles of free trade but such action would be extremely difficult. It would imply that the nation's status had changed (Krasner, 1978, p. 111).

In summary, the hegemonic powers seem indeed to be more protectionist, probably mainly on ideological grounds rather than for economic reasons. However, it is not at all certain that the existence of a hegemonic "system" is a sine qua non condition of the liberalization process.

Are there other variables that account for the national variations in tariff rates? Katzenstein (1980) claims that the smaller states are usually less protectionist, but Conybeare (1983, p. 460) stresses that the average tariff of the small states cited by Katzenstein does not differ from that of the larger states and that it is even higher if Australia and New Zealand are included among the small states. Conybeare examined four models which could explain the average manufacturing tariff of 35 countries in 1971. The model that gave the best results was that of "rational domestic economic policy," which assumed that "tariffs are primarily a function of the level of a country's economic development" (Conybeare, 1983, p. 450). However, this result is somewhat suspect because the sampling of countries selected by Conybeare was very heterogeneous, and this creates all kinds of difficulties, as stated in the Introduction. The size of the agricultural sector could be another relevant variable. We noted in Chapter 1 that "agricultural" countries received special treatment during the Kennedy Round negotiations.

In order to test these hypotheses, we traced the link between the average manufacturing tariff at the end of the 1970s[65] and the size, wealth, and employment of the agricultural sector.[66] We effected regressions including the 18 countries, and other regressions excluding New Zealand, where tariffs are particularly high, or excluding the United States, which might have a different behaviour inasmuch as it is a hegemonic state, or excluding both countries together. We also ran regressions comprising the three variables, or only two of them. All equations were found to be non-significant. Agricultural size, wealth, and employment thus have no direct link with protectionism.

Very little is known about the reasons why some countries are more protectionist than others. This is perhaps not surprising. Inasmuch as tariff protection is part of a historical continuum (Lavergne, 1983), any study that fails to take into account this historical dimension is bound to be rather unsatisfactory. Otherwise, we think that only one generalization seems reliable, namely that hegemonic powers are more favourable to trade liberalization, though this is for reasons that are more ideological than economic.

Interest Groups

Amerian Business and Public Policy is undoubtedly the most important study that has been made on the trade policy of any country. The main theme of the book is "a critique of an assumption that has been unduly shared by pluralists and antipluralists alike: that interest groups act rationally to serve their own interests" (Bauer, De Sola Pool and Dexter, 1972, p. viii). More specifically, this study shows that interest groups are much less organized than is often believed:

> Lobbies were on the whole poorly financed, ill-managed, out of contact with Congress, and at best, only marginally effective in supporting tendencies and measures which already had behind them considerable Congressional impetus from other sources" (Bauer, De Sola Pool and Dexter, 1972, p. 324).

The authors stress the even more basic fact that, in several instances, the interests of a firm or industrial sector were ambiguous so that "the pressure groups not only activated but defined the self-interest of the members of the coalitions" (ibid., p. 373). The authors concluded:

> The formal acts of economic calculation acquire their concrete content only through acts of communication and social influence. Neither a simple study of influence processes nor a simple study of economic interests without their interaction could have yielded much understanding of the behavior of our business respondents (ibid., p. 475).

A theme that keeps recurring in trade policy studies is the claim that protectionist forces are better organized than free trade forces. Protheroe, for example, noted that "the distribution of these resources among Canadian interest groups appears to have a protectionist bias on the making of Canadian trade policy" (Protheroe, 1980, p. 35). The logic is very well summarized by McKeown:

> A common observation about tariff politics is that since the gains from protection are concentrated while the gains from free trade are diffuse, it is easier for protectionists to organize and achieve their political demands than it is for free-traders (McKeown, 1984, p. 218).

This can be readily recognized as one of the main tenets of Olson's model (1965) on the formation of interest groups (see also Migué, 1979). Such a trend is usually presumed rather than demonstrated. On this point, too, the study of Bauer, De Sola Pool and Dexter is revealing. The authors found that protectionist businessmen were more likely to discuss trade policy with their colleagues and to write to their member of Parliament. Moreover:

> A mixed interest, for example on the part of a diversified company, stimulated action that could only with difficulty be distinguished from protectionist action. The protectionist component of the company's interest strongly dominated the export interest (Bauer, De Sola Pool and Dexter, 1972, p. 221).

Their analysis of lobby activities caused them to conclude:

> The protectionist tactic of mobilizing people and groups on the basis of direct self-interest is more effective in the short haul in producing political action than a more diffuse approach attempting to reach larger groups on the basis of the general interest (ibid., p. 397).

Baldwin's (1976) data corroborate this; they indicate that the way members of Congress vote on trade policy bills is influenced by the presence, within their constituency, of industries that are strongly affected by imports, but not by the presence of industries that are primarily export-oriented. This suggests that "workers and management who think they are being adversely affected by imports are apparently able collectively to persuade their congressmen to vote against trade liberalization. However, export oriented industries are not similarly successful" (Baldwin, 1976, p. 36). In spite of this, the period covered by our study was marked by a trade liberalization movement. This general trend can obviously not be explained by the impact of interest groups. As stated by Bauer, De Sola Pool and Dexter (1972, pp. 397–98):

> An image of the general interest which was diffused through myriad channels of mass media and citizen discussion promised in the end to triumph over rear-guard actions by even the cleverest of pressure groups.

This further supports the hypothesis that has already been proposed, to the effect that governments have a favourable prejudice toward free trade and that they can be fairly successful in resisting protectionist pressures.

More recently, a number of economists attempted to account for the tariff protection structure by using models that were more or less related to interest group theory (for Canada, see particularly Caves, 1976, and Helleiner, 1977). Their method is well summarized by Lavergne:

> Faced with a choice between "leverage" and "principled" explanation of tariffs, economists tend to favor the former, probably because it is consistent with their training and permits an extension of economic models of behavior to the political sphere. . . . These authors, among others, see

tariffs as being set in a political "market." These actors are rational, self-interested economic persons who form the demand and supply sides of that market. Demand is represented by the pressures exercised by interest groups who seek aid for their industries, whereas politicians, by virtue of their privileged positions, supply tariffs and other forms of assistance to the point where personal profit is maximized (Lavergne, 1983, p. 12).

Lavergne's data (which we saw, in Chapter 1, to be the most reliable) cast a great deal of doubt on the usefulness of this model:

> When all the analysis is done, the pressure group variables must be said to perform very weakly. As a group . . . they play a minor role in each of the regressions or tend to yield contradictory results. Experiments which were expected to enhance the likelihood of finding positive results for the group of variables also were disappointing (Lavergne, 1983, p. 155).

Lavergne concluded that "these results . . . constitute a fairly strong case against the likely importance of pressure group influence in tariff-setting" (1983, p. 184).

In Canada, businessmen have been the prime advocates of free trade with the United States, and this could be taken to mean that the issue is structured on the basis of class interests. However, a broader analysis of the stand taken by employers and unions in other countries shows that it would be risky to draw general conclusions. As regards the EEC, the study by Haas (1968) shows that the positions of the two groups varied substantially from one country to another and that one could not claim, overall, that employers were more (or less) favourably inclined toward economic integration than the unions were. The same applies to the United States, where "the defection of the labor movement from the cause of free trade" is a recent phenomenon (Bauer, De Sola Pool and Dexter, 1972, p. xviii; see also Baldwin, 1979; Allen and Walter, 1970). The orientation of business and unions is therefore far from cast in concrete, and it is strongly affected by the historical and national context. Unfortunately, we are not aware of any study that specifies the factors of those contexts which determine the way in which these two groups see their interests in this area.

The period covered by our study was marked by substantial trade liberalization. We believe that three main factors were responsible for the trend: the existence of a military alliance between the major capitalist countries, the fact that free trade has virtually won the ideological battle following a depression and two world wars, and the remarkable economic growth over the entire period. One might wonder how long this trend will continue. A great deal of caution is in order here. However, as we pointed out in Chapter 1, in spite of all the claims that a return to protectionism is occurring, the trend has not been reversed, even during very difficult economic times. This leads us to maintain the assessment made in 1981:

> We believe that this failure really to revert to mercantilism during a period of relative recession is highly significant. We believe it is the manifestation of a qualitative change in the operation and organization of capitalist production relationships. Since a large portion of production is widely scattered, the trend to growing trade is now part and parcel of the operation of the world system. We have reached the point of no return (Blais and Faucher, 1981, p. 24; translation).

The Canadian Case

The major issue in Canadian trade policy concerns the possibility of a free trade zone with the United States. The "American" option is not new (Granatstein, 1985) but it has gained a lot of ground recently, for reasons that should be examined. We believe that three factors are particularly relevant. The first factor is the Americans' fear of a return to protectionism:

> Ironically, one of the strongest arguments in support of bilateral initiative is U.S. protectionism. . . . Because of Canada's heavy reliance on the U.S. as an export market, the greatest international economic threat facing Canada is U.S. protectionism (Finlayson, 1985).

One must therefore recognize the large degree of Canadian economic dependence on the U.S. economy and the risks this entails if the United States ever decided to close its borders to Canadian goods. From this viewpoint, it is in Canada's interest to take refuge under the U.S. umbrella in order to preserve its main export market. We have stated that this new protectionism has not yet truly occurred and that it remains unlikely in the short and the medium term, barring a very serious economic or political crisis. Nevertheless, the dominant perception is that of an upsurge in U.S. protectionism, and this perception clearly influences the strategy of Canadian industrialists, bureaucrats, and politicians.

The second factor is the economic situation. The hard 1982 recession has shaken a lot of people and has triggered the search for new solutions. From a symbolic viewpoint, the American option provides a new "objective" to replace the National Policy which was adopted at the end of the last century and which remains very much an element in the public debate, although it is no longer in line with present practice. Recessions usually tend to reinforce protectionism, whereas the opposite seems to occur here. The Canadian reaction may thus seem surprising. This is not a new phenomenon. "Reciprocity discussions between Canada and the United States historically have intensified when times were bad" (Granatstein, 1985). This leads us to believe that in a "small" country such as Canada, the return to protectionism is excluded from the outset (thus confirming Krasner's hypothesis regarding the vulnerability of small states) and that the choice is between the status quo and greater trade liberalization (Blais, 1985b). Moreover, the American option is particularly attractive at a time when the Canadian economy is ailing and when the U.S. economic performance is better.

This brings us to the last factor, that of the political context. Inasmuch as "nationalist feeling among many English-speaking Canadians is closely tied to a negative reaction to American cultural and economic penetration of Canada" (Sigler and Goresky, 1974, p. 665), the Canadian people's image of U.S. society is no doubt important. In the 1950s, this image was extremely positive. Most Canadians believed that the Canadian lifestyle was not too influenced by the United States (Schwartz, 1967, p. 69). In the 1960s, the image of the Unites States deteriorated considerably (Sigler and Goresky, 1974, p. 641). As Sigler and Goresky point out (ibid., p. 666), "public moods in English-speaking Canada toward the United States are strongly affected by the drama of national politics in the United States. The Camelot to Watergate decade has left its traces on Canadian confidence in American leadership."

However, as events such as the Vietnam War and Watergate have gradually been forgotten, the image of the United States has improved.[67] The percentage of Canadians who think that American investment is a "bad thing" has been declining since 1974 (Murray and LeDuc, 1982, p. 221). In addition, since Quebec separatism no longer appears to be a serious threat to the national identity, the context seems fairly favourable to the American option.

One of the most difficult questions raised by the debate on a potential free trade zone with the United States is how real this option might be. The Canadian and U.S. economies are already highly integrated; tariffs on the products of the two countries will be virtually nonexistent by 1987, when the Tokyo Round agreements will have been implemented. One may wonder whether creating a free trade zone will really have a significant impact. The latest estimates of the effects of a multilateral cancellation of tariffs suggest a GDP increase of approximately 10 percent (Harris, 1985). We have already stated that this estimate is optimistic, as the impact of the EEC and EFTA was around 3 percent. Moreover, these estimates were made on the basis of the protection prevailing in the mid-1970s, and this will have diminished by approximately 40 percent by 1987. On the other hand, although (as we have already stated) the effects of free trade are political as much as economic, inasmuch as creation of a new jurisdiction weakens existing interest groups that oppose economic growth-generating innovations (Olson, 1982), the potential impact of the American option is not negligible.

The same problem arises regarding the potential consequences to the political sovereignty of Canada, which is the main concern of those who oppose the American option. Once again, things should be put in their proper perspective. The two economies are already so integrated that there could not possibly be any dramatic qualitative change. In many respects, the creation of a free trade zone would merely render official a situation that already exists. However, this is not a minor thing if one recognizes that symbols can be extremely important (Edelman, 1964). The problem is then considerably different, and explicit recognition of Canada's economic dependence might only serve to emphasize the need to affirm the uniqueness of Canada, inasmuch as it exists, politically and culturally (see Balthazar, 1983).

In summary, the American option gains attractiveness if the threat of U.S. protectionism grows, if the economic recovery is not too strong, if the U.S. economic performance exceeds the Canadian one,[68] and if the global image of U.S. society is not too negative.

Internal Aid: Intervention or Laisser-faire Policies

The choice between state intervention and non-intervention must also be made internally. We saw in Chapter 1 that aid to industry has grown throughout the period, with rapid expansion between 1970 and 1975. We also singled out certain groups of nations according to the magnitude of the aid granted. The main factors that could account both for the overall evolution and the differences between countries should now be discussed. As in the preceding section, we shall first examine the impact of government measures in this sector. Analysis will primarily cover grants to industry, on which we have more complete data and which, as shown in Chapter 1, constitute the main form of aid.

Impact of Internal Aid

Industrial policy is usually linked to growth and productivity objectives. Thus, according to an OECD document (1975, p. 7), "la politique industrielle a pour but de promouvoir la croissance et l'efficacité de l'industrie" ("the purpose of industrial policy is to promote industrial growth and efficiency"). Unfortunately, virtually no study has attempted to measure the actual effectiveness of industry aid programs (OECD, 1978, 1983e; Economic Council of Canada, 1983; Grant, 1983); thus the tendency is to hide behind general considerations or merely to quantify the cost of the programs.

Most economists seem fairly skeptical as to the effectiveness of state intervention in the industrial sector. The main guidelines proposed by Watson (1983) for politicians are clear: the state should only intervene if it is demonstrated that the market does not allow optimum resource allocation and that the government can really improve things. In summary, "government should probably do everything possible to avoid making detailed allocative decisions" (ibid., p. 104). The crux of Watson's argument is that although the market is not perfect, government intervention is not perfect either and its shortcomings may well be greater. On the one hand, there is no certainty that politicians and bureaucrats really want to maximize efficiency; instead, their policies may be based more on their desire to defend their own interests (ibid., pp. 26–29). On the other hand, it is more difficult for the government to assess its interventions, since it does not have a precise criterion — the equivalent in the private sector of profits and the ability to withdraw when a project is not profitable (ibid., p. 30).

Nevertheless, the notion that industrial policy is the key to economic development is still widespread. The reason for this is simple. The two countries where the state seems to intervene most systematically — Japan and France — have had remarkably high rates of growth. It is very tempting to discern here a cause-and-effect relationship. Thus, Zysman, although carefully noting that a government's interventionist measures can have unfavourable effects, claims that "government policies can create or maintain competitive advantage for firms in international markets and over time can reshape the comparative advantage of the national economy" (Zysman, 1983, p. 313).

Finally, according to another interpretation (Brenner and Courville, 1985), the impact of industrial policy varies depending on the context. Where there is already a certain social and political stability, state intervention usually has a negative impact on innovation and therefore on growth, for the reasons stated by Watson. On the other hand, stability is a prerequisite for innovation, and inasmuch as state intervention contributes to that stability, it may therefore be beneficial. The same reasoning, made by McCallum and Blais regarding social policy, could also apply to industrial aid:

> The welfare state may help to facilitate growth and change by compensating those who would otherwise be the losers in the growth process. If potential losers know that they will receive at least partial compensation for the losses, then they may offer less resistance to the resource reallocation that is required for economic growth (McCallum and Blais, 1985).

The impact of internal aid to industry may thus vary depending on the situation, on the instruments, and on the target involved. In Chapters 3 and 4 we shall examine in greater detail certain types of intervention. For the time being, we are looking only at the overall trends. On the one hand, as far as formulation is concerned, industrial policy is defined in terms of growth and efficiency. On the other hand, the economists are mostly skeptical as to its real impact. Where, in fact, does the truth lie?

A first step would be to simulate the impact of certain government measures, using a general equilibrium model. This is the approach used by Harris (1985), who thus estimated the effect of job, investment, and export subsidies, as well as the effect of production rationalization through the disappearance of one-half of firms (through mergers).

Except in the latter case, whose actuality is particularly doubtful, the consequences seem to be systematically negative. Carlsson (1983), in turn, simulated the impact of selective subsidies to a few firms, including general employment and export subsidies, using a microeconomic model comprising 140 firms. The verdict was fairly positive: "Compared to the laissez-faire case, the effects are very favorable in the short-run and yet not particularly costly in the long-run." However, the conclusion remains uncertain, because Carlsson added that "it is likely that the negative long-run effects of the selective subsidy policy relative to the laissez-faire policy are underestimated" (ibid., p. 18).

The conclusions of such simulations, which are based on a great number of assumptions, are very fragile. In our opinion, it would be useful to determine more directly whether there is a link between the size of a country's aid to industry and the economic performance of that country. We shall therefore once again use the data of the McCallum and Blais (1985) study on the economic growth of 16 OECD countries over three periods (1960–67, 1967–73, and 1973–79). Taking the four equations in Table 2-1 as our reference point, we have added a new variable, corresponding to the percentage of operating grants relative to the GDP at the beginning of each period (1960, 1967, 1973). The results are shown in Table 2-3. In each case, the overall impact of aid to industry seems nil. This tends to confirm the Brenner and Courville model, which would indicate that the effect of government measures is closely dependent on the social and political context. Certain types of aid probably have positive effects upon growth, while others have negative effects, so that the overall impact is more or less nil.

The Political Dynamics

Our primary goal, however, is to explain why aid to industry has been growing over time and why it varies from one country to another. There are virtually no studies on this issue.[69] Hence, we shall do an empirical analysis; although only exploratory, this should provide some interpretation elements. Table 1-12 showed the relative magnitude of grants to industry in the various countries. Our objective is to identify the variables that can account for the national variations in 1980.

Nine independant variables have been retained for the study. A first bloc of four variables pertains to the link between aid to industry and other aspects of government intervention. The first one is the size of the state (STATE). Aid to industry, indeed, could be seen as but one of many aspects of government intervention, and its magnitude is likely to rise if there is a strong tradition of government intervention. Thus, there would be "strong" and "weak" states (Katzenstein, 1983), this characteristic being apparent in aid to industry as in other fields. The same theme is broached in King's (1973) study on government policy in France, Great

TABLE 2-3 Impact of Grants to Industry on Economic Growth

	Impact Measured Over the 1960–67 Period (without Denmark and the U.K. for the 1973–79 period)	Impact Measured Over the 1960–73 Period (without Denmark and the U.K. for the 1973–79 period)	Impact Measured Over the 1960–67 Period (with Denmark and the U.K. for the 1973–79 period)	Impact Measured Over the 1960–73 Period (with Denmark and the U.K. for the 1973–79 period)
Convergence effect	−0.78 (1.38)[a]	−0.80 (1.43)	−0.78 (1.37)	−0.79 (1.40)
Change in total employment	0.59 (4.98)	0.62 (5.02)	0.59 (4.92)	0.62 (4.98)
Social security transfers	0.09 (3.32)	0.09 (3.13)	0.09 (3.35)	0.09 (3.24)
Institutional sclerosis	−0.03 (3.65)	−0.03 (3.71)	−0.03 (3.59)	−0.03 (3.72)
Period effect (1973–79)	−2.27 (6.54)	−2.16 (6.56)	−2.28 (7.60)	−2.21 (7.48)
Impact of free trade	0.04 (0.12)	0.15 (0.60)	0.02 (0.70)	0.12 (0.52)
Grants to industry	0.07 (0.85)	0.07 (0.80)	0.07 (0.84)	0.06 (0.79)
Constant	4.39 (5.65)	4.32 (5.72)	4.41 (5.86)	4.38 (5.90)
n	48	48	48	48
R^2	0.820	0.825	0.820	0.824

a. Student t test.

Britain, West Germany, the United States, and Canada. King shows that the differences between countries, particularly those between the United States and the European countries, do not vary from one intervention sector to another.

The second variable is the magnitude of social security transfers (SECURITY). The transfers could be seen as a substitute for industrial aid. Thus, Chandler (1985) and Trebilcock (1985) show that the West German state intervenes little in aid to declining firms or industries, and it emphasizes instead a general manpower policy. Within this perspective, the existence of a well-developed social security system would reduce the need for aid to industry.

Throughout Chapter 1, we also insisted on the interdependence of the internal and external components of aid to industry. Blais and Faucher (1981, p. 24) interpret the growth in financial aid "comme un mécanisme de compensation visant à maintenir la position concurrentielle, menacée par la réduction de la protection tarifaire" ("as a compensation mechanism designed to maintain the competitive position threatened by the reduction in tariffs"). This hypothesis supports the conclusion of Cameron (1978), according to whom the opening of the economy is the main cause of the growth of the state (see also Kirk Laux, 1978). The third variable is therefore the average manufacturing tariff (TARIFF).

The last "government" variable corresponds to the entirety of taxes levied upon firms (TAX). The logic behind the choice of this variable is described by Hager:

> The logic of industrial policy . . . may be described as the politics of compensation, . . . the state and society remove with one hand the resources (and conditions) that allow industry to prosper and give them back with the other. Both operations are carried out in the name of social objectives (Hager, 1982, p. 243).

Corporate tax could reduce profits and, indirectly, investment. Since governments are dependent on investment (Marsh, 1985) and since profit remains a taboo subject (Pinder, 1982; Lipset and Schneider, 1983), they are forced to adopt measures designed to stimulate investment when, for other reasons, they have decided to levy corporate taxes.

Next, there are four "socioeconomic" variables. First of all, there is the size of the country (SIZE), a variable on which authors such as Katzenstein place great emphasis. Katzenstein noted that it is in small countries that the growth in government expenditures has been greatest and that "their growth is due primarily to a substantial increase in transfer payments, primarily from government to households but also to producers" (Katzenstein, 1983, p. 109). The economy of small countries is usually more closely tied to international trade, so that once again this fits in with the thesis of Cameron (1978). The size of the agriculture (AGRICULTURE) comes next; we saw in Chapter 1 that this sector was the main beneficiary of government aid. The third variable is the level of wealth of a country (WEALTH). We should remember here the hypothesis of Gerschenkron (1962), according to which the governments of countries that have industrialized late tend to intervene more in economic development. However, we think that this hypothesis, which has already been seen to be inoperative as regards tariff protection, is highly doubtful. Government expenditure studies show that if one looks only at the most developed countries, the wealth of a country has no bearing on the size of its government (Cameron, 1978; Castles, 1982). The last socioeconomic variable is the unemployment rate (UNEMPLOYMENT). Since a large portion of government aid is devoted to declining industries and declining regions, and since this orientation is explained basically by employment concerns (see Chapter 3), the need for aid to industry will seem increasingly pressing as the unemployment rate rises.

Finally, we have included a more specifically political variable, namely the strength of the parties of the left (LEFT). While the prevailing trend in the 1970s was to conclude that political variables have no impact, a whole new string of studies has demonstrated that variables such as the party breakdown of government could be very important (Castles, 1982). In Canada, Chandler (1982) has also made an association between the political parties and provincial recourse to public entreprise.

Table 2-4 shows each of the independent variables. It provides a definition of the indicators and sources used. The theoretical expectations are also summarized in this table.

Before looking at the empirical results, the limitations of the exercise should be pointed out. The data cover only 17 observation cases.[70] Since we have nine independent variables, the number of degrees of freedom is quite small. In order to offset these shortcomings somewhat, we devoted greater attention to the solidity of the results by using different equations, excluding some variables or countries.

We saw in Chapter 1 that grants to industry were particularly high in Ireland and that this country should therefore be excluded. We conducted a whole series of "tests" including and excluding Ireland, and the results were systematically more interesting (with higher R^2) when Ireland was excluded. These are the results that will be used. We were also concerned by the possibility of "co-linearity" between the independent variables. Table 2-5 shows the correlation matrix between these variables. The only strong correlation was that between total government expenditures (STATE) and the social security expenditure (SECURITY). The conclusions regarding these two variables are therefore even more fragile.

Table 2-6 shows the relevant equations, with Ireland excluded. Each of the first two equations includes only one of the two highly correlated variables (STATE and SECURITY) while the third includes both these

TABLE 2-4 Information Regarding the Independent Variables

Variable	Definition	Source	Expectation
SIZE	Gross Domestic Product (GDP) in 1980	a	–
LEFT	Index from 1 to 5, score 1 being equivalent to a dominant position of left-wing parties. This classification is based on the proportion of ministries held by the various parties between 1974 and 1980	b	+
AGRICULTURE	Ratio of the active civil population engaged in agriculture (1980)	c	+
WEALTH	GDP per capita (1980)	a	?
TARIFF	Average manufacturing tariff, after the Kennedy Round (weighted by world imports)	d	–
TAX	Total income and labour tax levied from corporations, relative to GDP (1980)	Tables 1-15 & 1-17 of this study	+
STATE	Total public administration expenditures with respect to GDP (1980)	c	+
SECURITY	Total social security transfers with respect to GDP (1980)	e	–
UNEMPLOYMENT	Unemployment as a percentage of the total active population (1974–79)	f	+

Sources:

a. R. Summers and A. Heston, "Improved International Comparisons of Real Product and Its Composition, 1950–80," *Review of Income and Wealth* 30 (June 1954):207–62.

b. M.G. Schmidt, "The Welfare State and the Economy in Periods of Economic Crisis," *European Journal of Political Research* (March 1983), n. 7, p. 18.

c. OECD, *Investment Incentives and Disincentives and the International Investment Process* (Paris: OECD, 1983).

d. V.A. Deardoff and R.M. Stern, *An Economic Analysis of the Effects of the Tokyo Round of Multilateral Trade Negotiations on the United States and Other Major Industrialized Countries* (Washington, D.C.: U.S. Congress, Senate Finance Committee, June 1979).

e. OECD, *Textile and Clothing Industry* (Paris: OECD, 1983).

f. OECD, *Historical Statistics, 1960–82* (Paris: OECD).

TABLE 2-5 Correlation Matrix Between the Independent Variables

	SIZE	LEFT	AGRICULTURE	WEALTH	TARIFF	TAX	STATE	SECURITY	UNEMPLOYMENT
SIZE	1.00	−0.43	−0.20	0.41	−0.21	−0.03	−0.38	−0.19	0.29
LEFT		1.00	0.01	−0.18	0.20	0.04	0.42	−0.01	−0.40
AGRICULTURE			1.00	−0.41	0.06	−0.01	−0.20	−0.18	−0.15
WEALTH				1.00	−0.20	0.00	−0.07	−0.06	0.06
TARIFF					1.00	−0.14	−0.03	−0.14	0.23
TAX						1.00	0.50	0.61	−0.28
STATE							1.00	0.76	0.06
SECURITY								1.00	0.11
UNEMPLOYMENT									1.00

Note: This table excludes Ireland and New Zealand.

TABLE 2-6 **Grants to Industry: Factors Affecting National Variations**

	Equation 1	Equation 2	Equation 3
SIZE	−0.00 (2.42)[a]	−0.00 (2.62)	−0.00 (2.30)
WEALTH	0.00 (1.17)	0.00 (1.03)	0.01 (0.98)
AGRICULTURE	0.11 (1.15)	0.11 (1.14)	0.11 (1.02)
LEFT	0.82 (2.72)	0.68 (2.99)	0.73 (2.04)
TAX	0.24 (2.30)	0.25 (2.52)	0.26 (2.24)
TARIFF	−0.25 (2.30)	−0.24 (2.14)	−0.25 (1.97)
UNEMPLOYMENT	0.42 (1.92)	0.39 (2.16)	0.42 (1.79)
STATE	−0.04 (0.78)	— —	−0.02 (0.22)
SECURITY	— —	−0.08 (0.95)	−0.06 (0.53)
CONSTANT	−2.22 (0.65)	−2.26 (0.69)	−2.08 (0.57)
n	16	16	16
R^2	0.802	0.810	0.812
$\bar{R}^2$	0.577	0.593	0.529

Note: This table excludes Ireland and New Zealand.
a. Student t test.

variables. Let us consider, for the time being, only the other seven variables. In the case of the WEALTH variable, we had no theoretical expectation, and the value of the t was low. Moreover, to the extent that there was a trend, the richest countries provided the largest grants, which runs counter to Gershenkron's hypothesis. As regards the remaining six variables, for which we had expectations, the coefficients had unexpected signs. In Equation 2, which gave the best results (the adjusted R^2 being highest), the value of t exceeded 2.00, which yields a probability greater than 95 percent (single-queue test). It was only for the AGRICULTURE variable that the trend was weak, but we do not think it was sufficiently weak to reject the initial hypothesis.

Finally, let us return to our two highly correlated variables, STATE and SECURITY. It should be noted from the outset that the results are most satisfactory only when the SECURITY variable alone is included. The

STATE variable therefore seems inoperative. The case of the SECURITY variable is more ambiguous. The sign of the coefficient is the expected one, but the value of t is quite low (it is only significant at the probability threshold of 80 percent). In our own view, we should not reject the hypothesis which postulates that social security expenditures reduce grants to industry, though we are the first to acknowledge that this interpretation is debatable. In Chapter 3 we shall present additional data which tend to confirm the relevance of this variable.

As mentioned, we also looked at regressions by including Ireland. Overall, the results were not as interesting. The highest adjusted R^2 was only 0.48, whereas when we excluded Ireland it was 0.59. Therefore the value of t was lower. However, the signs of the coefficients are still the same as those shown in Table 2-6.

It would be impossible to overemphasize the fragility of these results. The number of observations is very limited. The overall thrust of the data is nevertheless very encouraging. For the six uncorrelated variables for which we had expectations, the coefficients had the expected sign, and for five of them the coefficients were significant at the probability threshold of 95 percent. There being no proof to the contrary, we therefore consider our hypotheses to be confirmed.

It is worth reiterating the scope of these results. Firstly, our thesis concerning the link between trade policy and domestic aid to industry has been confirmed. This should not come as a surprise if, as claimed by Ruggie, the philosophy prevailing in the aftermath of World War II was based on trade liberalization, counterbalanced if necessary by vigorous domestic policies:

> The task of postwar institutional reconstruction, . . . was . . . to devise a framework which would safeguard and even aid the quest for domestic stability without, at the same time, triggering the mutually destructive external consequences that had plagued the interwar period. This was the essence of the embedded liberalism compromise: unlike the economic nationalism of the thirties, it would be multilateral in character; unlike the liberalism of the gold standard and free trade, its multilateralism would be predicated upon domestic interventionism (Ruggie, 1983, p. 209).

That link is evident both in space and in time. In the manufacturing sector, the sector most directly affected by tariffs, the process is clear. In West Germany, Fels noted:

> During the 1960s, a shift occurred in West Germany's industrial assistance policy from assistance by trade barriers to domestic subsidies and tax allowances. The reason for this is obvious: trade policy was becoming subject to multinational agreements in which liberalization and significant tariff reductions were being achieved (Fels, 1976, p. 92).

Similarly, in Canada, the very first industrial assistance programs were aimed initially at the defence industry, following a trade liberalization agreement within the Defence Production Sharing Program; and then at shipyards, with respect to which customs tariffs were inoperative, in accordance with the British Commonwealth Shipping Agreement (Blais, Faucher and Young, 1983a). The fear of excessive production instability is one of the most important reasons for the proliferation of industrial assistance measures. We know that the destabilizing effect has probably been exaggerated. Nevertheless, inasmuch as the liberalization process introduces additional uncertainty in industrial organization, it can only promote greater government intervention. According to our data, *ceteris paribus*, a 4 percent reduction in the average tariff will cause a 1 percent increase in grants to industry. This is precisely the prevailing trend of the last 20 years. Since 1965, tariffs have dropped by somewhat more than 5 percent, while grants have risen by a little over 1 percent.

As a factor, the size of the country reinforces this trend. The smaller countries have a more open economy, and it is understandable that the governments of these countries are more tempted to intervene in industrial development. Moreover, the correlation between the size of the country and industrial grants ($r = -0.53$) is greater than the correlation with overall expenditures or with social security transfers, which are 0.38 and 0.43, respectively (Table 2-5). It would thus appear that industrial assistance is the aspect of government intervention that is most closely tied to the openness of the economy.

Thirdly, the relationship between grants and taxes should not be ignored. The countries in which firms receive greater financial assistance are also those where such firms are the most highly taxed. Industrial assistance should therefore not be seen as an outright gift to business. As suggested earlier, it is perhaps more in the nature of a compensation provided by government (concerned with promoting investment) to an industry that complains of being overtaxed. The compensation, however, is only partial: according to our data, each time taxes increase by 1 percent, grants rise by 0.25 percent.

The impact of unemployment upon industrial assistance is also very interesting. This merely confirms the crucial role played by "sectorial and regional" decline in industrial policy, a point upon which we shall dwell in the next two chapters. According to our data, when the unemployment rate is highest, demand for government intervention becomes strongest. The high unemployment rates that have prevailed over the last ten years or so could only contribute to the growth of government financial assistance to industry. Table 2-6 in fact suggests that the 1 percent rise in industrial grants during the 1970s could be explained almost entirely by the (approximately 2 percent) rise in the unemployment rate during that period.

The results regarding the size of government and the magnitude of social security transfers are more ambiguous. In particular, the size of government was not found to be a significant variable. Although the two variables were associated (a correlation of +0.57 was noted between industrial grants and overall government expenditures), the relationship fades when other factors are taken into account. This leads us to believe that the various areas of government intervention are not as closely linked as is sometimes presumed (Castles, 1982), a fact which cannot be accounted for by the strong states/weak states typology (Zysman, 1983, p. 348, n. 23). On the other hand, the hypothesis regarding the substitution effect between social security and industrial grants tends to be confirmed, albeit weakly. It therefore appears that a choice would have to be made between industrial assistance and assistance to the workers, and we shall discuss this choice later.

Finally, the only political variable included in the model was found to be relevant. This confirms the more recent research which has shown that political parties are not interchangeable and that they do influence government output (Castles, 1982; Blais and McRoberts, 1983; Kingdon, 1984). Industrial grants tend to be higher when the left is in power than when the right runs the government.

Conclusion

The main message that emerges from this chapter concerns the link between trade policy and domestic industrial assistance. Governments resort to the latter to a greater extent, in part because tariff protection has been substantially reduced. This is why a study of industrial assistance must start, as we have done, with the external components. Within this framework, we have questioned the validity of the interest group model which is used by many economists to account for protectionism.[71] On the one hand, the empirical data do not agree with the forecast of the model; on the other hand, the theory cannot explain the liberalization movement that has occurred over the last 40 years. This movement was facilitated by a favourable economic situation, but also by political and symbolic considerations: the Great Depression and the two world wars had made protectionism (which was associated with narrow nationalism) a suspect policy option that had to be attacked in order to maintain and consolidate the political and military alliance of the major capitalist countries.

Domestic industrial aid emerged to fill the gap left by the decline of classical protectionism. Such aid is increasing in the smaller countries, which are more exposed to the world economy. Industrial assistance tries to offset not only the lowering of tariffs but also the drop in profits due to the levying of corporate taxes. However, in both cases, compensation is only partial, since the rate of grant increase is below that of tariff reduction and tax increase. Industrial assistance is also greater in countries with high unemployment and with a less developed social security system. Finally, industrial assistance is part of the broader framework of the role of the state. Indeed, domestic industrial assistance is greatest in the countries where the left has a solid foothold.

Chapter 3

Choosing the Target

We have now seen what causes governments to intervene or not to intervene in order to support domestic production. We shall next look at what causes them to target their assistance in a given manner once the decision to intervene has been made. In this chapter, we look at the reasons why governments show more interest in certain types of industry or firms, or in certain aspects of economic activity. Chapter 4 will then deal more specifically with the types of intervention.

The starting point for our analysis will be a number of trends noted in Chapter 1. First, it was noted that the primary sector, and particularly agriculture, was a favoured government target, whereas services were largely neglected. Second, it was seen that declining industries were among the main beneficiaries of government intervention. Third, the state is very concerned with industrial development in outlying areas. Fourth, a great interest in activities related to innovation and technology was noted. Fifth, it seems that government assistance is targeted somewhat more at big business. Finally, the preferential treatment afforded the domestic industry is not as substantial as it seems. We shall look at each of these trends and shall attempt to identify the underlying sociopolitical dynamics in each case. As stated earlier, special attention will be devoted to the political calculations made by governments. Since the trends found in Chapter 1 seem to indicate little national variation, we assume that the parameters of political calculation are basically the same in all advanced capitalist democracies.

Resources, Manufacturing and Services

Why do governments appear to devote so much attention to the primary sector, and especially to agriculture, and so little to services? The first explanation relates to a theme already explored in depth in the previous chapter. Services are little affected by the trade liberalization that is often at the root of government intervention. Obviously, this explanation cannot account for aid to the primary sector, which is also little affected by the liberalization movement. In the latter case, it is probably the regional aspect that is the strongest determinant, since the primary sector benefits from its location in outlying areas. We shall have the opportunity to return to this regional dynamics aspect later.

It seems to us that there is a third, symbolic factor. The distribution of government aid reflects the image which society has of the value of various economic activities. It would thus seem that there is an "industrial" hierarchy that corresponds to the primary–secondary–tertiary typology. Some activities are considered more "essential" than others. As noted by Fels, "assistance measures have been provided to areas which produce for primary needs and/or whose survival is closely associated with traditional ideas of an autonomous nation" (Fels, 1976, p. 92).

Indeed, the place of agriculture in capitalist society is paradoxical: "La diminution de la place du secteur agricole dans l'économie des pays capitalistes . . . ne s'est pas accompagnée d'une diminution parallèle du pouvoir politique des paysans" ("The shrinking of the position of the agricultural sector within capitalist economies was not accompanied by a parallel reduction in the political clout of the peasants") (Gervais et al., 1969, p. 78). This paradox may be interpreted in several ways. Agricultural interests are perhaps easier to mobilize, although peasant organizations have numerous internal divergencies and their policy stands are often ambiguous (ibid., p. 79). However, it is clear that the symbolic aspect is paramount:

> In virtually every country, ideology is the peasants' major ally in their attempt to influence the powers-that-be. The peasant, the countryside and rural life often evoke favourable feelings throughout the population and among the elites, and they are oft-invoked ideological themes. . . . The ideological themes linked to the peasant are . . . very different depending on the country. . . . However, it is striking that the same prestige should be found in many countries and that there should be virtual unanimity in this respect within a given country. . . . This ideological agreement . . . greatly facilitates the role of peasant organizations (Gervais et al., 1969, pp. 135–36; translation).

The ruckus about "deindustrialization" is also highly revealing. There is nothing to indicate that such a process is starting either in Canada (Economic Council of Canada, 1983, p. 121) or in the United States (Lawrence, 1983), but the mere fact that people are talking about it proves that it is a matter of concern. Grant noted that in Great Britain, particularly within the Labour party "manufacturing jobs were seen as preferable to jobs in marketed services for a various mixture of economic and moral reasons" (Grant, 1982b, p. 11). There is an assumption, in most cases implicit, that industrial activity is "superior" or more basic than "mere" services. However, the countries where the services sector is more developed than elsewhere do not have a below-par rate of economic growth (McCallum and Blais, 1985).

The weight of these indices should not be exaggerated. The first two factors (liberalization and the regional aspect) are probably more important. Nevertheless, we believe that the symbols do play a non-negligible role.

Government and Industrial Decline

A large percentage of government aid is designed to support declining industrial sectors and to launch operations to salvage firms that are on the edge of bankruptcy. The main function of aid to industry, according to Corden (1977), would therefore be to provide some security against the fluctuations of the market. The insurance principle is the very basis on which the welfare state was built (Flora and Alber, 1981). It is paradoxical, though, that aid to industry, although based on the theme of growth as far as debate and theoretical justification are concerned, is in fact designed to slow down negative growth.

We must also define what exactly it is that the state is trying to preserve. The major concern is obviously employment. Denton has stated that "without doubt the one problem above all of these in provoking the growth of financial aid to industry has been unemployment" (Denton, 1976, p. 161). In addition, Denton, O'Cleireacain and Ash (1975) revealed, in the United Kingdom, a significant correlation between the size of grants and the unemployment rate within an industry. In the United States, as seen in Table 1-7, it is in those industries which face increased competition by foreign producers and which have a great number of employees that tariffs are diminishing the least. It is also in the industries that have many employees or in which employment is declining that retaliatory measures are most common (Herander and Schwartz, 1984; Finger, Hall and Nelson, 1982). Along the same lines, Kreile concluded that in Italy "the dominant pattern of industrial policy has been short-term crisis management ad hoc interventions that were aimed at safeguarding employment and ensuring the financial survival of floundering companies" (Kreile, 1983, p. 215).

One might wonder why job preservation plays such a large role in aid to industry. George, for example, claims that "more jobs is not really what people want. If it was, the unemployed would be prepared to work for nothing" (George, 1983, p. 67). Nevertheless, many data seem to indicate that work is indeed a central social concern. As a source of welfare, it is considered more important than the financial situation

(Campbell, Converse and Rodgers, 1976, Table 3-5, p. 85). The remuneration level, incidentally, is one of the job characteristics that is the least valued (ibid., p. 57): 84 percent of Canadians would prefer greater job security to a wage increase (*Decima Survey*, 1982, qn. 543). Although higher income may contribute to the feeling of well-being, the negative impact of unemployment is much greater:

> Unemployed men are particularly prone to remember affective experiences of a negative kind: feeling lonely and being bored, depressed, or upset by criticism. . . . Unemployment is associated with low levels of satisfaction, not only with life in general but also with the specific domains of life. . . . Men without jobs are much more concerned than employed men about meeting their bills, more often worried or frightened about something that might happen to them or their families, and twice as likely to say they sometimes worry about having a nervous breakdown (Campbell, 1981, pp. 120–21).

Moreover, "it is evidently not the low income that depresses these men; it is the psychological trauma of having no work and the diminished sense of controlling one's life that accompanies it" (Campbell, 1981, p. 122).

These concerns are not without political impact. Unemployment thus has a considerable impact on the popularity of governments (Frey and Schneider, 1981; Hibbs, 1982; Urspring, 1984; Albert, 1980). The fact of being unemployed necessarily affects electoral behaviour, but the perception that unemployment is an important problem also has an effect, and this perception evolves according to the unemployment rate (Kiewitt, 1983; see also Johnston, 1985). What, then, is the government strategy in this respect? On the one hand, a government cannot be indifferent, since unemployment affects its chances of re-election. On the other hand, the full-employment objective has obviously become obsolete over the past 20 years (Apple, 1980). As a result, a certain level of unemployment is tolerated; but at the same time, politicians insist on the need to create jobs (Ashenfelter, 1981). In the language of game theory, one would say that governments appear not so much to maximize employment as to minimize job losses. The aim is to avoid the worst and to prevent excessive unemployment. This theory is summarized very well by Mosley:

> Within the context of the "satisfying" theory we may interpret these changes as responses to the straying of a target variable into a "forbidden" region: when unemployment begins to take on "unsatisfactory" values, red lights, as it were, begin to flash and the authorities deploy their instruments in instinctive Pavlovian fashion until the offending target variable has moved back into the satisfactory region (Mosley, 1976, p. 65).

The goal is to ensure that the decline will be smooth, to spread it over a longer period so that it will be less painful. This procedure has considerable direct and indirect costs (Curzon Price, 1981, p. 121); but it is also quite attractive in view of the great importance which people attach to stability. Therefore:

> In an economy in which capital is sector specific, labour is imperfectly mobile and wage rates are sticky, intervention to ease the adjustment of an industry which is inefficiently large as a result of foreign competition can yield a better outcome than that resulting from market forces (Forster and Rees, 1983, p. 240).

According to this view, governments basically attempt to manage industrial decline by trying to ensure that the drop in employment is slow in the sectors that are in decline. The objective is, on the one hand, to prevent massive layoffs and, on the other hand, to hope that new firms will not emerge in the sectors involved. This second part of the equation should not be neglected, because new firms do arise in declining industries. According to the data of Baldwin et al. (1983), an average of ten new establishments (i.e., one per annum) were created in each of 26 declining industries in Canada between 1970 and 1979.

What exactly is the situation? Unfortunately, information on this is very scarce. On the one hand, very few studies specify the criteria on the basis of whether an industry is deemed to be in decline. On the other hand, production and trade data are much more abundant than employment data. The textile and clothing industries are probably the most classic cases of industrial decline. Table 3-1 shows the data on the evolution of employment in these industries. Between 1963 and 1979, there was a reduction in employment in the order of 30 percent, i.e., an annual rate of 3 percent. Overall, these results appear to support the thesis that decline is being managed. Furthermore, the drop in employment accelerated during the 1970s and was in fact twice as fast after 1973. According to the OECD (1983a), the preliminary 1980 data showed that the decline had once again, accelerated in most countries. Here again, the "new protectionism" theory seems very weak. In summary:

> Overall, the direction of change was in line with the changes undergone by the comparative advantage as a result of technological progress and movements in relative costs. Moreover, trade expansion remained very rapid, in spite of cyclical drops. . . . The steps taken by public authorities with respect to the textile and clothing industries primarily affected the rate of change, rather than the general direction of change (OECD, 1983a, p. 134; translation).

Some characteristics of employment in these industries must also be emphasized. A large proportion of the workers are female, accounting for approximately 50 percent of employment in the textile industry and 80 percent in the clothing industry (OECD, 1983a, pp. 78–79). Many of the workers are immigrants (Matthews, 1980), and the skill and profes-

TABLE 3-1 Evolution of Employment in the Textile, Clothing (including footwear) and Leather Industries in Various Industrial Countries

	Evolution of Employment 1963–73			Evolution of Employment 1973–79			Evolution of Employment 1963–79		
	Number	Percent	Composite Annual Percentage	Number	Percent	Composite Annual Percentage	Number	Percent	Composite Annual Percentage
Australia	+2,000	+1.25	+0.1	−43,000	−26.54	−5.0	−41,000	−25.62	−1.8
Austria	−59,000	+32.24	−3.8	−15,000	−12.10	−2.1	−74,000	−40.44	−3.2
Belgium	−60,000	−22.14	−2.5	−81,000	−38.39	−7.8	−141,000	−52.03	−4.5
Canada	+18,000	+9.10	+0.9	−23,000	−10.65	−1.9	−5,000	−2.53	−0.2
Denmark	−11,000	−19.64	−2.2	−14,000	−31.11	−6.0	−25,000	−44.64	−3.6
Finland	+8,000	+12.12	+1.2	−10,000	−13.51	−2.4	−2,000	−3.03	−0.2
France	−134,000	−13.89	−1.3	−164,000	−19.74	−3.6	−298,000	−30.88	−2.3
West Germany	−344,000	−24.95	−2.8	−173,000	−16.71	−3.0	−517,000	−37.49	−2.9
Italy	+61,000	+5.63	+0.5	−47,000	−4.10	−0.7	+14,000	+1.29	+0.1
Japan	−7,000	−0.72	−0.1	−206,000	−21.24	−3.9	−213,000	−21.80	−1.5
Netherlands	−96,000	−44.86	−5.8	−52,000	−44.07	−9.2	−148,000	−69.16	−7.1
Norway	−17,000	−36.96	−4.5	−1,000	−3.45	−0.6	−18,000	−39.13	−3.1
Sweden	−72,000	−48.98	−6.5	−21,000	−28.00	−5.3	−93,000	−63.27	−6.1
Switzerland	−31,000	−22.46	−2.5	−31,000	−28.97	−5.5	−62,000	−44.93	−3.7
United Kingdom	−388,000	−26.54	−3.0	−179,000	−16.67	−3.0	−567,000	−38.78	−3.0
United States	+215,000	+8.54	+0.8	−283,000	−10.36	−1.8	−68,000	−2.70	−0.2
Unweighted average		−16.04	−2.0		−20.35	−3.9		−32.20	−2.7

Source: OECD, *Textile and Clothing Industries* (Paris: OECD, 1983), table 31, p. 75.

sional training levels are low. Consequently, the workers are poorly organized for the most part (Hamilton, 1983, p. 20). It is therefore implausible that government assistance should result from structured pressures exerted by these groups. Nor is there anything to indicate that the employers are very powerful. Although there has been an increase in concentration in the textile industry, the legal structure is characterized by a large number of small and medium-sized firms, most of them family firms (OECD, 1983a, p. 29). Governments assist these industries because they believe that an excessively sudden drop in employment would cause too many upheavals and that social stability is required if the government is to be re-elected. From this viewpoint, the determining factor is probably the fact that employment is often concentrated in the areas where unemployment is above average. The Canadian case is a particularly interesting one. The clothing and textile industries are highly concentrated in the Province of Quebec (Matthews, 1980) and one could infer that, in the face of the separatist threat, the Canadian government made a greater attempt to cushion the decline of these industries. Thus, the decision to impose even more stringent quantitative restraints in clothing, in 1976, was made within two weeks following the victory of the Parti Québécois:

> The victory of the Parti Québécois in the Quebec election only a few days before had made the other ministers acutely sensitive to the "need" to use foreign economic policy to pursue national unity goals. In particular, the probable link between employment levels and the federalist cause was alluded to (Protheroe, 1980, p. 124).

Similarly, when Jean Chrétien was minister of industry, trade and commerce, he justified his decision to commit Canadair to the Challenger project by explaining, "Aucun membre du Parlement n'aurait voulu signer la mise à pied de 7000 personnes à Montréal, spécialement à cette époque du référendum" (*Le Devoir*, April 14, 1983, p. 1) ("No member of Parliament would have wanted to sign his name to the dismissal of 7000 people in Montreal, particularly at this point in the referendum").

Obviously, management of the decline is handled more liberally in some countries than in others. In the textile and clothing industries, it was in the Netherlands and Sweden that governments tolerated the greatest drop in unemployment (Table 3-1). As stated earlier with respect to industrial assistance as a whole (Table 2-6), it is in the countries with the lowest unemployment rate and the most highly developed social security system that government intervention should be the smallest and therefore that the loss of jobs should be the greatest; indeed, demand for protection should increase as the likelihood of finding another job diminishes and as the job-loss compensation mechanisms (particularly the unemployment insurance plan) become less numerous.

In order to test these hypotheses, we correlated the evolution of

TABLE 3-2 Evolution of Employment in the Textile, Clothing and Leather Industries, 1963–79: Factors Affecting National Variations

Unemployment[a]	0.69 (3.13)
Security[b]	−0.28 (3.43)
Initial employment[c]	0.10 (1.01)
Constant	−2.99 (1.61)
n	16
R^2	0.68
$\bar{R}^2$	0.60

Sources: Table 3-1, last column.
OECD, *Textile and Clothing Industries* (Paris: OECD, 1983), table 5, p. 17.
OECD, *Retrospective Foreign Trade Statistics*, 1960–80, 1960–81, 1960–82 (Paris: OECD).

a. Average unemployment rate, 1960–80.
b. Average social security transfers as a percentage of GDP, 1960–81.
c. Manufacturing employment share of the textile and clothing industries, 1963.

employment in the textile and clothing industries of the 16 countries for which we have data, noting the unemployment rate, the size of social security transfers, and the initial amount of employment in these industries (use of this last variable offsets the potential convergence or divergence effect). The results are shown in Table 3-2. Our hypotheses were thoroughly confirmed. It is in the countries where unemployment is lowest and social security transfers the most substantial that governments have allowed employment to drop farthest. It also appears that job losses were the greatest in the countries in which employment within these industries was lower at the outset. Although we must stress that the value of the *t* is low, this leads us to believe that management of the decline is more liberal when the sectors affected are not too substantial in terms of manpower. Lavergne similarly noted that, in the United States, industries with a large number of employees have seen their tariffs drop less (Lavergne, 1983, Table 7), which corroborates our results.

Despite assertions to the contrary, there is no doubt that the "defensive" strategy of assisting declining industries is paramount in virtually every country. Basically, this is because of the central role played by labour in capitalist society. The search for stable employment remains one of the major social concerns, and inasmuch as unemployment is high throughout a country or in a given region, it is virtually impossible for the state not to try to cushion industrial decline.

Regional Development

Since the 1960s, regional development incentives have been among the primary components of industrial aid. We believe that one of the reasons for this is the great legitimacy of regional development as a target for government intervention. For instance, 79 percent of Europeans agree that they should contribute, through their taxes, to the development of disadvantaged regions (Urich, 1983, appendix 7). Similarly, 83 percent of Canadians believe that the federal government should concentrate its efforts in the least favoured regions (*Decima Surveys*, 1981–83, qn. 375). There is therefore "demand" for a regional policy.

The reason for this demand is that there are very strong ties to the local community. In Europe, more people identify with their locality than with their country (Urich, 1983, appendix 9). In the United States, the great majority of people, especially in rural areas, do not want to switch to a different environment (Campbell, Converse and Rodgers, 1976, pp. 260–61). Therefore:

> Despite the shortcomings that can be found in almost every situation, most of us are at least moderately satisfied with our communities, our neighborhoods, and our dwelling units, and we change our location only with reluctance and under pressure of circumstances (Campbell, 1981, p. 159).

In Canada, the multiple geographic loyalties and individual attachment to one's province are almost as strong as attachment to the country (Johnston, 1985).

The issue of regional development presupposes that there is a regional "problem," and it is therefore important to determine how that problem is defined. Clearly, it is again employment that is the main concern, as shown by the comparative study of Ashcroft:

> The common perception of the regional problem as an unemployment problem suggests that the measurement of the impact of policy in unemployment in the assisted areas should be of prime concern. . . . Each of the six countries have to varying degrees tried to reduce the imbalance in regional unemployment rates by attempting to influence firm mobility and locations. . . . They have attempted to influence unemployment and employment by acting on one of the gross flows of net employment change (Ashcroft, 1980, p. 19).

The idea is thus that regional unemployment is a serious problem and that one of the potential solutions (namely, encouraging workers from one area to migrate to areas where the employment outlook is better) is unacceptable because of individual attachment to the local community. The sole remaining option is to encourage firms to migrate to where the workers are. In practice, the regional development objective coincides with the employment objective, except that jobs must be taken to the manpower instead of taking the manpower to the jobs.

Moreover, aid to industries in decline often has a strong regional component. We saw earlier that aid to the textile and clothing industries was justified primarily on the basis of regional unemployment considerations, the Canadian case being one of the most indicative examples in this respect. Miles (1976) noted that in Great Britain the footwear industry is less supported by the state than the textile industry, although both face similar problems. The former, however, is more scattered throughout the country and thus the political stakes are lower. Similarly, the favoured treatment of shipbuilding in almost all countries is largely explained by its geographic concentration. As de Closets noted about France:

> If shipbuilding had been scattered among a thousand small and medium-sized businesses located all over the place, it would no doubt have declined without receiving public assistance (de Closets, 1982, p. 243; translation).

In the United States, the data of Lavergne (1983) show that rurally located industry, whose survival is even more crucial to the region in which it is established, has seen its tariffs drop more slowly than urban industry.

Technology

Several government programs are aimed at industries with a strong technology component or, more broadly, at research and development activities. This may seem perfectly "normal," since technological capability is today considered one of the main motors of economic growth (Economic Council of Canada, 1983, p. 27). However, there has been a lively and ongoing debate about the role played by the creation or dissemination of technology and the government's role in this process. Aid to R&D is usually justified by the fact that the collective rate of return on applied research is higher than the private rate (ibid., p. 40). There would therefore appear to be an "externality" which would justify state intervention to promote this type of activity. On the other hand, within an international context in which technology can be disseminated cheaply, one could argue that it is in the interest of a given country, particularly a small country, to take advantage of technological innovation created elsewhere (McFetridge and Warda, 1983, p. 91; Mansfield, 1985). Another argument invoked in support of a vigorous government policy for technological innovation is Schumpeter's thesis regarding barriers to entry and, more particularly, the suggestion that technological competition is irreversible, inasmuch as a first successful innovation leads to further successes (Harris, 1985). However, the data on this point are sometimes contradictory. Thus, while acknowledging that some studies confirm the "success begets success" hypothesis, Kamien and Schwartz add:

> There is also some evidence that "success begets failure." Either initial success leads to complacency or the successful firm is not as hungry as the newcomer, or the behavior that led to the first success is maintained until it becomes obsolete in a changing environment (Kamien and Schwartz, 1982, p. 75).

Governments did not wait for the issue to be settled before they intervened. The underlying logic seems to have been as follows: during the 1960s, when governments agreed to play by the rules of world competition, and when each state therefore began to compare its productive structure with that of other countries, a feeling of profound insecurity emerged in many countries. The United States quickly emerged both as a reference benchmark and as a threat. The symbolic impact of the American "challenge," mainly during the 1960s but today as well, cannot be overemphasized. The presence of an economic giant in the forefront of technological development leaves no choice to the governments of other countries: something must be done in order to avoid being "swallowed up" by American power. Zysman is unequivocal on this point, observing that in France "simple insecurity was at the bottom of the technology gap debate" (Zysman, 1977, p. 143). Warnecke also noted this emulation effect: "The industries they [governments] wish to emulate at home are frequently those they believe enhance other nations' political and economic power" (Warnecke, 1975, p. 9). At a time when world competition is increasing and when technology tends to play a growing role, governments want at least to ensure that their country's industry will not suddenly be outclassed by foreign producers.

There is no proof that the reasoning has been sound. For instance, the benefits ascribed to high technology industries during the early 1960s appear to have vanished quickly. "The differential between the high returns in technologically advanced industries and the earnings of others disappeared between 1965 and 1970" (Bergsten, Horst and Moran, 1978, p. 266). Although all governments "have to some extent made attempts to discover which industries are likely to become winners" (George, 1983, p. 41), this is a delicate exercise in that "success" factors change over time. Similarly, the countries which invested the most in R&D activities have had growth rates no higher than those of other countries:

> Statistically, in fact, there is a weak negative association, i.e., the countries who have devoted an above-average share of the output to research and development have, if anything, experienced below-average rates of growth" (Norris and Vaizey, 1973. p. 123).

Whatever the case may be, it is difficult for governments to resist the temptation to intervene in the technological innovation process, due to the very great uncertainty in that field. Given the nature of technological development, governments are concerned that a given innovation may have the potential to jeopardize a whole sector of domestic production, particularly within the context of trade liberalization.

The interest shown to high technology sectors may also be linked to considerations of national security. As Jéquier points out, the French computer policy was partly the result "of the refusal of the U.S. State Department to grant an export licence in 1966 for two of Control Data's largest computers," though this incident may not be the main reason, because similar policies were adopted in Great Britain, West Germany, and Japan, "where there had been no takeover of a prestigious national firm by an American company and no disputes with the State Department" (Jéquier, 1974, p. 202).

According to another interpretation, governments are motivated by the prestige of high technology:

> Computers have come to symbolize the essential power of the second industrial revolution; and the efforts . . . to preserve a national computer industry in the face of immense technological and economic odds are not so much a fight against the apparent rationality of industrial specialization as an attempt to retain some form of real power by preserving the symbol of power (Jéquier, 1974, p. 195).

Moreover, since the larger countries, which are prone to comparing themselves with the United States, are more likely to be concerned with prestige, there should be no surprise in the finding that "the drive for an independent computer industry is closely linked with a country's size" (Jéquier, 1974, p. 202).

Such concerns are not the exclusive preserve of the elite. About 80 percent of Canadians want the federal government to invest a great deal of money in developing new technology (*Decima Surveys*, 1981–83, qn. 373). Technology and research have a rather special status in our societies. The fact that the social status of researchers is very high is extremely revealing (Hodge, Siegel and Rossi, 1966; Treiman, 1977). Science, medecine, and higher education are the institutions that inspire the greatest degree of confidence (Lipset and Schneider, 1983, pp. 68 and 383). Research and innovation are perceived as valid objectives in themselves.[72] Collectively, a society has a need to perceive itself as having a certain excellence. The pride evoked by the achievements of national athletes at the Olympics is but a symptom of this (see also Goode, 1978). Thus, a government can hardly afford not to have a technology policy.

Demand for vigorous government intervention in the field of technology usually stems from the associations of scientists and technical experts. In Canada, the Science Council has assumed the role of spokesman for this option (Blais, 1985a). This should not be surprising because "the main beneficiaries of research and development aimed at producing significant technical advances are likely to be scientists in the jobs thereby created." (Daly and Globerman, 1976, p. 6). Although it seems plausible that researchers are not impartial observers, their real influence is doubtful. As we have just seen, the demand is far from being limited to this group alone.

We believe that the interest shown by governments toward technology is based primarily on symbolic considerations. The idea that there is a technological race, and that the countries which fail to participate in this race can only be losers, leads governments to the conclusion that they cannot afford not to intervene. "Smart thinkers" are those who think of the future rather than of the past and those who are on the side of innovation and technology. Who would dare to claim that research and development is not a good thing and that it should not be encouraged by governments? Moreover, the uncertainty linked to technological development is such that the risk of non-intervention appears prohibitive. From this viewpoint, aid to the high technology industry is "defensive," since the government's goal is primarily to avoid a situation in which the country's industry would suddenly be outclassed by foreign competitors as a result of technological innovation.

Big Business and Small-sized Firms

We saw in Chapter 1 that big business benefits from government aid more than small business does. However, the favourable treatment of big business is limited and mainly takes the form of grants. Furthermore, the preference was greater during the 1960s. As emphasized by Grant (1983), "the 'merger mania' of the late 1960s has now been replaced by a fashionable belief that small firms are the key to economic revival." The OECD (1983b, p. 18) noted that since the mid-1970s, there has been a tendency to prefer measures favouring small business"). Similarly, Blais, Faucher and Young (1983a, pp. 81–82) noted that as regards direct financial aid by the federal government of Canada, "Le désavantage dont souffrent la petite et la moyenne entreprises s'amenuise toutefois légèrement avec le temps" ("The disavantage of small and medium-sized firms has been diminishing slightly over time"). Finally, it is in the United States that the bias in favour of big business is the smallest. The United States is also the only country that seems to have set up a program to guarantee small business a "reasonable" share of public contracts (Peterson, 1977, p. 152).

Why does big business tend to be a slight favourite of the government? First of all, we should ask whether this bias is intentional. In some cases, it is obviously unintentional. Thus, national security concerns cause governments to favour the defence industry, which is highly concentrated; in this case, big business is favoured even though this is not the primary goal of government intervention. Similarly, government needs usually require large-scale production (OECD, 1978, p. 165), and thus governments are more likely to rely on big business for their procurement. The basic issue, though, is not whether the result is intentional or unintentional. If we assume that the result is known — which seems highly plausible — we must wonder why governments have taken so long to remedy this situation; this brings us back to the initial question.

Two main interpretations account for the position taken by the state with respect to big business and small business. The first approach, an instrumentalist one, emphasizes the organizational power of the factors involved. Better-organized big business can therefore better impose its views. Although attractive, this thesis is highly unconvincing. The fact that big business invests a great deal in its government lobbying (Grant, 1982b; Bauer, De Sola Pool and Dexter, 1972; Gollner, 1983) does not mean that large firms are better organized and more powerful. The big business organizations, such as Roundtable Business (in the United States), the Association des grandes entreprises françaises (in France), and the Business Council on Issues of National Interest (in Canada) are relatively recent and their political weight is largely unknown.

The few studies available tend to suggest that there is a tendency to overestimate the organizational power of big business. In the case of U.S. trade policy, for example, the automotive giants, the Wall Street bankers, and a multinational such as Du Pont did not dare to intervene in the debate:

> The practice of "corporate restraint" by large firms came as something of a surprise. To a great extent, we shared the common notion that bigness and potential power are unmixed blessings in controversy. But, even before we began our community studies, we ran into evidence that very large firms were reluctant to appear to be throwing their weight around too much. In the oil industry, for example, representatives of small oil interests told us that the giant companies went to great pain to appear not to be using their full power. Of course, the representatives of the small firms painted a picture of subtle sub rosa use of power by the large companies. But the appearance of virtue requires some part, at least, of the practice thereof. The representatives of large companies knew that there were severe limits to what they could do by way of manoeuvring behind the scenes (Bauer, De Sola Pool and Dexter, 1972, p. 317).

A second approach deals with the political calculation of governments. The state would thus tend to favour big business because government decision makers would perceive it as having greater potential than small business, given the objectives sought. What, therefore, are the relative advantages and disadvantages, for the government, of big and small business?

Let us first consider employment which, as seen earlier, is at the very heart of aid to industry. In this respect, small business creates more work and would from the outset be more attractive. Incidentally, some advocate it as a source of jobs. In Canada, small establishments were responsible for almost 90 percent of net job creation in manufacturing between 1971 and 1980 (Table 3-3). The same phenomenon was noted in the

United States, where the establishments with 20 employees or less created two-thirds of the jobs between 1969 and 1976, and those with 100 employees or less created approximately 80 percent (Birch, 1981). It should be stressed, however, that small establishments are also more likely to go out of business (Table 3-3) and thus small establishment employment is less stable. Moreover, these data pertain to establishments rather than to firms. Although the vast majority of firms have only one establishment, the exceptions are not negligible. In the United States, 9 percent of firms with several establishments employ 62 percent of the private-sector workforce (Armington and Odle, 1982). Furthermore, at least in the United States, "a significant portion of the growing small establishments are branches or subsidiaries of large firms" (ibid., p. 14). When we look at the size of firms rather than of establishments (Table 3-4), we see that between 1978 and 1980 large firms created the most jobs, in addition to causing a relatively smaller number of terminations. It should be noted, though, that while small firms only created 39 percent of jobs during this period, small establishments created 78 percent (ibid., p. 15). In summary, small establishments have the advantage of providing new jobs and they have the disadvantage of providing less stable jobs. Small firms have only the disadvantage.

Also, governments are more concerned by the closing (or risk of closure) of a large establishment than they are by the shutdown of a small establishment, because the impact on regional unemployment is much greater. The state is only worried by the decline of small establishments if they are concentrated within a given territory. Large firms are thus more likely to be "saved" than small ones.

Another criterion is economic growth. It could be that the government is more interested in large firms because they are more efficient and are thus a "growth vector." The studies on the relationship between the size of firms and their performance (return on investment, efficiency, innovation) tend to conclude that there is no clear relationship. On the other hand, there is no doubt that during the 1960s, particularly in Europe, the prevailing perception was that trade liberalization would expand the markets, that economies of scale would increase, and that big firms would be in a better position to take advantage of the new situation (Blais and Faucher, 1981, p. 26). This perception had a considerable impact on the policies of several governments in favour of corporate mergers. It is easy, in retrospect, to criticize the shortcomings of this analysis, but it is equally arguable that this position seemed quite plausible at the time. One of the reasons why large firms were favoured in the 1960s was therefore the perception that they were more likely to grow within a trade liberalization context, and one of the reasons why this preference has diminished over time is that mergers have rarely yielded the expected results (OECD, 1984b, p. 8). This therefore shows that governments can correct at least some of their mistakes.

On a more specifically political level, one might think that govern-

TABLE 3-3 Evolution of Employment in the Canadian Manufacturing Sector by Establishment Size, 1971–80

	Total Employment in 1971	Loss of Jobs Due to the Closing of Establishments (1971–80)	Variation in Percentage	Job Creation Due to the Expansion of Establishments (1971–80)	Job Creation Due to the Founding of New Establishments	Total Job Creation (1971–80)	Total Variation in Percentage	Net Employment Change (1978–80)	Distribution of Net Job Creation (percentage)
Small establishments[a] (0–49)	291,732	−101,094	−34.7	94,027	180,239	274,266	+94.0	173,172	87.8
Large establishments[a] (50 and over)	2,270,159	−168,797	−13.3	77,595	115,363	192,958	+15.2	24,161	12.2
									100.0

Source: Canada, Department of Regional Industrial Expansion, *Executive Summary — Combined Impact of Old and New Establishments, 1971 to 1980* (Ottawa: The Department, March 1984), p. 11.

a. Number of employees.

TABLE 3-4 Evolution of Employment in the United States by Firm Size, 1978–80

	Total Employment in 1978	Loss of Jobs Due to the Closing of Establishments (1978–80)	Variation in Percentage	Job Creation Due to the Expansion of Establishments (1978–80)	Job Creation Due to the Founding of New Establishments	Total Job Creation (1978–80)	Total Variation in Percentage	Net Employment Change (1978–80)	Distribution of Net Job Creation (percentage)
Small firms[a] (0–99)	29,177,000	−2,336,000	−8.0	28,000,000	2,317,000	5,117,000	+17.5	2,780,000	39.1
Large firms[a] (100 and over)	52,231,000	−2,623,000	−5.0	2,930,000	4,016,000	6,946,000	+13.3	4,234,000	60.9
									100.0

Source: Catherine Armington and Marjorie Odle, "Small Business — How Many Jobs?," *Brookings Review* 1 (2) (Winter 1982), table 1, p. 15.
a. Number of employees.

ments prefer to negotiate with firms over which they can exert a greater degree of control. From this viewpoint, small business is more attractive. According to the "divide and conquer" precept, the government can more easily exercise leadership by dealing with many small firms than by arguing with a single large one. However, other considerations seem more important. The heads of large firms are indeed more likely to understand the government's viewpoint and to enter into government-industry negotiations. For example, Bauer, De Sola Pool and Dexter (1972, p. 1939) showed that:

> Interest in export markets appeared to have no relationships to attitudes toward tariffs among the heads of the larger firms, but . . . it did have a perceptible relationship among the small firms.

The authors' interpretation of this is particularly interesting:

> It does not mean that the heads of the larger firms are less motivated by self-interest, but rather that their self-interest is more complicated and therefore seems less dependent on a single factor.

Therefore:

> The new situation of big business in American society demands qualities of mind on the part of the leaders of these big firms that make them generally closer in attitude and thinking to the intellectual community than are the heads of small firms. In general, the larger the firm the more the head of the firm is forced by his role to think in broad economic, political and social terms (Bauer, De Sola Pool and Dexter, 1972, p. 488).

In summary, the position of the leader of a large firm is structurally more akin to that of the politician, and thus it is probably easier for the two parties to exchange services.

In addition, Krasner expressed the view that the means by which politicians can influence industrialists tend to be more effective when targeting the leaders of large firms. He recalled, first, the paramount role of social status, both in business and in politics: "Prestige, personal power, and the attainment of dominating positions are much more important than material rewards, even in the development of commercial organizations" (Krasner, 1978, p. 78). He then argued that governments can alter the perceptions of businessmen "by defining problems and by appealing to the notion that managers are trustees of social resources, or to their loyalties as citizens, or to their private drive for status and prestige" (p. 81). Since "large corporate managers who accede to the entreaties of public officials are likely to be recognized" (p. 82), which is not the case with small entrepreneurs, government has more to offer to leaders of large firms (ambassadorships or appointments to task forces, commissions of inquiry, etc.) and can thus extract more concessions from them.

There is, though, another dimension in which small business is ahead: the legitimacy dimension. Ever since David and Goliath, there has been virtue in smallness and vice in bigness. Small business is not shy about invoking this mythology. It likes to present itself as the true representative of genuine capitalism, often undermined by the unfair practices of big bankers and industrialists. In the United States, the data in this respect are very clear:

> Big corporations were given highly favorable ratings by 10-16%, while the percentages having such positive feelings about small business companies range from 35 to 46%. About a third of the respondents . . . gave big business corporations either not too favorable or unfavorable ratings, compared to the one-twentieth who evaluated small companies in a negative light (Lipset and Schneider, 1983, pp. 81–82).

It is therefore politically impossible for government to defend big capital:

> The decision-makers are extremely anxious to avoid any suggestion that they favor large firms over small ones; they are, of course, painfully aware that rival politicians and the mass media are always ready to pounce upon even the slightest hint of an instance of favoritism (Braam, 1981, p. 264).

Even the British Conservative party "has to appeal to a broad electoral base and too close an identification with big business might run counter to the populist suspicion of 'bigness' among many of the voters likely to support the Conservatives" (Grant, 1980, p. 151).

Obviously, this has not prevented government aid from favouring big business somewhat, which shows the limits of symbolism. On the other hand, there are also limits to the discrepancy between language and reality, and it is not surprising that the favoured treatment of big business has diminished over time. It is also indicative that it is in the United States, where liberal ideology is deeply rooted, that small firms receive the best treatment.

In summary, the advantage enjoyed by big business is most clearly evident in the steps related to industrial decline, the main reason being that large firms are more likely to destabilize regional employment. In addition, political leaders have a tacit agreement concerning preference with the heads of large firms, who are more sensitive to social and political concerns; but the politicians must take care not to give the impression that they are discriminating against small business, in view of the traditional virtues which the prevailing ideology ascribes to small business. Finally, the favourable treatment granted to big business during the 1960s is explained by the idea that trade liberalization carried the risk of eliminating a substantial proportion of small firms. Since this view has become questionable, there has been renewed interest in developing "entrepreneurship."

The Domestic Firm and the Foreign Firm

We have seen that, to some extent, governments have tended to favour domestic capital at the expense of foreign capital, particularly in the sectors which have a large technological component or which are linked to security, though this "nationalist" preference has been quite limited overall. Obviously, a foreign firm is usually a large firm, and the observations made regarding large firms will apply here. We shall stress, however, the characteristics that distinguish multinationals from large domestic firms.

We shall look first at the behaviour of multinational firms, in terms of two aspects whose political consequences have already been discussed: employment and technology. The goal is to assess the advantages and disadvantages of a multinational firm, based on these two criteria, as far as the political leaders of the host country are concerned. We shall then look more specifically at the multinational dimension of these firms and its impact on the calculations of governments. In this respect, the relative mobility of multinationals and the political consequences of this mobility must be examined. We must also determine whether a multinational firm tends, to a greater extent, to further the interests of its country of origin or the interests of the host country. Finally, we shall look at the multinationals' ability to exert influence, which is greatly dependent upon their legitimacy as well as on their political ability.

Let us look first at the multinationals' role with respect to technology and employment. Multinationals are particularly active in sectors with a large technological component: "The most valuable regression studies have indicated that size of firm and a measure of technological intensity are the most important determinants of investment abroad" (Hood and Young, 1979, p. 45). On the other hand, although they are active in research and development, R&D tends to be centralized at the parent company, and thus subsidiaries make less use of R&D than domestic firms do (Economic Council of Canada, 1983; Rugman, 1981). Nevertheless, subsidiaries are quicker to adopt technological innovation that has been produced elsewhere (Economic Council of Canada, 1983, p. 61); but this is little consolation since, for the reasons already stated, governments are interested in the production of new technology. In this respect, domestic firms are therefore more advantageous.

As regards employment, both multinationals and large firms tend to be capital-intensive. However, we do not have the data required to determine whether they create a greater or a smaller number of jobs and whether these jobs are more or less stable. Finally, the wages paid by multinationals are no different from those prevailing in the domestic industry, provided that other variables such as the industrial sector and the size of the firm are kept constant (Caves, 1982, p. 152).[73] As regards employment, there is therefore no indication that domestic firms are either more or less attractive.

Perhaps the most salient characteristic of a multinational is its mobility. As emphasized by Marsh, "large TNCs by definition operate in a number of countries and as such can more easily move capital and production between countries" (Marsh, 1985). This mobility should not be exaggerated, however. Bergsten, Horst and Moran have noted:

> Most production runs in most industries are based on long-term investments which cannot be easily shifted, excess capacity is frequently unavailable in alternative sites, and large investment losses and large severance payments would be incurred by precipitate shifts (Bergsten, Horst and Moran, 1978, p. 101).

The fact remains, though, that "the MNE makes its investments and financial decisions on a global basis, so that its rate of capital expenditure in one country will tend to fall when its expected returns rise for investment somewhere else" (Caves, 1982, p. 193). Shapiro's (1983) data on the mobility of domestic and foreign firms in Canada support this. All things considered, we feel that the well-pondered statement by Hood and Young sums up the situation correctly:

> In reality, MNEs may only be slightly less subject to locational inertia than other companies. Moreover, not all MNEs are in "footloose" industries; indeed, many have high fixed capital investment on each side. Even so, they have more flexibility than the single plant or national company (Hood and Young, 1979, p. 124).

This greater mobility is an invaluable asset. Since a government's re-election is to a large extent dependent on investment, it tries to attract such firms to its territory by offering "appropriate" incentives. Once a firm decides to invest in a given region, it can announce its intent to invest and then sit back and await offers. This can be highly profitable (Marsh, 1985).

A multinational, however, does not hail from outer space. There is a parent company established in a given country, and the question arises as to whether multinationals tend to favour the economic development of their country of origin or that of the host country. This issue has several aspects, particularly the distribution of R&D, which has already been mentioned, as well as pricing and the repatriation of dividends. Although the data are fragmentary, they seem to indicate that, overall, the host country is not clearly favoured or discriminated against. The most systematic study on American multinationals concluded that "foreign direct investment . . . does not have a single, preponderant net impact . . . on the economy of the United States" (Bergsten, Horst and Moran, 1978, p. 492). Similarly, according to Hood and Young, "the empirical evidence indicates that the postulated adverse affects of MNE operations have perhaps been overstressed, but equally the gains for foreign investment appear to be less hypothesized" (Hood and Young, 1979, p. 180).

We saw earlier in this chapter that the image of the large firm is fairly unfavourable. One might suspect that the image of the multinationals would be even worse. This is indeed the case. Multinational firms are one of the types of institution that Canadians trust least. Only unions have an image that is more negative. The general perception of multinationals is even less favourable than that of the federal government and of public administration (Johnston, 1985). However, the attitude of the elites is less antagonistic, the dominant trend being "a moderately favorable overall appraisal" (Fayerweather, 1982, p. 4). although, always "simmering behind the surface are basic nationalistic views" (p. 18). Much like the citizens themselves, governments cannot fail to feel vulnerable in the face of these seemingly all-powerful juggernauts (Black et al., 1978; Graham, 1982). This is a threat that should be taken seriously.

This lack of legitimacy is sometimes aggravated by clumsy strategies. The heads of multinationals are often ill-informed regarding the social and political context, and this causes them to make gross mistakes which are no help to their cause:

> In the same way that U.S. corporations tend to criticize their home government wherever it intervenes into their economic affairs, they tend to take a similar stand abroad. At home, they can rely upon trade associations, lawyers, and press releases in dealing with public affairs. Abroad, however, these instruments are either unavailable or are not nearly as effective as in the United States. At the same time, U.S. MNCs are obviously not flexible enough to develop personal relationships with governmental bodies abroad (Goldberg, 1983, p. 17).

Very little is known about the political finesse or clumsiness of multinationals, but although anecdotal, the information cited by Goldberg suggests that such firms can bring to bear relatively little direct influence upon governments.

In summary, governments are fairly distrustful of multinationals, which are perceived as a potential threat to their autonomy (Bonin, 1985). The nationalist reaction, however, cannot be too pronounced, inasmuch as multinationals provide the jobs governments want. Their mobility gives them additional leeway, which governments can only ignore at their peril. This is why multinationals are not discriminated against when employment is the main consideration, as with aid to declining sectors and regional development.[74] On the other hand, the nationalist orientation is stronger in the field of technology, where the concerns are different. In addition, the bias in favour of domestic industry seems to be more prevalent during periods of relative prosperity. Murray and LeDuc noted that, among the Canadian population, "a more favorable attitude toward foreign investment or toward closer ties with the United States may be seen by some as necessary in a period of economic slowdown" (Murray and LeDuc, 1982, p. 233).[75]

Finally, the nationalist reaction is more muted in countries where there are several parent companies of multinational firms (Kiesl, 1981, p. 143; Black et al., 1978, p. 14), because the government is worried about the way in which the subsidiaries established abroad will be treated and about the impact of its own policies on those of other governments. Since the range of capital-exporting countries has been growing, the pressure for a "neutral" treatment could grow. Nevertheless, this factor should have no more than a marginal effect. Krasner (1978), for example, has shown that the U.S. government has intervened but little to protect the interests of American multinationals (see also Vernon, 1985).

Conclusion

The selectivity shown by governments in allocating their aid is not a random occurrence. A number of trends can be discerned, and we consider two of them to be basic. The first is the importance given to social, economic, and political stability. This concern is very evident in the aid to declining sectors and in aid for regional development, but it is also discernible elsewhere. Even the support to technology can be interpreted in part as an attempt to prevent excessive instability. We find here a theme already developed in the previous chapter; internal aid is designed as an instrument for offsetting the impact of trade liberalization. The primary goal is job stability, in view of the crucial role of work in our society, but there is also the goal of regional stability because people are rooted in their local environment.

Secondly, our analysis would seem to indicate that the choice of goal largely reflects the preferences of the population. The paramount place of aid to declining industries is due to the fact that a majority of citizens value stability and expect that the government will intervene to slow down the rate of decline. The extent of regional development aid arises from the fact that a majority of citizens do not want to move to another community or area in order to find a job. Technology is favoured partly because it is considered a legitimate, important activity by the population as a whole.

Of course, these "demands" are not translated automatically into government measures. Nothing happens by itself. The clothing industry must exert pressure to obtain government aid. However, such pressure is more effective when it is in line with certain "needs" or prejudices of the population. The organizational strength of an industry does not seem to be the most determinant variable. Undoubtedly, pressure may play a crucial role in certain cases, but it cannot account for the overall trends. The data in this respect are clear. The two most systematic studies on U.S. trade policy, those by Bauer, De Sola Pool and Dexter (1972) and Lavergne (1983), concluded that the pressure group theory had little explanatory value. In addition, it is difficult to see how that theory could be plausible if it is true — as we hope we demonstrated in the previous chapter — that the industries most favoured by the state are agriculture, textiles, and clothing. It is difficult to see how and why these industries might be better organized than others. In fact, it is likely that they are less well organized. The fact that they are industries in decline and are concentrated in outlying areas (and are thus particularly important from the viewpoint of social stability) seems more relevant.

Nor do we believe that the assumption that the demands of the population are "manipulated" by the political or industrial elites is more plausible. The local roots of individuals, for example, are obviously a constraint to governments. Things would be much easier if people were fully mobile and would readily agree to move to areas where the job supply is greater. It is difficult to see why the elites might be interested in creating or fostering this local attachment. The case of the small firm is also interesting. If our analysis is correct, politicians tacitly grant an advantage to the leaders of large firms. However, the image of big business, like that of all large institutions, has deteriorated (Lipset and Schneider, 1983), and these perceptions have forced governments to pay more attention to small firms.

It would be naive to claim that the choice of target is fully explained by the demands of the population. These demands are sometimes contradictory and often so vague as to leave the government a great deal of elbow room. We believe, however, that they determine the broad parameters of state intervention. In summary, we think that the trends noted are accounted for better by the "democratic" model rather than by any of the other proposed models, particularly that of interest groups.

Chapter 4

Choice of Instrument

In Chapter 2, we looked at the reasons why governments intervene, or abstain from intervening, in industrial development. In Chapter 3, we tried to explain why, once the decision to intervene has been made, governments show more interest in some industrial sectors or some types of firm. In this chapter, we examine the reasons why, once the decision to aid a given type of industry has been made, governments prefer some instruments over others. We shall begin by stressing the underlying political calculation involved in these choices. Our analysis is based on the assumption that such choices are largely inspired by political "rationality." Our approach on this point is related to that of another study (Trebilcock et al., 1982). However, unlike the approach of these authors, ours will be basically inductive, no specific hypothesis being established at the outset to be checked or tested later. Instead, we shall attempt to determine the major parameters of the political strategy, case by case, and we shall only attempt to establish the dominant features of the political rationality in the conclusion.

We should perhaps reiterate here the limitations of this exercise. On the one hand, the instruments which we want to study are many: tariffs, quantitative restraints, voluntary restraint agreements, grants, loans, guarantees, tax advantages, public contracts, and technical assistance. It is simply not possible to compare all these instruments with one another. The analysis can therefore not be as systematic as that of Woodside (1979, 1983), which specifically makes a comparison between grants and tax advantages. On the other hand, the instruments considered are limited. We shall not deal with Crown corporations or with regulations — instruments which are also available to governments. We shall therefore examine only one aspect of political strategy.

We could have structured this chapter so as to study each instrument in turn and to discuss its political advantages and drawbacks. This is the approach taken by Woodside (1979, 1983) and by Trebilcock et al. (1982). However, as our study unfolded, it became increasingly obvious that political calculation varies a great deal from one target to another. For example, grants have different advantages and disadvantages depending on whether the goal is to promote regional development or to foster R&D. We therefore decided to base the discussion on the broad orientations identified in the previous chapters. Chapters 1 and 2 dealt with the trade liberalization process within the framework of GATT and its considerable impact. We believe that it should now be explained why GATT focussed its effort on some instruments instead of others. We shall then examine four trends dealt with in the previous chapter: aid to sectors in decline; regional development; innovation and technology; and aid to small business. For each of these targets, we shall explain why governments choose a given type of aid over another. Obviously, it would be impossible, for each case, to consider all instruments available. We shall therefore limit ourselves to the main instrument, with a view to accounting for the most marked trends.

The Orientation of GATT

Since GATT's purpose is the liberalization of trade, its role is to reduce barriers to international trade. We should therefore try to determine the "political" obstacles on which GATT has focussed its action, as well as the reasons why it has done so.

The scenario is fairly clear. Initially, priority was given to abolishing quantitative restraints: "Much of the first fifteen years of the history of GATT centers on the effort to get quota systems of protection dismantled" (Jackson, 1969, p. 307). During the 1960s at the time of the Kennedy Round negotiations, significant tariff reductions were agreed on, the next decade saw a broadening of interests; during the Tokyo Round, tariffs were again reduced, but there was also interest in non-tariff barriers, within the framework of codes on customs values, on grants and offset duties, on standards, on government purchases, and on procedures for the import of licences (Jouanneau, 1980).

What logic underlay this strategy? In many respects, it seems to have been "economic." While economists generally agree in decrying protectionism, most of them also feel that quantitative restrictions have the most harmful effects, followed by tariffs, then by subsidies:

> Economists generally prefer direct subsidies to tariffs and quotas. Subsidies do not disturb the structure of relative prices and are therefore more efficient (less inefficient) than trade measures . . . then it is the tariff and not the quota that gives greater certainty that benefits exceed cost in the face of falling foreign costs (Pearson and Salembier, 1983, pp. 25, 27; see also Breton, 1974; Lal, 1980).

It appears highly significant that GATT did indeed tackle quantitative restrictions first, and then tariffs. In each decade, stress is laid on the instrument which poses the most serious problems. Once the system of quantitative restrictions was breached, tariffs became the next target. Recent strategy, however, has been more ambiguous, with the action being fought on several fronts at once. It was nonetheless in the area of tariff reductions, still the major barrier (see Chapter 1), that the Tokyo Round agreements were most significant.

We must not exaggerate the "economic" rationality behind GATT's strategy. There was also some symbolic significance in the early stress that was laid on the abolition of quantitative restrictions, which were viewed with a jaundiced eye because of their identification with the catastrophic period of the 1930s:

> Tariffs evoked the golden days before World War I. . . . Other barriers, such as quantitative restrictions, reminded the draftsmen of the gloomy interwar period . . . and were considered to have been contributory causes of World War II (Dam, 1970, p. 26).

GATT devoted its first decade to the abolition of quantitative restrictions. The battle was finally won in 1957 when, after two years of struggle, West Germany was persuaded to give up quotas which were no longer justifiable in terms of the balance of payments. This victory had considerable impact on other governments (Jackson, 1969, pp. 709–10; Kock, 1969, p. 143). GATT thus strengthened its authority by proving that freer trade was well and truly ensured.

Lastly, we might question GATT's ability to contain measures other than tariffs and quantitative restrictions. Pessimists hasten to stress the limitations of the various codes adopted under the aegis of GATT and to tick off the cases in which the rules have not been respected. Optimists remember that, despite everything, "the extent of compliance . . . has in fact been reasonably good" (Finlayson and Zacher, 1983, p. 299). As for ourselves, we consider GATT's ability to tackle each decade's most serious obstacle to trade to be quite remarkable. The task will likely be all the more difficult in future as the stakes increase, with no one measure appearing to be clearly more important than the others.

Declining Industry

There are many ways in which the government helps declining industry. Certain sectors, such as clothing and footwear, have been spared from reductions in tariff protection. In addition, there have been voluntary restraint agreements, such as the Multifibre Arrangement on textiles. There are also grants for businesses, which are of particular importance to industries such as shipbuilding, and which might also involve modernization or restructuring projects. For rescuing foundering businesses, loans and guarantees are probably the most popular measures. Lastly, financial aid is sometimes provided to employees who have been laid off by their companies, in order to encourage mobility, retraining, or even early retirement. There is every indication, however, that tariffs are still favoured and that voluntary restraint agreements are being used more and more frequently. For this reason, we shall first turn our attention to these agreements. Later we shall look at a little-used formula in which there has been a recent revival of interest on the part of certain economists, i.e., grants to workers (Glenday and Jenkins, 1981; Burton, 1979; Curzon Price, 1981; Trebilcock, 1985). We shall ponder the fact that governments offer help to businesses rather than to employees.

In Chapter 1 we saw that voluntary restraint agreements have become rather significant in the past few years. Products covered by such accords represent 3 to 5 percent of international trade (Hindley, 1980). Although their real significance is usually exaggerated, there is no doubt whatsoever of their growing importance. Naturally, we want to explain why this is so. We must, though, first make a few comments on the status of quantitative restrictions within GATT and on the voluntary nature of these bilateral agreements.

GATT's Article 19 permits the adoption of safeguarding measures (a supplementary tariff or quantitative restriction) in order to protect an industry that is being "severely" injured by increased imports. In return, the importing country must compensate all the exporting countries concerned, or else they may take reprisals. These conditions are relatively stringent, with the result that unilateral safeguarding measures are rare. It is more usual for an importing country to threaten safeguarding action in order to negotiate a voluntary restraint agreement. The fact that there is a threat makes the use of the term "voluntary" rather ironic; but Yoffie shows that it is a question of real negotiations, during which both parties make concessions: "Bilateral negotiations usually lead to higher imports, greater flexibility and more growth than unilaterally imposed programs" (Yoffie, 1983b, p. 25). Moreover, the mere fact that these agreements are reached proves that governments rarely contravene Article 19, despite the argument that there is no respect for GATT's rules (Lazar, 1981).

Why are there not more of these voluntary restraint agreements? In a manner of speaking, we have already answered this question. In Chapter 2 we saw that pressure for protectionism grows stronger in tough economic times, and the rise in quantitative restrictions indicates a trend toward protectionism. This answer fails to explain, however, why this particular approach is chosen. We must still show that these agreements respond more sensitively to the economic climate than other forms of intervention do. The reasons for this emerge if we study their advantages and disadvantages.

Let us begin with the advantages. In the previous chapter we saw that the first purpose of helping declining industry is to maintain employment, a goal that is part of an overall concern with social, economic, and political stability. From this viewpoint, quantitative restrictions look very appealing. By stabilizing imports, one stands a good chance of stabilizing employment in the industry in question: "With quotas, the employment effect is certain" (Pearson and Salembier, 1983, p. 27). Since the majority of the population is "risk-aversive" (Johnston, 1985), quantitative restrictions offer a tempting solution to the problems of an industry. From this point of view, a voluntary restraint agreement, because it is limited to one or more countries, is less effective than a unilateral quota. It has the symbolic advantage, however, of pinpointing the country which is perceived as the source of the industrial problem. Restrictions are aimed essentially at countries where wages are much lower than in the importing country, and they reflect the "moral" indignation of the importing country's population that competition from these other countries is "unfair." As Cable points out, this ideological dimension is crucial:

> There is no mechanical process by which politicians weigh notes and bureaucrats defer to economic power and good organization. There is also an important ideological component; lobbies need to capture a sense of what is both "fair" and in the national interest (Cable, 1983, p. 228).

It is therefore not surprising that voluntary restraint agreements are generally well accepted by the population. A significant majority of Canadians and Americans approve (to varying degrees) of restrictions on the importing of Japanese cars (*Decima Surveys*, Autumn 1982, qn. 515; *Public Opinion*, April–May 1985, p. 30). Furthermore, an opinion poll by the Conference Board of Canada (Adamek, 1984), conducted among the heads of European companies, reveals that voluntary restraint agreements are the one measure that the majority would like to see used more often. Industrialists prefer this form of intervention (which does not affect the way they run their business) to grants, which come with all kinds of strings attached — conditions which are more or less constraining and which might favour one kind of business over another (Edmonds, 1983; Aggarwal and Haggard, 1983). With such advantages, one might well wonder why quantitative restrictions are not more common. The obvious answer is that they come with a large price tag.

Tyson and Zysman nicely summarize the negative effects of voluntary restraint agreements:

> OMAs tend to have three main consequences. The first is well understood: the restriction of imports from one country encourages new producers to spring up quickly in other places. The second is even more serious: if one limits the volume of imports, it is in the interest of foreign producers to move into higher-value goods to achieve the largest possible value of total sales. Finally, foreign producers may alter the composition of the goods they produce to escape the quantitative limits on certain imports (Tyson and Zysman, 1983, p. 53).

As a result, "sectoral problems may actually get worse — not better — in the long run" (Yoffie, 1983a, p. 347). Moreover, this policy costs dearly. Jenkins (1980) calculates that voluntary restraints in the clothing industry cost Canadian consumers nearly $200 million in 1979, which means a subsidy of $33,000 for every job preserved. American restrictions on Japanese cars have added nearly $1,000 to the price of imported cars and about $400 to the price of domestic ones (Maskus, 1984; Crandall, 1984). In 1983, it cost $160,000 to preserve each job (Crandall, 1984).

If the negative effects are so "terrible," why do governments choose such measures? Tyson and Zysman offer the classic explanation:

> Because the groups benefiting from protection are organized, whereas the groups paying for it are diffuse, protection tends to be a politically expedient choice. The costs of alternative policies, such as tax and credit policies, to other industries or consumers (or both) can be more easily observed and resisted. Thus although protection is a second-best strategy by economic criteria, it is a workable and often superior strategy (Tyson and Zysman, 1983, p. 53).

The explanation is the view of the school of "interest groups," whose limitations we noted earlier. The cost of quantitative restrictions is perhaps less discernible than the cost of financial aid programs, although we have no data on this subject. What Tyson and Zysman fail to explain, however, is why industrialists support such measures which, in any event, do nothing to solve the industry's problems. Either they are shortsighted or else the negative effects are not as severe as they claim. The truth is probably a mixture of both. Despite everything, voluntary restraint agreements reduce industrial decline. In the textile industry, "plant closings have been avoided, jobs have been saved" (Aggarwal and Haggard, 1983, p. 308), with the result that reduction of the employment rate is done slowly. The expectations of management and labour are thus satisfied. The workers can keep their jobs. As for industrialists, many of them identify with their businesses and fiercely want to see them survive, even with minimal profits, until they retire.[76]

The economic cost of quantitative restrictions is enormous. That is why they are only used in exceptional circumstances, when the economic climate is particularly unfavourable, to avoid too sudden a loss of jobs in industries where wage competition is deemed "unfair."

We must also stress the transient nature of voluntary restraints. Critics rush to point out their tendency to last unnecessarily long or even indefinitely (Aggarwal and Haggard, 1983). This is undoubtedly the case in the textile industry. But in other sectors, even if their use is prolonged, these measures are still, by definition, temporary (Faucher et al., 1985) and their life expectancy is much shorter than that of direct financial aid programs (Blais, Faucher and Young, 1983a). The snowball effect is therefore not as systematic as some critics like to pretend.

Voluntary restraint agreements are a radical and expensive measure, used sparingly in times of great economic difficulty in order to prevent a severe drop in employment in a given industry. Because of the harmful effects which they produce, the desired objective is only partially attained. Nevertheless, it is hard to see how governments could renounce this instrument if the preservation of employment is the objective of industrial policy:

> Safeguard clauses are accepted by most observers of international commercial diplomacy — even the most liberal — as an essentiel precondition of obtaining liberalising trade agreements. Behind this acceptance lies the idea that an unduly rapid contraction of a domestic industry due to imports is politically embarrassing, and socially costly. . . . It is believed that governments will not commit themselves to liberalisation unless they are assured that they can avoid such costs should they arise (Hindley, 1980, pp. 315–16).

Quantitative restrictions are the most likely means of ensuring stability:

> A quota stabilises the circumstances of domestic producers for any downward shift of the foreign supply curve. . . . Thus in a situation in which there is considerable uncertainty as to the future position of the foreign supply curve — even in its position in the immediate future — there is a case for a protectionist government to choose a quota system rather than a tariff (Hindley, 1980, p. 326).

Another indication of the political need for voluntary restraint agreements is the fact that, by and large, they are tolerated, even though they contravene the fundamental GATT standard that all safeguard measures must be multilateral and not discriminatory (Merciai, 1981; Lipson, 1983). Thus, "because VERs and OMAs single out individual exporters for restrictions, they violate the spirit if not the letter of GATT's first and most important article" (Yoffie, 1983b, p. 5). This kind of bilateral agreement, moreover, can affect third countries, whose markets are in danger of invasion by exporters in search of new outlets (Merciai, 1981). These third countries, however, do not complain to GATT. There is, thus, a "complicity which exists between governments when one of them is forced to take unpopular trade measures because it has a domestic problem on its hands. All governments know what it is to be subject to such pressures, and they are usually prepared to be indulgent with each other because they do not know when they will be forced to ask for sympathy and understanding themselves" (Curzon and Curzon, 1976, p. 222).

Since voluntary restraint agreements are aimed at the newly industrialized countries, they are quickly brought into the debate on the Third World. According to some authors, underdevelopment is being maintained for the sake of short-sighted domestic political considerations. The most deprived people on the planet thus pay the price of this shameless protectionism:

> The few developing countries which have allowed development to proceed along the lines of comparative advantage find that their export outlets are blocked. All this represents a tragic misallocation of resources and loss of output especially for poor countries which can least afford it (Curzon Price, 1982, p. 104).

It is not as simple as this. On the one hand, the poorest countries are not the most affected by voluntary restraint agreements, which in fact are usually aimed at Japan. On the other hand, as we have already pointed out, we must not overestimate the efficiency of this protectionism: "There are political and economic weaknesses in the structure of modern protectionism . . . the politics of trade have paradoxically created opportunities for the 'weak' to beat the 'strong' at their own game" (Yoffie, 1983b, p. 9).

Next to quantitative restrictions (and tariffs), financial aid to businesses is the most important measure with regard to declining industries. Here there would seem to be a paradox. Since employment is the targeted objective, would it not be more logical to help employees directly, rather than to help businesses? More and more economists are coming round to this way of thinking (Glenday, Jenkins and Evans, 1982; Saunders, 1984; Watson, 1983; Burton, 1979; Curzon Price, 1981). There are several suggestions: termination bonuses or transferable benefits for employees laid off, retraining programs, mobility aid, or early retirement incentives. Nor are the political and economic repercussions always the same. The underlying logic is in fact relatively simple. Looking at it fairly, the employees' adjustment problems are greater than the employers':

> Employees will often find it easier than investors to secure compensation, on the one hand because . . . their job prospects are reduced and they are perhaps less able to negotiate risk premiums even if they are rather well aware of the danger of finding themselves without work, and on the other hand because investment in human capital is harder to diversify than any other type of investment (Trebilcock, 1985).

If this is the case, one wonders why governments do in fact usually subsidize businesses rather than employees, within the framework of restructuring or modernization projects. Trebilcock (1985) suggests the following reasons. First, the real cost of government intervention can more easily be hidden in the case of aid to businesses: it can be offered in the form of loans and guarantees, the cost of which is not obvious. But is this an important consideration? Newspaper headlines seldom make a fuss over the budgets set aside for different government programs, but they do mention the figures when loans or guarantees are given to rescue a business. It is quite likely that people fail to realize that it is only a loan (or guarantee) and that the real cost of such government intervention is thus exaggerated. It is far from certain, therefore, that the government can really hide the cost of helping industry, since such help has a more "spectacular" appearance than programs such as unemployment insurance. In fact, the opposite would appear to make more sense.

In the second place, aid to industry, according to Trebilcock, has the added advantage of "buying" the support of both management and labour, which is obviously not the case when aid is given directly to employees. This observation is certainly to the point. What has not been proven yet is whether the support of industrialists in declining industries, or of leaders of businesses in difficulty, is essential or important to government strategy. We possess no sure information on this subject. However, insofar as management's power lies in its ability to invest or not to invest (Marsh, 1985), "shaky" industrialists would have little political clout unless they formed coalitions with other groups. The advantage mentioned by Trebilcock would therefore not be a determining factor.

Thirdly, according to Trebilcock, "assistance to firms permits targeting on the marginal firms in an industry whose failure would have direct and immediate employment consequences" (Trebilcock, 1985). This presupposes that aid to businesses can be more selective than aid to employees, a proposition which is not proven. It is possible, nonetheless, that the existence of a general system of unemployment insurance might make it difficult to adopt specific measures regarding workers in certain types of business. This third argument appears to be more relevant.

Fourthly, "industrial assistance programs focussing on firms in declining sectors rather than labour can be justified by symbolic reassurances to the public (taxpayers) in terms of 'modernization' and 'industrial renewal'" (Trebilcock, 1985). This is an interesting hypothesis if we admit the crucial role played by symbols in politics. Having both "adjustment" and "modernism" in a single program is the "ultimate" policy, one that is competent but also sensitive to industrial problems. However, the scope of this factor must not be exaggerated. Another form of assistance to labour encourages mobility and retraining, both of which can nicely be given symbolic significance.

In summary, Trebilcock's interpretation undoubtedly holds some interest, but it seems to us insufficient in some areas and ultimately rather incomplete. We believe the problem should be formulated in different terms. First and foremost, if industrial decline stems essentially from the problem of employment, as we argued earlier, it is not obvious that giving money to labour would "buy" its support, especially if there is a high unemployment rate. The lengthy miners' strike in England is significant in this respect. It is businesses which provide employment, and it is not surprising that it is with them that the government deals. On the other hand, for the reasons of equity which have already been mentioned, aid to business is considered less legitimate than aid to individuals. It is pertinent to recall the success of the 1972 NDP campaign on the theme of "Corporate welfare bums" (Blais,

Faucher and Young, 1983a). In Quebec, aid to business is one area in which increased government spending is considered highly undesirable (*La Presse*, April 11, 1981, p. C-5). The same phenomenon has been observed in Great Britain (Grant, 1982a, p. 52). Industrialists themselves express certain reservations concerning the aid they are offered, in Quebec (Sales, 1983) as well as in the rest of Canada (Litvak and Maule, 1974) and in the United States (Edmonds, 1983) and Great Britain (Wilks, 1983). Yet although industrialists may express reservations, they use government programs and rarely refuse grants. There is a clear distinction here between rhetoric and actual behaviour. Nonetheless, there is every reason to believe that industrialists would really prefer to do without government aid and, in return, to pay fewer taxes (see Table 2-6).

Aid to business offers (political) benefits, but at a price. Its net benefits are probably greater than those of aid to employees, which is one reason governments prefer it. Aid to employees, though, has its attractions, which have perhaps been underestimated by politicians until now. The optimal strategy is probably a combination of the two types of intervention, as found in the policy of the Canadian Industrial Renewal Board, which includes grants for mobility and retraining (Trebilcock, 1985).

This entire discussion presupposes a choice between two options, either aid to business or aid to employees. Yet political considerations clearly prove that these are not the only options. Industrial decline often affects an entire region, leading to united efforts by interested groups on a regional basis. In the United States, for instance, "in addition to industry and labor activity, this pressure came from a newly created Steel Communities Coalition composed of public officials representing two dozen communities in traditional steel working areas" (Walters, 1982, p. 112). From this perspective, compensation must be envisaged for all the citizens of the region in question. Let us therefore turn our attention to the question of regional development.

Regional Development

Regional policy, like sectorial policy, includes a wide range of programs. Yuill, Allen and Hull distinguish five types of incentive: investment grants, preferential credits, tax credits, accelerated write-offs, and employment grants. Their analysis clearly indicates that in the countries of the EEC, "capital grants are the mainstay of most regional incentive packages" (Yuill, Allen and Hull, 1980, p. 117). McAllister (1982) and Ashcroft (1980) make the same point. Similarly, in Canada the regional aspect is of great concern in the federal government's financial aid programs (Blais, Faucher and Young, 1983a), but it is of less importance in the case of tax benefits. The legitimacy of regional policies, which was noted in the previous chapter, influences the choice of intervention programs. Governments are anxious to show that they are doing something for regional development and want their efforts to be visible. From this point of view, grants to specific firms have much to offer (McAllister, 1982; Lewis, 1984, p. 144).

The real impact of investment incentives is a hotly debated issue. The extent to which incentives really influence a firm's decision has yet to be determined: if a firm has invested even without these incentives, there is not really any supplement. In Canada, studies based on interviews seem to indicate that the supplement rate is between 30 and 80 percent (Economic Council of Canada, 1975, p. 174). Moreover, the creation of the Department of Regional Economic Expansion (DREE) coincided with a reduction of 1 percent in the gap between the unemployment rate in the Atlantic provinces and that in the rest of Canada (ibid., p. 168). Of course, there is no proof that DREE's policies were entirely responsible for this situation (Usher, 1983), but such data tend at least to confirm the hypothesis of a significant impact. This led the Economic Council to conclude:

> DREE's expenditures within the framework of the regional development seem to be effective; in other words, a sufficient number of firms are encouraged by the grants to move their plants, thereby contributing to increased national production, which would not occur otherwise, and at the same time employing workers who would otherwise be unemployed (Economic Council of Canada, 1975, p. 186).

The same conclusion seems to have been reached concerning other countries as well. Ashcroft's assessment of econometric studies on the impact of regional incentives in six European countries is as follows:

> Regional policies had induced 13.6 percent of assisted investments in the GA areas of Germany, 16.0 percent of total investment in the Northern Region of the Netherlands and 20.0 percent of total investment in the three main DA regions of the United Kingdom. For employment it appeared that regional policies had raised employment by 1.26, 1.23 and 1.19 jobs per annum per thousand of the population in respectively the GA areas of Germany, the Designated Areas of Ireland and the four main DA regions of the United Kingdom. In Denmark and Belgium no quantitative studies of the effect of policy were available. However, for Denmark, one study could be interpreted as indicating that 0.79 jobs per annum per thousand of the population had been created by regional policy in Jutland. In Belgium there was evidence that suggested a redistribution of investment in favor of the assisted areas (Ashcroft, 1980, p. 102).

Ashcroft even feels that "the effect appears to be substantial" (Ashcroft, 1980, p. 53). Along the same lines, an OECD study (1983d) concludes that, in general, incentives have little influence on investment decisions but that their impact on the pace of investment, within a given large economic region, is more significant. The OECD study also advances the theory that this impact has been increased recently as businesses have become more aware of production costs.

Thus, two other questions come to mind. First, since the regional problem is one of employment, why not stimulate job creation directly, instead of stimulating investment? Secondly, why turn to grants instead of to tax concessions? The fact that regional incentives are aimed at investment rather than at employment is often presented as inconsistent. Woodward's argument on this score is a classic:

> The capital bias of DREE's maximum-incentive formula, of the constraint affecting most industries, and of the majority of offers is inconsistent with the department's primary objective: employment. The inconsistency occurs because a capital bias implies that the designated regions' extra employment attributable to the grant program is less, and investment more, than would have occurred if the incentive had been neutral or labor biased (Woodward, 1974, p. 173).

However, government strategy is perhaps not as inconsistent as it at first seems. Even if employment is a government's top priority, the government must count on the private sector to create the jobs. Since the thinking of business leaders is oriented toward investment, not employment, governments must take this into account when attempting to influence their decisions. This explains why incentive grants for job creation seem to be less effective than investment incentives. Employers, in any case, find them less appealing and take less advantage of them than they might (OECD, 1982, p. 47); as well, the budgetary cost per job tends to be inflated (see McKerrie and Sengen Berger, 1983). Moreover, "there is no satisfactory evidence that policy has induced firms to substitute the factor subsidized for a non-subsidized factor" (Ashcroft, 1980, p. 104).

Yet why do governments favour grants rather than tax concessions? Unfortunately, the existing literature does not allow us to compare the relative effectiveness of the two approaches (Ashcroft, 1980, p. 104). According to the OECD (1983d), it seems that, next to the importance of incentive programs, it is their foreseeability that business generally values most. From this point of view, the advantage of grants is that one can get the money quickly and in full, whereas tax measures are only worthwhile once a business begins to make a profit. Such measures have fewer constraints, however, and this makes them appealing to investors (OECD, 1983d; Woodside, 1979). Overall, however, industrialists seem to be biased toward tax concessions. In Canada, businessmen want reduced taxes, not grants (Blais, Faucher and Young, 1983a). The same attitude is found in Europe:

> Despite being relatively minor in expenditure terms, it is often claimed that these allowances have an impact greater than their monetary value would suggest. . . . Tax concessions, too, have a significant psychological

> impact, suggesting, as they do, that awarding bodies take an especially positive stance to recipient firms (Yuill, Allen and Hull, 1980, p. 230).

This leads us to believe that tax concessions are probably more effective than grants.

Thus, it is not out of concern for economic efficiency that governments favour grants. The choice is essentially political. As we have already shown, grants have a higher profile. A minister or a member of Parliament can announce that the government is spending a specific amount to encourage the establishment of a certain industry in a given region. From the vote-seeking point of view, this seems like a clever plan. But is it really? A strong dose of skepticism seems to be called for here. For, in fact, there is every reason to believe that the electoral impact of very selective interventions is rather marginal. Agricultural policy, for instance, is often criticized because of its "vote-seeking" nature. However, a systematic analysis of the effect of agricultural policy on election results in Quebec concludes that this effect is negligible and that the government's popularity depends more on the overall agricultural picture and its short-term fluctuations (Blais, 1978). Moreover, a study on the allocation of facilities in London and New York indicates that this had very little effect on voting in the next election (Glassberg, 1973). This result is particularly surprising in the case of New York, where all observers took it for granted that this was a crucial element in local politics. Any electoral advantage that a government might gain from regional grants can easily be exaggerated by politicians themselves. This does not mean that visibility is not important. Politicians want their interventions in regional politics (whatever form these may take) to be widely advertised. But it is in their best interests to see that these interventions are effective, in other words, that they encourage investment and reduce unemployment. It is therefore not obvious that grants are preferable to tax measures if, as we have already seen, investors are more sensitive to tax benefits.

In the context of regional development, the principal advantage of grants as opposed to fiscal aid seems to us to be something else. Here again, public perception is all-important. Everything seems to suggest that tax measures are even more badly perceived by the public than grants are; 63 percent of Canadians are opposed to the federal government reducing taxes in the business sector in order to stimulate economic growth (*Decima Surveys*, 1981–83, qn. 374); 68 percent of Americans favour increased taxation of corporate profits in order to reduce the deficit, whereas only 24 percent are in favour of increased personal taxes (*Public Opinion*, vol. 8, February–March 1985, p. 27). There are angry outcries about companies which succeed in making stupendous profits and avoid paying any taxes. The *Wall Street Journal* (November 20, 1984) related the following "disturbing" facts on its front page:

> General Electric Co. is one company reaping the benefits of changes in the corporate tax. Last year, it earned a hefty $2.4 billion on its domestic operations but didn't have to pay a penny to the federal government in income taxes. Nor did the company pay federal taxes in 1982 or 1981, in spite of $2 billion in domestic earnings each year. And it has been able to claim large refunds of taxes paid in earlier years. It accomplished that by taking full advantage of rapid write-offs and investment tax credits for purchases of new plant and equipment.

Despite these reactions, tax benefits are still offered. We shall see shortly that in an area such as research and development they offer many advantages. But in order to avoid a situation like the one that arose with General Electric, it is in a government's interest to ensure that the tax benefit is not too large. However, in regional development the incentives must be substantial in order to obtain the desired effect. As we have already shown, the nominal rate of grants is 25 percent. The actual rate is often much lower (Ashcroft, 1980), though the amounts involved are significant. Tax incentives have to be very generous to be of equal financial value and must be spread over several years. Grants, on the other hand, are directly related in time to investments.

Lastly, we must comment briefly on the orientation of regional policy. Several economists believe in encouraging geographic mobility. Trebilcock, for instance, recognizes the political necessity of compensation for localities that are severely affected by industrial decline, but he stresses measures which "induce members to forego the stay option and exercise the exit option" (Trebilcock, 1985). It is not clear whether he means the option to exit from the industry or from the region, but any policy that gives priority to geographic mobility is in danger of arousing vehement opposition, since there is a strong attachment to the local milieu, as we saw in the previous chapter.

Innovation and Technology

In the area of innovation and technology, the most substantial government aid is probably the preferential tax treatment given to R&D. Several countries allow R&D costs to be written off over a shorter time, sometimes in the same year in which they were incurred. In addition, there are special deductions and tax credits pegged to the level of expenditure of an earlier period or to the changes in that level (McFetridge and Warda, 1983). Several of these measures are relatively recent. In the United States, for instance, which is the most generous developed nation next to Canada (ibid., Table 5-4, p. 72), it is only since 1981 that there has been a tax credit for the excess R&D expenditures (ibid., p. 46). The Canadian example is interesting as well. In 1976 the federal government abolished its R&D grant program and two years later reintroduced a more or less equivalent tax deduction (Blais, Faucher and Young, 1983a; Blais et al.,

1983). This gives a good idea of the general tendency to favour tax measures in this area, contrary to what occurs in regional development. This tendency will be the first object of our attention. Later we shall look at government contracts which, as we saw in Chapter 1, are particularly important in highly technological industries.

Let us begin with the tax concessions for research and development. The government's interest in this type of activity is probably exaggerated:

> Some countries tend to exaggerate the importance of research and development within the framework of their technology policy. In many respects, it is innovation and technological change that is important, not R&D, which, in itself, is of little value, if any. It only becomes important when it extends into production and marketing. Moreover, in several sectors, many innovations do not result from structured, complex R&D efforts (Mansfield, 1985).

It seems to us that government policies have to be explained by two types of considerations. The first are symbolic considerations. R&D is an activity which lends itself easily to quantification, and in most discussions of technology it is the statistics on the amounts allocated to R&D that are usually quoted. In Canada, the insignificant sums spent on R&D and the meagre contributions in this area by multinationals are important issues in the debate on industrial policy (Blais, 1985a). Insofar as every government has to be seen to be highly interested in technology (as we saw in the previous chapter) governments must spend and cause the spending of "sufficient" sums on R&D. From this point of view, it is not surprising that the Canadian tax system is so generous (McFetridge and Warda, 1983) given that Canada's performance is so poor in this area (Bernstein, 1985, Table 1-1). There is strong pressure exerted on the government to correct this "abnormal" situation.

Governments would be making a mistake to resist this pressure, particularly as there are good reasons to believe that these incentives are somewhat beneficial. Studies on the impact of tax incentives indicate that they do in fact contribute to increased research and development, although at high cost (tax loss) (Mansfield, 1985; McFetridge, 1977). Moreover, R&D seems to increase the number of patents, the surest indication of innovative activity (McFetridge, 1977).

Secondly, governments have realized that they stand to gain by adopting the least selective approach possible, for it is probably in the technological sector that industrial policy has known its worst defeats. Westcott reports that "the return from research and development tends to be lower in those fields where much of it is supported by the U.S. government" (Westcott, 1983, p. 112). Zysman's study (1977) of French computer science shows how government intervention merely weakened the commercial position of firms that depended on public aid. Ilgen's analysis of the chemical industry concludes that "an industry that relies on innovation as its engine of growth needs a setting where individuals and firms have maximum freedom to pursue their innovative instincts" (Ilgen, 1983, p. 680). If, in fact, commercial failures like the Concorde are the rule rather than the exception, we cannot but agree with Trebilcock when he states that general incentive measures form the best economic policy toward industrial R&D that is attainable in our political system (Trebilcock, 1985). On the same lines, Mansfield states:

> It appears that governments are more successful in stimulating civil technology when they limit themselves to general policies without trying to decide precisely the kind of product to develop or how fast a particular product should be marketed (Mansfield, 1985).

This seems to be the conclusion eventually reached by most governments. To be sure, aid measures to certain industrial sectors or to specific projects are not abolished overnight; but the infatuation with "national champions" has lost its early glow. Governments seem to undergo a learning process, during which they correct certain errors in judgment, especially the most glaring ones. In an area in which the dangers are so great, governments must be careful not to become associated with any specific project, since they stand to lose much more from a dismal failure than they might gain from a resounding success.

The fact that research and development is encouraged by tax measures rather than by grants is another indication of this desire to take a non-selective approach, since in general there is less likelihood of discrimination with their use (Woodside, 1979). Tax measures have another advantage, one that is not insignificant in a period of budget restrictions, namely that they can mask the total cost of government intervention (Bird, 1980, p. 14). Yet this should not be the determining factor. We must remember that tax concessions as a whole have not increased over time (see Chapter 1). It is thus in the area of technology that fiscal measures are favoured, and we feel that the reason for this is essentially that governments opt for a less selective approach to this sector.

Supporters of a strong technology policy often stress the crucial role of government contracts: "The most important way in which government . . . has influenced technological innovation is through demand" (Rothwell and Zegveld, 1981, p. 50). Data on the impact of preferential government purchasing are almost nonexistent (Bernier, 1984). Dalpé has observed that most Canadian firms offering products of medium- or high-level technological intensity have taken advantage of protectionist purchasing policies in Canada (Dalpé, 1984, p. 171); but we must also, logically, consider cases in which businesses suffered through government contracts (Zysman, 1977), as well as the cost of such policies. The only available studies deal with government contracts and suggest that the effect is minimal:

> Two recent U.S. studies have concluded that the magnitude of spin-off benefits . . . is very small indeed. Goldberg found that spin-off benefits accruing to recipients of federal R&D contracts in the United States have

> amounted to 2 percent of the value of the contract. Terleckyj found that federally funded R&D had either no effect or a negative effect on the subsequent growth in total factor productivity of U.S. R&D contractors. The implications of Terleckyj's work is that spin-off benefits are non-existent (McFetridge and Warda, 1983, pp. 79–80).

Be that as it may, it appears that government contracts are a rather popular instrument of industrial policy in industrial circles. In Quebec, nearly all industrialists favour a policy of preferential purchasing (Bernier, 1984: Sales, 1983). In fact, of all possible measures of intervention, the policy of purchasing is perceived as the most acceptable (Bernier, 1984). Bernier also states that the same attitude can be observed in the rest of Canada. This measure is all the more popular in that it is supposed to preclude any kind of discrimination or constraint upon firms' decisions and behaviour. It has a symbolic value as well: since foreign suppliers do not pay taxes in the country, local industrialists do not see why they should receive any kind of benefits from the government.

The stance of governments is cautious. On the one hand, they cannot ignore pressure from the industrialists: "Most governments perceive themselves as being highly vulnerable to the charges of 'neglecting national interests,' 'exporting jobs,' and failing to 'protect' domestic industry" (De Mestral, 1982, p. 172). On the other hand, they try to resist this pressure. The minister responsible for government contracts is generally concerned with efficiency, and the policies adopted try more or less to reconcile the objectives of efficiency and of industrial development. The minister will agree to turn only to local suppliers so long as their numbers are sufficient to guarantee some competition among them (Bernier, 1984). The adoption of a code on government contracts at the time of the Tokyo Round is another indication of the desire of governments to restrict the use of this instrument and to protect themselves against the pressure of certain protectionist demands.

In short, aid to technology tends to be less and less selective: "It seems that governments are turning towards more horizontal policies" (OECD, 1982). Governments have more faith in fiscal incentives of a more general nature. This new direction corresponds to a learning stage, since several governments have been burned by unfortunate experiences when they were closely associated with projects that turned out very badly.

Aid to Small Business

Aid to small business is primarily in the form of loans and technical services. It is the financing aspect that concerns us here. We shall first consider why the government favours loans in its policies on small business. We shall then look at the relative advantages and disadvantages of guarantees and loans as a form of aid.

It is not at all obvious that the financing of small businesses is a "serious" problem. A poll taken among Canadian business leaders reveals that financing is ranked sixth in the order of their concerns, after marketing, operational costs, the recruiting of skilled labour, inflation, and production (Canada, Department of Industry, Trade and Commerce, 1982). The same results are found in a study of owner-operators of firms of manufactured goods in Quebec (D'Amboise, 1983). Overall, the operators of small businesses express satisfaction with services provided by the banks (Hatch, Wynant and Grant, 1982, p. 7; Canada, Department of Industry, Trade and Commerce, 1982, p. 31).

There is nothing to suggest, in fact, that small businesses suffer when they deal with the banks. Hatch, Wynant and Grant make this very clear:

> Our results argue that small businesses are not treated in a substantially different fashion than are larger firms. Small businesses, in fact, receive more favourable treatment by the banks in terms of the amount of financing obtained, the loan conditions imposed on the business and the time taken by the banks to reach a decision (Hatch, Wynant and Grant, 1982, p. 8).

Of course, small businesses must generally pay higher interest rates, but the difference is entirely due to the higher risks and administrative costs involved (Hatch, Wynant and Grant, 1982, p. 11). Financial institutions also insist upon personal guarantees more often, but again this practice can be justified by certain features of small business. The only real problem seems to be the banks' hesitation to lend money to high-risk firms:

> There is some anecdotal evidence that the chartered banks simply do not wish to become involved in potentially high loss rate types of business. The implication is that being involved in bankruptcies and foreclosures on a recurring basis . . . increases the cost of an intermediary's normal business (McFetridge, 1984, p. 12).

The economical rationale behind aid for financing small businesses is therefore rather doubtful (Gagnon and Papillon, 1984).

What of the political rationale, though? At first glance, the need for government intervention is not at all obvious. In Canada, banks inspire a good deal of confidence; they rank third in a list of the trustworthiness of 20 institutions (Johnston, 1985). In the United States, their image is even brighter. According to surveys by the Opinion Research Corporation, banks rank second only to churches in inspiring confidence (Lipset and Schneider, 1983, p. 60, Table 2-3, p. 60). According to a survey in the *U.S. News and World Report*, banks are considered the most efficient and honest of 26 institutions examined (Lipset and Schneider, 1983, Figure 3-2, p. 75). They are also the most highly esteemed industry.

In this context, government intervention comes as a surprise, all the more so since small firms themselves prefer banks as lenders of short-

and long-term loans (Facsym Research Ltd., 1981, p. xii). The explanation is that confidence in banks is not total. Their image was somewhat tarnished by the end of the 1970s, following the increase in interest rates (Lipset and Schneider, 1983, p. 367). As well, the activities of the banks themselves engender a good deal of distrust. The price of a loan is interest, and "interest rates do not enjoy the same respectability as other market prices" (Facsym Research Ltd., 1981, p. 19). This distrust is increased by the fact that the borrower is perceived as being poor and the lender as being rich (ibid., p. 21). In the situation that concerns us here, the poor borrower also possesses the virtue of being small, while the rich lender's vice is that he is big.

As a result, the satisfaction expressed with regard to banks is not wholehearted:

> Despite the fact that banks are perceived to be the small businessman's best ally, almost all respondents registered the same complaints. Most felt "under the thumb" of their bank managers, described as an uneasy alliance; that loan decisions are at best arbitrary; that most bank managers have little business sense or acumen, and are not truly sympathetic to the problem of small business (Thorne Riddell, Thorne Stevenson and Kellogg, 1981, p. 23).

The reason for credit programs for small business can be explained by the fact that the government is constrained by political necessity to prove that it is doing something for small business, especially as big business is favoured in other ways. As McFetridge notes, "it is quite possible that federal assistance to small business merely compensates for other federal benefits bestowed on 'big' business for which small firms, by force of circumstances, are not eligible" (McFetridge, 1982a, p. 28). In Canada, moreover, the federal government established the Federal Business Development Bank in 1944 instead of modifying the *Bank Act*, which prohibited banks from taking real estate as security and which limited the interest rates they could charge their clients (Hatch, Wynant and Grant, 1983, p. 366).

Now that these restrictions have been removed, could the government not simply withdraw from this field of intervention? Abolishing aid programs to small business just when small business is so popular would be rather rash and would send the wrong signal. Governments must show that they are concerned with the problems of small business, and giving assistance in financing offers several advantages in this respect. On the one hand, as we have seen, there has always been latent mistrust of the banks on the part of small businessmen. On the other hand, government intervention is relatively inexpensive. In 1979, the cost to the treasury of Federal Business Development Bank loans was only $20 million, while that of guarantees provided within the framework of the *Small Business Loan Act* was a mere $1.5 million (Economic Council of Canada, 1982, Tables A-2 and A-4). Ultimately, this is a fairly inexpensive way for the government to show that it is doing something for small business.

What are the respective advantages and disadvantages of loans and guarantees as a means of intervention? Hatch, Wynant and Grant (1982) are in favour of loans. Their argument is essentially that the only real problem in financing is in dealing with high-risk firms and that an institution like the Federal Business Development Bank is more likely to deal with such clients. McFetridge (1984), on the other hand, prefers guarantees because they involve lower administrative costs. On the political level, direct loans have the "advantage of being highly visible. For this reason, loans offered by the Federal Business Develoment Bank are by far the best-known program of aid to small business (Canada, Department of Industry, Trade and Commerce, 1982, p. 26). This advantage must not be exaggerated, however; it is certainly possible to increase the visibility of guarantees. Another important difference is that loans require the establishment of institutions like the Federal Business Development Bank, whereas in the case of guarantees the administrative authority is delegated to the private institution which advances the loan (Economic Council of Canada, 1982, p. 15). Loans thus lead to the creation of a bureaucracy which has its own interests at heart; most notable of these, of course, is its own survival as an institution. A good example of this is the way the Federal Business Development Bank reacted when demand for its services as a financing institution decreased: it created new programs, such as the financial liaison service, which brings together investors and businesses in search of capital (Federal Business Development Bank, *Annual Report*, 1984, p. 7). The existence of this bureaucracy makes it harder to abolish loan programs.

Yet if, as we claim, the first objective of government is to provide symbolic satisfaction to small businessmen, at insignificant cost, then guarantees seem to offer many advantages. For the same price, guarantees provide aid to a greater number of businesses anywhere within the country.[77] A suggestion such as that of Hatch, Wynant and Grant (1983), who propose that more government aid be directed toward high-risk businesses, has little appeal politically (as the authors are the first to admit) insofar as this would require higher interest rates. After all, the political target of intervention is the small business in all its ideological virtue, not the risky enterprise. The importance recently attached to guarantees in Canada suggests that the same view is held by the politicians. The number of loans guaranteed under the *Small Business Loan Act* increased fivefold between 1977 and 1983 (Department of Regional Industrial Expansion, *Small Business Loan Act*, 1984, p. 7).

Conclusion

The considerations behind the choice of an instrument vary widely according to its target (aid to declining sectors or small businesses, regional development, or innovation and technology). We must now try to determine some general trends. Our analysis leads us to propose the seven generalizations which follow.

The calculations of politicians are rarely optimal. It is in fact very easy to overestimate the rationality of political thinking and to present decisions, a posteriori, as if they were part of a perfect strategy. Politicians, for example, tend to exaggerate the political dividends of regional development grants. Their timetable is very heavy and the information they are given is often fragmentary (Winn, 1985). They seldom have the time to weigh the pros and cons of various options, with the inevitable result that their conclusions are approximate and pragmatic. As Latouche (1985) points out in the case of the constitutional debate, government strategies are often characterized by a certain subjectivity, and casual events can assume enormous importance.

Political calculations improve somewhat with time. Although the calculations which lead initially to the choice of one instrument over another are sometimes shaky, one might imagine that the strategy would develop a certain logic over time. In some cases one can perceive just such a learning process. The most obvious example is aid to innovation and technology: failures in what was known as the strategy of "national champions" led to serious reassessment of the policy. At the same time, the learning process has been very slow. It was only recently, for instance, that the Canadian government began to favour securities over loans as a form of aid to small businesses. The re-evaluation of former decisions does not go very far, partly because the political agenda is limited (Cobb and Elder, 1972; Kingdon, 1984) and partly because politicians tend to overestimate their own ability to appreciate the political impact of existing measures[78] and thus see no need for a systematic analysis of profitability.

Politicians take into account the calculations of industrialists. Since industrialists are the ones who make investments, they wield considerable power, and politicians cannot disregard their strategy or their psychology when it comes time to select an instrument of intervention. Even if they wish to stimulate employment, politicians must subsidize investments, because it is from this angle that industrialists conceive their projects. Even if politicians wish to aid labour and not management, they must still subsidize business, because it is business which creates (or maintains) jobs. Because industrialists are concerned about their administrative independence, they prefer less discretionary forms of intervention, particularly tax concessions. All else being equal, politicians would thus do well to use tax concessions; but all else is not always equal and, for reasons of legitimacy (which we shall discuss in the next point), tax concessions cannot always be used on a wide scale. This fact suggests that the power of industrialists is limited to certain specific parameters and that it is far from being the main determinant of the choice of instrument.

Politicians consider the legitimacy of the various instruments. Government contracts, quantitative restrictions, and the financing of small business are perceived as particularly legitimate forms of aid, while tax concessions are viewed as being particularly unfair. This explains the limited use of the latter instrument. The case of quantitative restrictions is also interesting. We have seen that politicians resist protectionist pressure but turn to voluntary restraint agreements when this pressure becomes too strong, since these agreements have the advantage of pinpointing the "guilty" country, which then bears responsibility for the industrial problem.

Politicians consider the effectiveness of the various instruments. GATT's choices are made largely for economic reasons. The limited use of voluntary restraint agreements shows that governments are conscious of the harmful effects of such agreements. Disenchantment with the strategy of "national champion" can be viewed in the same light. On this point, our analysis differs considerably from that of Trebilcock (1985), according to whom, the political framework yields a set of positive policy implications that are in many respects diametrically opposed to those implied by the economic framework. This dichotomy between the economic and political cannot be overemphasized, considering that, as we have seen, the performance of the economy is a major factor in elections. If governments wish to be re-elected they must see that their policies are as effective as possible, i.e., that they reduce regional unemployment, encourage growth, and stimulate research and development. This is not the only concern, as the other generalizations attest, but it is nonetheless an important one.

Politicians consider the flexibility of the various instruments. Since the effects of a given policy are largely uncertain at the outset, "it may be rational to choose an instrument that maximizes sensitivity and flexibility, so that continuous marginal adjustments in the balancing of interests can be made over time" (Trebilcock et al., 1982, p. 33). From this point of view, instruments such as grants and loans seem less flexible, because they require the support of a bureaucracy, which will subsequently resist the abolition of the program it directs. Programs of direct financial aid, moreover, have a fairly long life expectancy (Blais, Faucher and Young, 1983a). However, grants are the most substantial form of aid next to tariffs, and their use has grown the most over the past 20 years. There is nothing to suggest, therefore, that the flexibility of the various instruments influences the politicians' decisions, partly because other criteria are more important and partly because their reasoning is imperfect and they tend to think of the short term only.

Politicians attach too much importance to the visibility of the various instruments. Politicians want the benefits of their policies to be as discernible as possible, while keeping the costs as invisible as possible. As a result, according to Trebilcock et al., the benefits must be concentrated so that they will be more visible, while costs must be dispersed to reduce their visibility. Moreover, "it is in the interest of a governing party to choose policies that confine the benefits to marginal voters" whose loyalty can be changed and whose vote can be manipulated (Trebilcock et al., 1982, p. 33).

Overall, our analysis tends to show up the weaknesses of these hypotheses. However, they do have a certain validity which we must recognize from the outset. Obviously it is in the government's interest if the benefits of their programs appear to be considerable, at minimal cost. It is equally obvious that politicians are worried about the visibility of their policies, the best example being regional development grants. Lastly, the costs of government measures are well dispersed and are thus less easily discerned. Yet this is true no matter what the instrument, and we are skeptical about politicians' ability to reap benefits from the greater visibility of some forms of aid compared with others.

On the one hand, we know too little about the way that government measures are viewed and about the source of these perceptions, so it is difficult to decide upon the optimal strategy. For instance, Trebilcock (1985) expresses the opinion that guarantees, which do not involve budget spending, are less visible than grants. This is not obvious. In the case of rescue operations in particular, where there are apt to be newspaper headlines citing facts and figures, more is known about the amounts loaned or guaranteed by the government than about the amounts involved in grant programs, which receive less publicity. Moreover, since many people fail to make the distinction between the amount of the guarantee (or loan) and the real cost of the operation (the implicit subsidy), this cost could be greatly exaggerated. In addition, tax concessions are perhaps less visible, but if the media report cases of businesses which manage to avoid paying taxes, the effect is the opposite, and people begin to imagine a whole series of tax shelters just for the benefit of business.

Moreover, government measures (such as a particular grant to a particular business in a particular district) are not visible in themselves. Visibility comes when the results of the measures are publicized by the media. In the electronic age that we live in, it is not the first spadeful of earth announcing a new factory that counts so much as the monthly or quarterly headlines about the growth of the Gross National Product, unemployment, or inflation. In Great Britain, for instance:

> A regression in which the values of unemployment and inflation reported by the *Daily Mirror* are used as independent variables explains a greater part of the variance in government popularity than a regression in which the values of unemployment and inflation reported by the Central Statistical Office are read as explanatory variables (Mosley, 1984, p. 128).

With the media insisting so much on results, the possibility for symbolic manipulation is greatly reduced.

The proposition concerning marginal voters is even more doubtful. First of all, there is no real evidence that we can empirically distinguish marginal voters (or districts) from non-marginal and infra-marginal ones. In Canada, especially, party loyalty wavers easily:

> Canadians do alter their party ties, . . . they do abandon the loyalties of their fathers; and do reach out to new parties. Thus Canadian parties cannot count on stable following in the electorate for decades (Jenson, 1975, p. 553).

In most democracies, moreover, there are greater changes in voting patterns (Flanagan and Dalton, 1984). Even "loyal" voters rarely stay with one party unconditionally; if they feel their interests are no longer being represented, they change their vote (Jenson, 1976), and for this reason they can never be taken for granted. As Winn (1985) points out:

> To be pre-occupied with allocating benefits to marginal voters is time consuming; . . . it is wasteful when ministers need to distribute largesse within their own party; and it is electorally dangerous.

In addition, elections are increasingly concerned with national issues (Wilson, 1980), and local variations of the voting pattern often depend on the candidates' strategy, which is in turn greatly influenced by the overall state of the economy (Jacobson and Kernell, 1981). A strategy aimed specifically at a particular electoral district will likely fail.

To be sure, governments want to proclaim the benefits of their interventions while disguising the costs. Our analysis indicates, however, that people are not fooled and that visibility cannot be masked or exaggerated at will. The media play a crucial role here. The importance which politicians attach to this aspect would therefore seem to have been exaggerated. The psychology of industrialists and the legitimacy, effectiveness, and flexibility of the measures are much more important considerations. Once again, political calculations are often faulty.

Conclusions

Throughout this study, we have attempted to define the broad characteristics of industrial aid and its sociopolitical dynamics. We have tried to paint as full a picture as possible in order to highlight the most significant parameters of government intervention in this area. The available information was fragmentary, and the picture is less complete than we could have wished; but we believe it to be more complete than the one given in the various studies we consulted. Our approach does entail a few disadvantages. We were unable to analyze problems which were specific to a given industry or a particular country. In addition, we could not discuss the government measures in detail. Yet it seemed to us at the time, as it seems to us now, that it was more important to provide a global perspective, which is the only way we can view sectorial or national particularities in their real context.

We were also very careful to measure the amount of the various forms of industrial aid, as well as giving a breakdown of this aid according to the type of industry or business. Our insistence on this point is the result of our methodological position, according to which a solid description of government output is essential to the analysis of its causes, a condition seldom respected in the literature on industrial policy.[79] This is why we spent so much time in Chapter 1 on a description of the principal trends and orientations of industrial aid. Since these were summed up at the end of that chapter, there is no need to repeat them here. Nonetheless, we would like to stress three conclusions which call traditional interpretations into question. A central thesis of this text is that the process of freeing trade is the backdrop to industrial aid. This thesis might seem surprising at a time when more and more observers are proclaiming the emergence of a new protectionism. First of all, we have maintained that the strongest trend is toward freer trade. Our evaluation is based on two kinds of data, the growth of international trade which is continuing to expand, and the results of studies on the amount of various forms of aid, which indicate that the increase in grants and quantitative restrictions is much smaller than the reduction of tariff protections. These data are not complete, but both sets of information point to the same conclusion. Some will claim that studies quantifying the range of the various instruments contain gaps, but our reply is that the figures given in these studies are more believable than those of the "neoprotectionists" who mostly cite specific examples. It is also possible that recent trends have not yet been measured, since research is always several years behind reality. The possibility must not be dismissed a priori, but we must not overlook the fact that data on international trade point to this same conclusion and that the trend to protectionism is supposed to have "emerged" since 1972 (Balassa, 1978, p. 413). Like most predictions, the truth of this one may well be confirmed by the facts . . . in five, ten, twenty, or fifty years' time.

It is understandable that liberal economists and international bodies who believe that free trade among nations is beneficial should be strongly moved by the number of barriers set up by governments and should tend to exaggerate them. Talking about them a great deal and making sure that they are discussed at international conferences is a good way of helping to contain these barriers. The entire discourse on protectionism, therefore, can be seen as a method of encouraging the lifting of barriers.

Secondly, we have stated that tariffs are still the most substantial form of aid, when every other study on the subject conveys the impression that tariffs have fallen into disuse and that it is non-tariff barriers that will be significant henceforth. We have continued to stress the necessity of dropping the empty typology of this tariff/non-tariff dichotomy and of basing the classification of instruments on their form and place. While it is true that tariffs are less important than all the other forms of aid together, they are still the instrument which offers the greatest protection. We could certainly name industries where this is not the case, but the overall tendency seems clear to us. This fact could have important political ramifications. Skepticism about GATT is generally based on the double hypothesis, according to which GATT is more effective in reducing tariffs than in combatting non-tariff measures and that these measures must be tackled now (Grey, 1981). By contrast, our analysis indicates that tariffs are still a major barrier and that there is room for another program for reducing tariff protection within the framework of GATT.

Thirdly, we have established that big business is only slightly privileged by government measures as a whole. Its only real advantage is in the area of grants. Moreover, this advantage is reduced with time.

Actually, it is agriculture, the bastion of small business, which receives the most government aid. Despite this, the thesis of collusion between government and big money seems to be accepted in works on this subject. Obviously it is a central theme of the orthodox Marxist school, which pays particular attention to the dominant role of the large industrial and financial groups (Le Pors, 1977, p. 7). Analyses of big business adopt the same point of view, the best example being the classic study by Vernon, where we learn that "there has been a growing tendency to use large national enterprises in an effort to solve specific problems, as if they were agencies of the state" (Vernon, 1974, p. 3). Even authors praising the virtues of small business tend to convey the same image, namely that government measures place the small and medium-sized businesses at a disadvantage (see especially Peterson, 1978, pp. 112 ff). The same impression reigns among the population (Lipset and Schneider, 1983, p. 168). While the data we collected did not completely invalidate this thesis, they certainly made us modify it considerably.

However, the most basic characteristic of industrial aid is the movement toward freer trade, attenuated by a whole series of measures designed to slow down the rate of decline in industries, businesses, and regions in difficulty. In many respects, this strategy might be considered optimal, since it combines the citizens' desire for growth with strong stability. A society which has the impression that it is "going somewhere," even if not at top speed, while managing to avoid the biggest jolts, will be relatively happy. From this perspective, political systems produce the output which the majority wants.

This evaluation of industrial aid might seem unnecessarily positive. Surely government measures entail all kinds of harmful effects? No doubt they do. We have mentioned them several times, particularly when discussing voluntary restraint agreements. But the scope of these negative effects is largely unknown. On the one hand, profitability studies are practically nonexistent (Grant, 1983; Ashcroft, 1980; OECD, 1983d). On the other hand, impact is almost never measured in terms of job preservation, which is obviously the prime objective. Our own data tend to show that government intervention is not as harmful as one would have thought. In Chapter 2 we were able to claim that grants to industry, on the whole, do not appear to lower a country's economic growth (Table 2-3).

Is our conclusion therefore to be that existing policies are near perfect? Researchers rarely consider existing government policies to be wholly satisfactory, and we shall not break with this tradition here. Two thorny questions have been raised, we feel. The first concerns the relationship between industrial aid and other aspects of government intervention. We have seen that in countries where social security payments are higher, industrial aid grants are lower (Table 2-6) and that governments are less concerned with unemployment in the textile and clothing industries (Table 3-2). Would an equitable social security system not be preferable to industrial aid? There are good reasons to think so. McCallum and Blais (1985) have shown that social security payments could even have a positive influence on economic growth by contributing to the social consensus and reducing resistance to change, since "losers" are assured of some form of compensation. This is why, according to Trebilcock (1985), the key to an effective adjustment policy is found in manpower programs.

We must, however, stress the limitations of social policy in general, and of manpower programs in particular. Industrial aid differs from social policy in that it tries to preserve jobs, rather than to provide financial compensation to those who lose their jobs. While the principle of compensation is, a priori, more advantageous, it loses some of its appeal at a time of high unemployment when there is a strong demand for preserving jobs. In countries where unemployment is highest, there are sizable industrial aid grants (Table 2-6) and very few jobs are lost in the textile and clothing industries (Table 3-2). Social policy is therefore only an effective substitute for industrial aid when unemployment is not a problem.

The obvious question is whether the most effective solution might not be to attack unemployment directly, through corporatist institutions for instance,[80] or by eliminating taxes on manpower (Rousseau and Taurand, 1984). This question obviously lies beyond the scope of this study, but we should keep it in mind when evaluating industrial aid.

A second consideration concerns the concrete mechanisms used to control industrial decline. For some time now, quantitative restrictions have attracted the most attention — and the most criticism. Our own evaluation is much less negative. We consider these restrictions to be a kind of safety valve, essential to the process of freeing trade. This safety valve is orientated directly toward job preservation. Its symbolic effectiveness is enormous, since it identifies the countries responsible for national industrial problems. It is obviously a very expensive safety valve, but so far no one has gone too far. The most fashionable proposals recently have dealt with measures for compensating workers. Our main quarrel with these proposals is that they are diametrically opposed to the principle of government intervention itself, which is the control of decline. Encouraging mobility is desirable, of course, and all governments have adopted this kind of program. But such programs should not form the basis of an adjustment policy. Especially at a time of high unemployment, people look for stability, not mobility. This can lead to rigidities, which in turn reduce economic growth; but there is no real problem as long as greater value is placed on stability than on growth.

From our point of view, the biggest problem with adjustment measures is their failure to be resolutely regionalist. On the one hand, attachment to the local milieu is much stronger than to the place of employment. On the other hand, political dynamics are based on regionalism. The problem only becomes political if a business or industry is having difficulties which might increase local unemployment. Governments recognize this reality, of course, and regional policies play an important role in industrial aid. Our analysis would suggest, however, that governments should probably make the regional aspect the linchpin of their policy. From this point of view, experiments such as the Canadian Industrial Renewal Board are very attractive.

In the Introduction, we said that we would follow two avenues of research in this study. First, we stressed the need to place industrial aid within a social context and to take industry's political power into account. We also announced our intention to see government intervention from the perspective of politicians. We would like to a take a brief look at these points again.

Let us begin with the power of the social actors. We have, on several occasions, mentioned data or studies which confirm that industry has an important power. In Chapter 2 (Table 2-6), we saw that when businesses are taxed more heavily, they receive more industrial aid as compensation. Similarly, in Chapter 4, we saw that governments cannot ignore the fact that industrialists prefer tax concessions as an instrument of intervention. Yet the power of these industrialists was shown to be less significant than we had foreseen. Despite their demands, for instance, there has been no increase in tax concessions. The thesis that businessmen enjoy a privileged position because they control investments must therefore be modified. The mobility of investors is not as great as is generally supposed, as we noted in the section regarding multinationals. Moreover, the workers possess a certain power, since they can paralyze production (Kaufman Percell, 1981). Finally, even if the image of business is less "bad" than that of government and the unions, anti-business feelings are far from negligible (Lipset and Schneider, 1983, chap. 6), and this naturally limits the potential influence of business.

We are also interested in the influence of bureaucrats. Unfortunately, we can say little about this question. There are virtually no studies[81] on the relationship between politicians and bureaucrats as they create and set in motion the various industrial aid programs. This is one of the worst gaps in the documentation.

Even if we were trying to define the role of industrialists and bureaucrats, our main concern would be the calculations of politicians. Believers in public choice generally suppose that these calculations are essentially vote-seeking and that a politician's main concern is re-election (Blais, 1982). This position can be criticized as being overly reductionist. Winn (1985), in particular, states that vote-seeking is only one of nine roles played by ministers. The objection is certainly valid, and we shall return later to the eight other non-vote-seeking motives. But we also have good reasons to believe that re-election is the prime concern of governments, a point which even Winn (1985) seems to concede. Where we disagree with the usual analysis of public choice, represented in Canada by the works of Trebilcock, for instance, is regarding the recipe for electoral success. Trebilcock et al. (1982) suggest that optimal strategy consists in rewarding target groups. Yet the literature on election results appears to us to prove that these groups depend, on the one hand, on the global economic picture and, on the other, on dramatic or spectacular events, such as scandals or international conflicts (Mackuen, 1983). As a result, vote-seeking calculations on the part of governments lead them to be concerned with the economic effectiveness (in the broad sense of the term, which includes the objectives of income and job stability) of their interventions. Political rationality is therefore not opposed to economic rationality, and this explains to a large extent why the liberalization process has endured.

This overlapping of economic and political rationales tends, moreover, to become accentuated, partly because of the growing importance which the media give to the economy:

> Reporting of economic data has become much more regular, and more importantly conspicuous headlines must have a ratchet-effect in making people permanently aware of phenomena that were not previously significant to them. Concern about inflation during the 1950s in Britain was largely confined to academic and government circles, and even in the late 1960s as the inflation rate rose to 7 and 8 percent annually the mass media paid it little attention. Suddenly, in 1971, as the inflation rate hit double figures for the first time, things changed, and for the first time it hit the headlines of both the *Mirror* and the *Sun*. . . . It seems highly likely that the popular newspapers were the crucial influence which triggered off anxiety about the state of the economy in the minds of very many voters (Mosley, 1984, p. 123).

It is evident that one of the major vote-seeking concerns of governments is the visibility of their interventions. One of the most widespread theories on this subject is that it is in a government's interest to turn to tax concessions as a way of hiding the real cost of aid measures. We do not think this theory has been proven. On one hand, contrary to what is often said, our data indicate that the volume of tax concessions has not increased over time. On the other hand, strategies for hiding information might prove ineffectual or might event backfire. Since tax concessions have low political legitimacy (we recall that a large majority of Canadians are opposed to lowering the tax burden for businesses) and since citizens know vaguely that tax concessions exist, and since the media sometimes make headlines out of instances where large firms manage to avoid paying taxes — for all these reasons, it is quite likely that the extent of tax measures has in fact been exaggerated by the population. Since the tax system inspires so much distrust, it is in the government's interest to adopt a system that is as clear (and simple) as possible, without a complicated set of specific measures that the people will immediately imagine were created to provide special shelters for business. The great interest aroused by proposals for a simpler tax system (Hall and Rabushka, 1983) seems to prove the point.

Politicians are not entirely motivated by vote-seeking. Are there some general motives which our study reveals? The most significant prejudice we identified was a preference for free trade. We have seen that, up to a certain point, politicians resist protectionist pressure. Why is this so? The most plausible explanation is that free trade is perceived as running in the direction of the national interest (Bauer, DeSola Pool and Dexter, 1972, pp. 397–98). The "national interest" is obviously a nebulous concept which masks serious conflicts, conflicts that are at the very heart of the political process. But politicians are nonetheless sensitive to its implications, and they behave accordingly. Politicians may not be saints, but they are not sinners either. Insofar as they are concerned with what posterity will have to say about them,[82] they must at the very least appear to be patriots who are motivated by noble ideals.

It was also apparent that politicians do not automatically yield to the demands of interest groups. The almost exclusive preference shown by economists for the "interest group" model seems unjustified in this respect. It is not that pressure by these groups has no effect; but political leaders also respond, probably more so, to the general demand for good economic performance as well as to their perception of the national interest.

On the whole, industrial aid reflects the wishes of the majority of the population. It tries to accommodate both growth and stability. It takes into account the fact that people are deeply rooted in their local milieu, with a strong dislike of geographic mobility. The orientation of government policies can also be partly explained by a predilection for agriculture, small business, and technology. This preference influences policies only indirectly, but it is worth noting that not a single case of government intervention runs wholly counter to it. The situation of small business seems relevant here. While big business does start out with much greater resources, it seems plausible that it is because of its legitimacy that small business manages to come out well at the end of the game.

The analysis thus tends to confirm the relevance of the democratic model as an explanation for government industrial aid. On the one hand, there is a close connection between output and the wishes of the majority of the public. On the other hand, the amount of government aid depends on the party in power (as seen in Chapter 2) and this suggests that the choices offered to voters are not artificial. It is true that the democratic model can only provide a partial explanation. But, on the whole, industrial aid seems to us to be determined more by the indirect influence of the voters than by the secret games of pressure groups or by the "structural" power of industry. In this we agree with Kingdon's conclusion that "the complex of national mood and elections seems to create extremely powerful impacts on policy agendas, impacts capable of overwhelming the balance of organized forces" (Kingdon, 1984, pp. 171–72).

Throughout this study we have stressed the stabilizing role which devolves upon the government in capitalist societies. The "spontaneous" development of capitalism creates a whole series of social imbalances which the government tries, with some success,[83] to attenuate. In closing, we must recognize that stability can quickly lead to a dull existence, as Scitovsky points out:

> It is also possible that with increased affluence, they were gradually lured into a new way of life by their love of comfort, unaware at first of the costs involved and finding themselves fully accustomed to their new ways by the time they "realize the extent of the loss of pleasure suffered" (Scitovsky, 1976, p. 73).

Moreover, stability comprises several dimensions, some of which might be in conflict. A major problem, for instance, is the choice to be made between job security and a secure income. If it is true that the salary level can affect jobs (Malinvaud, 1982) and that jobs are prized more than income, then we must attack the rigidity of salaries. De Closets leaves us with this very important message:

> Let us adopt the principle that any division which gives certain parties a winning hand in the form of acquired rights — standard of living, guaranteed income, job security — is unfair. If we admit that our wealth is linked to the market economy, no one can claim a right to it without accepting on the other hand certain constraints in the system. We must therefore necessarily agree to be penalized on one of the master trumps in our hand. . . . Social justice would take a giant step forward if salary insecurity gradually replaced job insecurity in the work of wage earners (de Closets 1982, pp. 306–307; translation).

There is no question of elevating stability to the status of an absolute good. Change, with all its uncertainties, is also indispensable. But if it is true that the family — the nuclear family first of all, but the extended family as well — is the chosen centre of satisfaction for the vast majority of citizens (Bénéton, 1983, chap. 12; Campbell, Converse and Rodgers, 1976), then we can appreciate the crucial importance of the feeling of belonging.

Appendix A

Estimated Evolution of the Average Rate of Nominal Tariff in the Advanced Capitalist Democracies

We thought it useful to provide an approximation of the average level of tariff protection in all the advanced capitalist democracies, as well as of its evolution over time. Unfortunately, this turned out to be a highly complex task. First of all, almost all studies are narrowly focussed and cover only a precise time or, at best, two such times (before and after the Kennedy Round or the Tokyo Round). Secondly, the estimates of the various studies are not mutually comparable, since the weighting criteria and the scope of each study are not the same (it is sometimes the manufacturing sector alone, sometimes the "industrial" sector, including the primary sector but excluding agriculture, and, more seldom, the primary and secondary sectors as a whole).

In view of these difficulties, we opted for the following strategy. First of all, we retained the specific estimate that we believed was the most valid. In this respect, the data of Hawkins for the year 1972 (1972, Table 3-1, 3rd column, p. 43) are clearly the most interesting because they include both the primary sector (including agriculture) and the secondary sector, and because they are weighted by the combined imports of the countries involved. For the eight regions studied (Austria, Japan, United Kingdom, EEC, United States, Norway, Denmark, and Sweden), the average nominal protection rate was 6.79 percent. On the basis of this first estimate, which we believe to be the most reliable, we made other estimates of three other specific times, based on the average rate of reduction reported by various authors. Thus, Lazar (1981, p. 3) and Hawkins (1972, p. 52) mention a 35 percent drop in nominal protection during the Kennedy Round, which yields an estimate of 9.16 percent prior to the Kennedy Round. The third specific time that we chose was the year 1979, immediately prior to the implementation of the reductions negotiated in the Tokyo Round. A single adjustment was made here to account for the unilateral reduction in Japanese tariffs, of the order of 20 percent during that period (Corbet, 1979, Table 1, p. 328). Finally, the estimates for the period after the Tokyo Round are based on a 33 percent lowering of the nominal protection rate, a figure quoted by Lazar (1981, p. 8) and Corbet (1979, Table 1, p. 328).

Appendix B

Agreement Between the Results of the Various Studies on the Average Tariff in the Advanced Capitalist Democracies

Clearly, the estimate of the average protection rate varies greatly from one study to the next, as can be seen from Tables 1-3 and 1-5, in Chapter 1. In fact, though, the differences are more apparent than real. The estimates of Hawkins, which we retained for the reasons given in Appendix A, are usually lower than those of Corbet and of Deardoff and Stern. The higher result obtained by Corbet is attributable, on the one hand to the inclusion of New Zealand, which is clearly a deviant case, and on the other hand to the exclusion of agriculture from Corbet's estimates. Deardoff and Stern gave even higher rates because they only considered the manufacturing sector, which is more protected than the primary sector.

Notes

1. The same bias is found in the works on the "barriers" to Canadian economic union.
2. We ignore government interventions designed to correct problems stemming from other measures of the same government or foreign governments (Breton, 1974).
3. The criterion assumed by Castles and McKinlay (1979) was a per capita GDP in excess of US$2,000 in 1974. In our case, all the countries retained had a per capita GDP in excess of US$5,000 in 1982.
4. They are: Australia, Austria, Belgium, Canada, Denmark, Finland, France, West Germany, Ireland, Italy, Japan, the Netherlands, New Zealand, Norway, Sweden, Switzerland, the United Kingdom, and the United States.
5. Throughout this text, the term "domestic industry" means the industry belonging to the investors of the country where a product or service is produced.
6. Since Hawkins (1972) did not have a reliable estimate for Canada, we have used for this country the data of Faucher et al. (1985). These data had the dual advantage of including the primary (including agriculture) and secondary sectors, like the data of Hawkins (1972), and of covering a long period (1961–78). The estimates are virtually identical to those of Wilkinson and Norrie (1975), which covered the period 1961–70. However, the data of Hawkins (1972) and Faucher et al. (1985) are not strictly comparable, since they are based on different weightings.
7. Unfortunately, no author sees a need for making his own results agree with those of other studies.
8. Deardoff and Stern (1979) and Corbet (1979) presented estimates of the average nominal rate. In both cases, the Japanese and the American rates were close to the Swedish rate.
9. The discrepancy seems smaller in the data of the Economic Council of Canada (1975, Table 2-1, p. 13). See also Balassa (1965, p. 591), Oulton (1976, p. 81), and Hiemenz and Rabenau (1976, p. 61). Lavergne (1983) noted that with the other variables held constant, this factor only has an effect on the tariff protection that existed in 1979 (and not on that of 1964 or 1972).
10. In 1987, in 16 of the 18 countries studied by Deardoff and Stern (1979), it ranked first among the 19 manufacturing industries. The average rate in the 18 countries was 23 percent, as against 17 percent for footwear, which came second.
11. The mean correlation between the nominal tariff structures of the various countries, within the manufacturing sector, was 0.82.
12. By applying the principle of linear reduction, the tariff structure remains intact. Among the 19 manufacturing industries studied by Deardoff and Stern (1979), there was a correlation of 0.99 between the average protection rate in the 18 countries retained as a whole, before and after the Tokyo Round.
13. For the 19 manufacturing industries studied by Deardoff and Stern (1979) the variation factor of the average protection rate (for the 18 countries retained) rose from 0.55 to 0.65 between 1979 and 1987.
14. Lavergne (1983) found that industries located in rural areas as well as in the poorest states, in the United States, were more protected in 1979.
15. The following studies should be mentioned: Ball (1967), Caves (1976), Cheh (1976), Corbo and Martens (1979), Helleiner (1977), Jones and Caudadio (1984), Oulton (1976), Postner (1976), Ray (1981a, 1981b), Saunders (1980).
16. For example, in Canada, Helleiner (1977) found that the most protected industries were the labour-intensive, unskilled ones. In turn, Saunders (1980) noted no relationship. Finally, Corbo and Martens (1979) reported positive, significant correlations for skilled and unskilled labour in the Quebec manufacturing sector. It is regrettable that these contradictory results are not discussed by the authors of the studies.
17. However, tariffs are dropping *faster* in the industries where there is already a great deal of competition. Lavergne explained this contradictory result on the basis of the change, over time, in the comparative advantage.
18. Of the 133 surveys made between 1975 and 1979, 86 cover these five industries (Ehrenhaft, 1979, p. 1375).

19. Of the 108 surveys covering the demands for countervailing duties between 1975 and 1979, 79 pertain to these four industries.
20. An increase in the number of anti-dumping cases in Canada was also noted (Faucher et al., 1985).
21. In the three studies (Finger, Hall and Nelson, 1982; Herander and Schwartz, 1984; Finger, 1981) which examined the factors responsible for the success (or failure) of the various industries, the employment variable was the only one to be determined unequivocally.
22. The quotas on wheat, cotton and peanuts had a negligible effect (Cline et al., 1978, p. 178).
23. This is the case in Canada at least. Dam (1970, p. 257) has stated that in general: "not only is effective protection in all likelihood higher on average than in any other sector of the international economy, but there are indications that the rate of effective protection is increasing."
24. This measure may take the form of a quantitative restraint or a supplementary tariff.
25. Morici and Megna (1983, Table 2-1, pp. 29–30). We exclude here two cases that involved voluntary restraint agreements.
26. The rise in imports must be an *important* reason for the difficulties of the industry, whereas it ought to be the main cause, according to the 1962 *Trade Expansion Act* (Lazar, 1981, p. 38).
27. On the other hand, the 1962 *Trade Expansion Act* reduced by six the number of complaints per year and led to one fewer positive decision per annum.
28. Between 1975 and 1979, only 3.8 percent of U.S. imports were affected by unilateral actions within the framework of Article 19 (Finger, Hall and Nelson, 1982, Table 5, p. 465).
29. Following its initial five-year term, this agreement was extended twice for an additional period of three years, in 1967 and 1970 (Morici and Megna, 1983, p. 22).
30. The 1974 agreement (MFA I) was renewed in 1978 (MFA II) and in 1982 (MFA III).
31. When dealing with guarantees, we shall include credit insurance, which closely resembles a guarantee, except that it is not limited to a specific transaction and that "un grand nombre d'entreprises peuvent en bénéficier sans qu'elles aient un lien de parenté avec l'établissement qui l'accorde" ("many firms may receive it without their having any corporate link with the establishment granting it") (Economic Council of Canada, 1982, p. 2).
32. The "loans" category includes investments. The latter amounted in 1982 to approximately 15 percent of total credits. The data of the Economic Council of Canada (1982) do not allow a distinction to be made between loans and investments for the years 1950 to 1970.
33. The $700 million constitutes the implicit subsidy of the loans, computed on the basis of the social opportunity cost method. Based on the cash flow cost method, the implicit loan subsidy is of the order of $196 million. Regardless of the method used, the guarantees include no implicit subsidy. No estimate is given for investments, but we believe that the implicit subsidy is negligible. We prefer the social opportunity cost method, which has the advantage of accounting for "les bénéfices dont nous nous privons, en tant que collectivité, en investissant des ressources financières dans des agences publiques plutôt que de les placer sur le marché privé" ("the benefits that we forgo, as a community, by investing financial resources in public agencies rather than in the private sector") (Economic Council of Canada, 1982, p. 138).
34. Thus, payments to oil importers benefit both individuals and firms.
35. Jenkin (1983, p. 171) also noted that "l'administration fédérale consacre des montants en moyenne trois fois plus élevés au développement du commerce et de l'industrie que l'ensemble des 10 provinces" ("the federal government devotes to the development of industry and trade on average amounts three times greater than all of the ten provinces").
36. Aid programs were virtually nonexistent before the late 1950s at the federal level, and before the mid-1960s in Quebec and Ontario.

37. We are referring here to the payments to the railways under the *National Transportation Act*, and to the payments to importers of crude oil and oil products.

38. The Economic Council of Canada (1982, Table 13-2, p. 144) also gives data on the geographic breakdown of federal government loans and guarantees, which likewise show that Ontario firms are at a disadvantage. In this case, the Atlantic provinces also appear to be favoured, as well as British Columbia, but not Quebec.

39. The concepts of centre and periphery do raise some questions, particularly as regards the status of Quebec, which is ambiguous to say the least. We assume here that Ontario alone constitutes the industrial centre.

40. The variation factor is higher than in the case of tariffs.

41. In 1971, the West German primary sector received over 80 percent of grants (Corden and Fels, 1976, Table 4-4, p. 100), whereas the French agricultural sector obtained 47 percent of total grants in 1968 (Le Pors et al., 1971–72, Table 10, p. 43). See also Bobe (1983, p. 15, Table 8).

42. Stoffaës (1978, p. 539); Denton (1976, p. 23); Corden and Fels (1976, Table 4-4, p. 100); Curzon Price (1981, chap. 4); Carmoy (1978); Krugman (1984).

43. Aid to the automotive sector only materialized when that sector was in decline.

44. See also Vernon (1974, p. 13), and Grant (1983, p. 371).

45. Corden and Fels (1976, Table 4-4, p. 100); Carmoy (1978, Table 2-1, p. 42); Morici and Megna (1983, Table 5-2).

46. The usual distinction will be made between taxes on the basis of the tax base. From this viewpoint, social security premiums are labour taxes (OECD, 1984c, p. 60).

47. We prefer the data in Tables 1-15 and 1-17, where the GDP is the reference criterion.

48. We are concerned here primarily with the average for the 1955–80 period.

49. The correlation for 1980 was -0.14, but it rose to -0.29 when Norway (a deviant case) was excluded.

50. Although it is true that this tax penalizes to a greater extent labour-intensive firms, it can be assumed that that is not the prime objective. In addition, this tax is only exceptionally subject to special provisions, as in the case of corporate income tax.

51. We are not taking into account here the studies on the marginal rate of investment taxation (Auerback, 1983; Boadway, Bruce and Mintz, 1984), since "marginal effective tax rates embody fewer aspects of the tax code than do average rates" (Hulten and Robertson, 1984, p. 328).

52. Several of the tax advantages granted to industry are now being questioned. See the *Wall Street Journal*, November 20, 1984, p. 1.

53. Estimates based on the data of Smith (1979, p. 44).

54. The transport and communications sector also seems to have a low tax rate, but this is basically due to the warehousing industry, which comprises a large number of cooperatives, which can deduct from their profits the refunds paid out to their members.

55. The agricultural sector also seems highly taxed, but this situation is explained by the magnitude of the tax losses that can be deducted from income (Boadway and Kitchen, 1980, p. 118).

56. Study effected within the framework of the Blais, Faucher and Young project on industrial policy in Canada. A first analysis was effected in the summer of 1983. The data cited here are preliminary.

57. This is what we have shown in the Canadian case. In the United States, a study of Congress (United States, Joint Committee on Taxation, 1983) showed that the paper and lumber sector was the least taxed, in 1982, of the 20 sectors studied. However, the industries in that sector were among the most highly taxed in 1963 (Siegfried, 1974, Table 1, p. 254).

58. Unpublished data (Blais, Faucher and Young research and study).

59. No distinction seems to be made, however, between domestic firms and foreign firms located in Canada.

60. However, services are not covered, nor are purchases related to defence and R&D (de Mestral, 1982, p. 178).

61. The grant and protection rates can be compared because "une subvention à la production du produit final a sur la production le même effet qu'un droit de douane du même taux" ("a subsidy to the production of the final product has the same effect on the production as a customs duty at the same rate") (Corden, 1977, p. 37).
62. We chose Equation 4 in Table 4, excluding however the DGT variable (expenditure growth), the theoretical status of which is ambiguous (see McCallum and Blais, 1985).
63. Protheroe (1980, p. 141) claims that bureaucrats tend to be even more in favour of trade liberalization than politicians. Messerlin (1983), on the other hand, claims that they are more protectionist, but he gives no data in support of his position.
64. Frey (1978) has stated the view that the highs and lows in popularity of a government affect the level of public expenditures, but Alt and Chrystal (1983, p. 23) have shown that this variable is inoperative once the effect of the GDP is controlled. Similarly, the fact that the Progressive Conservative party was clearly dominant in Ontario for a long time did not prevent the government from manipulating the budget according to the election cycle (Blais, McRoberts and Nadeau, 1983).
65. The data are from Deardoff and Stern (1979, Table C-5, p. 151).
66. These variables are described in Table 2-4. For the size and wealth data, however, we have used the data of Kravis, Heston and Summers (1980) relative to the year 1977.
67. This image has been somewhat tarnished by the foreign policy of President Reagan (Granatstein, 1985).
68. In this respect, one should also take into account the level of information on these performances. The popularity of the American option might be due particularly to the fact that, through their travel or through the media, Canadians are better informed about the price gap between Canadian and U.S. products.
69. Zysman (1983) and McKay and Grant (1983) have examined the different forms that industrial policy assumes depending on the country, but not specifically the relative magnitude of aid to industry. For a critique of these two studies, see Blais (1985a).
70. On this point, we follow the same procedure as Hicks and Swank (1984, p. 97): "Variables with slopes that at least attain the minimal support of F-statistic values greater than or equal to 1.00 are retained, even when they fail to attain the 0.05 level of significance. This is done to reduce the chance of eliminating variables without truly zero-effects." For studies covering a small number of cases, we believe this procedure is the most appropriate.
71. As noted by Cable (1983), it is at least surprising that economists are so concerned with "political" models whereas political scientists are particularly interested in the "economic" variables: "There is a certain irony in the fact that political scientists are now looking at essentially economic explanations of protection while economists are falling back on political explanations; and, moreover it is the former who have tried harder to integrate an understanding of 'macro' economic tendencies with industry specific phenomena" (ibid., p. 196).
72. However, opinions on this issue are not free of contradictions. Thus, a majority of Canadians think that society is excessively machine- and technology-oriented (*Decima Surveys*, 1980–82, qn. 67). This does not prevent them from supporting a technology policy (for a more systematic discussion, see Blais, 1985b).
73. In Quebec, the average remuneration in foreign firms is higher than in francophone firms, but it is no different from that in anglophone firms (Raynauld and Vaillancourt, 1984).
74. Ashcroft (1980, p. 86) mentions several studies indicating that a large proportion of regional development grants go to multinationals.
75. While a small recession favours the multinational firm, a stronger recession could have the opposite effect, by exacerbating the latent hostility toward foreign capital. For a discussion of the "scapegoat" role of the multinationals, see Fayerweather (1982), p. 332.
76. Miles (1976) noted this phenomenon among textile industralists in Great Britain in the late 1950s.
77. One of the arguments used when the *Small Business Loans Act* was passed, was that

the Industrial Expansion Bank (forerunner of the Federal Business Development Bank) had no branches in rural areas (Blais, Faucher and Young, 1983a, p. 16).

78. "Ministers see themselves as relatively skilled in matters of mood and sentiment" (Winn, 1985).

79. The book by Zysman (1983) provides a good illustration of this shortcoming. The author manages to present clearly an original interpretation of the industrial policy of five countries without analyzing that policy in depth. For critical discussion of that study, see Blais (1985b).

80. See Schmidt (1982 and 1984). Schmidt demonstrated that it is in "corporatist" countries that the unemployment rate is the lowest. Unfortunately, the analysis does not indicate the intermediate variables, i.e., the government policies that produce these results. We believe, however, that this should be an essential part of the argument.

81. An important exception is the study by Winham (1978) on the role of the Canadian bureaucracy in the Tokyo Round negotiations.

82. For example: "Un jour de janvier 1984, Mulroney avait confié à son premier conseiller politique qu'il voudrait que l'histoire se souvienne de lui. Brian ne veut pas seulement être Premier Ministre, souligna un jour son ami Lucien Bouchard, il veut passer à l'histoire" ("In January 1984, Mulroney had mentioned to his closest political adviser that he would like history to remember him. According to his friend Lucien Bouchard, Brian does not only want to be prime minister, he wants to pass into history") (MacDonald, 1984, p. 371).

83. There seems to be a relationship between the size of the state and economic stability (Montmarquette, 1981; Alt and Chrystal, 1983, p. 200; McCallum and Blais, 1985).

Bibliography

Abramovitz, Moses. 1983. "Notes on International Differences in Productivity Growth Rates." In *The Political Economy of Growth*, edited by Dennis C. Mueller. New Haven: Yale University Press.

Adamek, Josef. 1984. *Business Leaders Views' on Protectionism in Western Europe*. Ottawa: Conference Board of Canada.

Aggarwal, Vinod K., and Stephan Haggard. 1983. "The Politics of Protection in the U.S. Textile and Apparel Industries." In *American Industry in International Competition: Government Policies and Corporate Strategies*, edited by John Zysman and Laura Tyson. Ithaca: Cornell University Press.

Albert, Alain. 1980. "Conditions économiques et élections : le cas de l'élection provinciale de 1976 au Québec." *Canadian Journal of Political Science* 13 (June): 325–47.

Allen, Robert Loring, and Ingo Walter. 1970. *The Formation of United States Trade Policy: Retrospect and Prospect*. New York: New York University, Institute of Finance.

Alt, James E., and K. Alec Chrystal. 1983. *Political Economics*. Brighton: Harvester Press.

Apple, Nixon. 1980. "The Rise and Fall of Full Employment Capitalism." *Studies in Political Economy* 4 (Fall): 5–41.

Armington, Catherine, and Marjorie Odle. 1982. "Small Business — How Many Jobs?" *Brookings Review* 1 (2) (Winter): 14–18.

Ashcroft, Brian. 1980. *The Evaluation of Regional Policy in Europe: A Survey and Critique*. Glasgow: Centre for the Study of Public Policy.

Ashenfelter, Orley. 1981. *What Is a Full Employment Goal in the 1980s?* Ottawa: Task Force on Labour Market Development.

Auerback, Alan J. 1983. "Corporate Taxation in the United States." *Brookings Papers on Economic Activity* 2: 451–515.

Bairoch, Paul. 1976. *Commerce extérieur et développement économique de l'Europe au XIXe siècle*. Paris: Mouton.

Balassa, Bela. 1965. "Tariff Protection in Industrial Countries: An Evaluation." *Journal of Political Economy* 73: 573–94.

______. 1978. "The 'New Protectionism' and the International Economy." *Journal of World Trade* 12: 409–36.

Baldwin, J.R., P.K. Gorecki, J.S. McVey, and J. Crysdale. 1983. *The Relationship Between Plant Scale and Product Diversity in Canadian Manufacturing Industries*. Ottawa: Economic Council of Canada.

Baldwin, Robert E. 1970. *Non-tariff Distortions of International Trade*. Washington, D.C.: Brookings Institution.

______. 1976. "The Political Economy of Postwar U.S. Trade Policy." *The Bulletin* 4 (New York University).

______. 1979. "Protectionist Pressures in the United States." In *Challenges to a Liberal International Economic Order*, edited by Ryan C. Amacher, Gottfield Haberler and Thomas D. Willet. Washington, D.C.: American Enterprise Institute.

Ball, David S. 1967. "United States Effective Tariffs and Labor's Share." *Journal of Political Economy* 75: 183–87.

Balthazar, Louis. 1983. "Les relations canado-américaines : nationalisme et continentalisme." *Études internationales* 14 (March): 23–49.

Bauer, Raymond S., Ithiel De Sola Pool, and Lewis Anthony Dexter. 1972. *American Business and Public Policy: The Politics of Foreign Trade*. Chicago: Aldine.

Bélanger, André J. 1985. *Framework for a Political Sociology*. Toronto: University of Toronto Press.

Bénéton, Philippe. 1983. *Le fléau du bien : essai sur les politiques sociales occidentales*. Paris: Robert Laffont.

Bénoun, Marc, and Patrick Sénecourt. 1980. *L'aide à la création et au développement des entreprises nouvelles : comparaison internationale*. Paris: École supérieure de commerce.

Bergsten, Fred C., Thomas Horst, and Theodore H. Moran. 1978. *American Multinationals and American Interests*. Washington, D.C.: Brookings Institution.

Bernier, Ivan. 1984. "L'économie québécoise face à la concurrence extérieure : les fondements scientifiques de la politique d'achat préférentiel du Québec." *Études internationales* 15 (March): 61–93.

Bernstein, Jeffrey J. 1985. "Research and Development, Patents, and Grant and Tax Policies in Canada." In *Technological Change in Canadian Industry*, volume 3 of the research studies prepared for the Royal Commission on the Economic Union and Development Prospects for Canada. Toronto: University of Toronto Press.

Binhammer, H.H., L.C. McDonough, and G. Lepore. 1983. *Government Grants to Private Sector Firms*. Ottawa: Economic Council of Canada.

Birch, David L. 1981. "Who Creates Jobs?" *Public Interest* (Fall): 3–14.

Bird, Richard M. 1980. *Tax Incentives for Investment: The State of the Art*. Toronto: Canadian Tax Foundation.

Black, Robert, Stephen Blank, and Elizabeth C. Hanson. 1978. *Multinationals in Contention: Responses at Governmental and International Levels*. New York: Conference Board.

Blais, André. 1974. "Power and Causality." *Quality and Quantity* (August): 54–64.

______. 1978. "Politique agricole et résultats électoraux en milieu agricole au Québec." *Canadian Journal of Political Science* 11: 333–82.

______. 1980. "Orientation de la recherche." In *Introduction à l'analyse des politiques*, edited by Réjean Landry. Quebec: Presses de l'Université Laval.

______. 1982. "Le Public Choice et la croissance de l'État." *Canadian Journal of Political Science* 15 (December): 783–808.

______. 1985a. "The Debate on Canadian Industrial Policy." In *Canadian Industrial Policy*, volume 44 of the research studies prepared for the Royal Commission on the Economic Union and Development Prospects for Canada. Toronto: University of Toronto Press.

———. 1985b. "Industrial Policy in Advanced Capitalist Democracies: An Overview." In *Canadian Industrial Policy*, volume 44 of the research studies prepared for the Royal Commission on the Economic Union and Development Prospects for Canada. Toronto: University of Toronto Press.

Blais, André, and Philippe Faucher. 1981. "La politique industrielle dans les économies capitalistes avancées." *Canadian Journal of Political Science* 14 (March): 3–35.

Blais, André, Philippe Faucher, and Robert Young. 1983a. *L'aide financière directe du gouvernement fédéral à l'industrie canadienne 1960–1980*. Montreal: Université de Montréal, département de science politique. Mimeographed.

———. 1983b. *L'aide financière directe du gouvernement fédéral à l'industrie manufacturière : dynamique et contraintes*. Montreal: Université de Montréal, département de science politique. Mimeographed.

Blais, André, Philippe Faucher, Robert Young, and Roger Poupart. 1983. *Les avantages fiscaux du gouvernement fédéral à l'industrie manufacturière canadienne*. Montreal: Université de Montréal, département de science politique. Mimeographed.

Blais, André, and Kenneth McRoberts. 1983. "Public Expenditure in Ontario and Quebec, 1950–1980." *Canadian Studies* 18 (Spring) 28–54.

Blais, André, Kenneth McRoberts, and Richard Nadeau. 1983. *Dépenses gouvernementales et cycles électoraux au Québec et en Ontario, 1950–1980*. Paper presented at the annual meeting of the Canadian Political Science Association, Vancouver.

Bloom, H.S., and H.D. Price. 1975. "Voter Response to Short-Run Economic Conditions." *American Political Science Review*: 1240–54.

Boadway, Robin W., Neil Bruce, and Jack M. Mintz. 1984. "Taxation, Inflation and the Effective Marginal Tax Rate on Capital in Canada." *Canadian Journal of Economics* 17 (February): 62–80.

Boadway, Robin W., and Harry M. Kitchen. 1980. *Canadian Tax Policy*. Toronto: Canadian Tax Foundation.

Bobe, Bernard. 1983. *Public Assistance to Industries and Trade Policy in France*. Washington, D.C.: World Bank.

Bonin, Bernard. 1985. " Une boîte noire à manipuler soigneusement : l'analyse des coûts et des bénéfices sociaux de l'entreprise multinationale. " *Études internationales* 16 (June): 261–81.

Borrus, Michael. 1983. "The Politics of Competitive Erosion in the U.S. Steel Industry." In *American Industry in International Competition: Government Policies and Corporate Strategies*, edited by John Zysman. Ithaca, N.Y.: Cornell University Press.

Bosworth, Barry. 1982. "Capital Formation and Economic Policy." *Brookings Papers on Economic Activity* 2: 273–317.

Bowles, Samuel, David M. Gordon, and Thomas E. Weisskopf. 1983. *Beyond the Waste Land: A Democratic Alternative*. Garden City, N.J.: Anchor Books.

Braam, Geert P.A. 1981. *Influence of Business Firms on the Government: An Investigation of the Distribution of Influence in Society*. The Hague: Mouton.

Brenner, Reuven, and Léon Courville. 1985. "Industrial Strategy: Inferring What It Really Is." In *Economics of Industrial Policy and Strategy*, volume 5 of the research studies prepared for the Royal Commission on the Economic Union and Development Prospects for Canada. Toronto: University of Toronto Press.

Breton, Albert. 1974. *A Conceptual Basis for an Industrial Strategy*. Ottawa: Economic Council of Canada.

Breton, Albert, and Ronald Wintrobe. 1982. *The Logic of Bureaucratic Conduct: An Economic Analysis of Competition, Exchange and Efficiency in Private and Public Organizations*. Cambridge: Cambridge University Press.

Brown, Douglas, Julia Eastman, and Ian Robinson. 1981. *The Limits of Consultation*. Ottawa: Science Council of Canada.

Burton, John. 1979. *The Job Support Machine*. London: Centre for Policy Studies.

———. 1983. *Picking Losers? The Political Economy of Industrial Policy*. London: Institute of Economic Affairs.

Buzelay, Alain. 1983. "Intégration européenne et fluctuations économiques." *Revue d'économie politique* 93: 576–89.

Cable, Vincent. 1983. *Protectionism and Industrial Decline*. London: Hodder and Stoughton.

Cameron, David. 1978. "The Expansion of the Public Economy: A Comparative Analysis." *American Political Science Review* 72 (December): 1243–62.

______. 1982. "On the Limits of the Public Economy." *Annals of the American Academy of Political and Social Science* 459 (January): 46–63.

Campbell, Angus. 1981. *The Sense of Well-Being in America: Recent Patterns and Trends*. New York: McGraw-Hill.

Campbell, Angus, Philip E. Converse, and Willard L. Rodgers. 1976. *The Quality of American Life: Perceptions, Evaluations and Satisfactions*. New York: Russell Sage.

Canada. Department of Finance. 1978. *The Tax Systems of Canada and the United States*. Ottawa: The Department.

______. Department of Industry, Trade and Commerce. 1982. *An Overview of Small Business Financing*. Ottawa: The Department.

______. 1983. Federal Task Force on the Canadian Motor Vehicle and Automotive Parts Industries. *An Automotive Strategy for Canada — Report*. Ottawa: Minister of Supply and Services Canada.

______. Department of Regional Industrial Expansion. 1984. Small Business Secretariat. *Incidence des anciens et nouveaux établissements de 1971 à 1980*. Ottawa: The Department.

Carlsson, Bo. 1983. "Industrial Subsidies in Sweden: Macro-Economic Effects and an International Comparison." *Journal of Industrial Economics* 30 (September): 1–23.

Carmoy, Guy de. 1978. "Subsidy Policies in Britain, France and West Germany: An Overview." In *International Trade and Industrial Policies*, edited by Steven J. Warnecke. New York: Holmes and Meier.

Castles, Francis G. 1982. "Introduction Politics and Public Policy." In *The Impact of Parties: Politics and Policies in Democratic Capitalist States,* edited by Francis G. Castles. Beverly Hills: Sage.

Castles, Frank, and Robert D. McKinlay. 1979. "Does Politics Matter: An Analysis of the Public Welfare Commitment in Advanced Democratic States." *European Journal of Political Research* 7 (June): 169–86.

Caves, Richard E. 1976. "Economic Models of Political Choice: Canada's Tariff Structure." *Canadian Journal of Economics* 9 (May): 278–300.

______. 1982. *Multinational Enterprise and Economic Analysis*. Cambridge: University Press.

Caves, Richard E., and Ronald W. Jones. 1977. *World Trade and Payments: An Introduction*. Boston: Little, Brown.

Chandler, Marsha. 1982. "State Enterprise and Partisanship in Provincial Politics." *Canadian Journal of Political Science* 15 (December): 711–40.

______. 1985. "The State and Industrial Decline." In *Canadian Industrial Policy*, volume 44 of the research studies prepared for the Royal Commission on the Economic Union and Development Prospects for Canada. Toronto: University of Toronto Press.

Cheh, John H. 1976. "A Note on Tariffs, Non-tariff Barriers, and Labor Protection in United States Manufacturing Industries." *Journal of Political Economy* 84: 389–94.

Cline, William R., Noboru Kawanabe, T.O.M. Kronsjö, and Thomas Williams. 1978. *Trade Negotiations in the Tokyo Round: A Quantitative Assessment*. Washington, D.C.: Brookings Institution.

Cobb, Roger W., and Charles D. Elder. 1972. *Participation in American Politics: The Dynamics of Agenda-Building*. Boston: Allyn and Bacon.

Conybeare, John A.C. 1983. "Tariff Protection in Developed and Developing Countries: A Cross-Sectional and Longitudinal Analysis." *International Organization* 37 (Summer): 441–67.

Corbet, Hugh. 1979. "Importance of Being Earnest about Further GATT Negotiations." *World Economy* 2 (September): 319–41.

Corbo, Vittorio, and André Martens. 1979. "Effective Protection and Factor Inputs in Quebec Manufacturing." *Canadian Journal of Economics* 12 (August): 426–38.

Corden, Warner M. 1977. *La théorie de la protection*. Paris: Economica.

Corden, Warner M., and Gerhard Fels. 1976. *Public Assistance to Industry: Protection and Subsidies in Britain and Germany*. Boulder, Col.; Westview Press.

Crandall, Robert W. 1984. "Import Quotas and the Automobile Industry: The Costs of Protectionism." *Brookings Review* (Summer): 8–17.

Curzon, Gerard, and Victoria Curzon. 1976. "The Management of Trade Relations in the GATT." In *International Economic Relations of the Western World, 1959–1971*, vol. I, edited by Andrew Shonfield. London: Oxford University Press.

Curzon Price, Victoria. 1981. *Industrial Policies in the European Community*. London: Trade Policy Research Centre.

______. 1982. "The Spirit of Geneva and the International Trade Order." In *Annales d'études internationales*, edited by Otto Hieronymi. Geneva: Institut universitaire de hautes études internationales.

Dalpé, Robert. 1984. "L'accès des firmes canadiennes du transport public et des télécommunications aux marchés publics américains." *Études internationales* 15 (March): 157–73.

Daly, D.J., and S. Globerman. 1976. *Tariff and Science Policies: Applications of a Model of Nationalism*. Toronto: Ontario Economic Council.

Dam, Kenneth W. 1970. *The GATT: Law and International Economic Organization*. Chicago: University of Chicago Press.

D'Amboise, Gérald. 1983. "La recherche sur les P.M.E. : de l'importance de mieux connaître et comprendre les P.M.E." *Options politiques* 4 (May–June): 34–37.

Das, Bhagirath L. 1983. "The GATT Multi-Fibre Arrangement." *Journal of World Trade Law* 17 (March/April): 95–105.

Davenport, P., C. Green, W.J. Milne, R. Saunders, and W. Watson. 1982. *Industrial Policy in Ontario and Quebec*. Toronto: Ontario Economic Council.

Deardoff, V. Allan, and Robert M. Stern. 1979. *An Economic Analysis of the Effects of the Tokyo Round of Multilateral Trade Negotiations on the United States and Other Major Industrialized Countries*. Washington, D.C.: U.S. Congress, Senate Finance Committee, June.

de Closets, François. 1982. *Toujours plus*. Paris: Grasset.

de Mestral, A.L.C. 1982. "The Impact of the GATT Agreement on Government Procurement in Canada." In *Non-Tariff Barriers After the Tokyo Round*, edited by John Quinn and Philip Slayton. Montreal: Institute for Research on Public Policy.

Denton, Geoffrey. 1976. "Financial Assistance to British Industry." In *Public Assistance to Industry*, edited by W.M. Corden and G. Fels. Boulder, Col.: Westview Press.

Denton, Geoffrey, Seamus O'Cleireacain, and Sally Ash. 1975. *Trade Effects of Public Subsidies to Private Enterprise*. London: Trade Policy Research Centre.

Dye, Thomas R. 1976. *Policy Analysis: What Governments Do, Why They Do It, and What Differences It Makes*. University, Ala.: University of Alabama Press.

______. 1978. *Understanding Public Policy*. Englewood Cliffs, N.J.: Prentice-Hall.

Economic Council of Canada. 1975. *Looking Outward: A New Trade Strategy for Canada*. Ottawa: Minister of Supply and Services Canada.

______. 1982. *Intervention and Efficiency: A Study of Government Credits and Credit Guarantees to the Private Sector*. Ottawa: Minister of Supply and Services Canada.

______. 1983. *The Bottom Line: Technology, Trade and Income Growth*. Ottawa: Minister of Supply and Services Canada.

Edelman, Murray. 1964. *The Symbolic Uses of Politics*. Urbana, Ill.: University of Illinois Press.

Edmonds, Martin. 1983. "Market Ideology and Corporate Power: The United States." In

Industrial Crisis: A Comparative Study of the State and Industry, edited by Kenneth Dyson and Stephen Wilks. Oxford: Martin Robertson.

Ehrenhaft, Peter D. 1979. "What the Antidumping and Countervailing Duty Provisions of the Trade Agreements Act [Can] [Will] [Should] Mean for U.S. Trade Policy." *Law and Policy in International Business* 11: 1361–1404.

Facsym Research Limited. 1981. *Small Business Financing and Non-Bank Financial Institutions*. Ottawa: Department of Industry, Trade and Commerce.

Faucher, Philippe, André Blais, and Robert Young. 1983. "L'aide financière directe au secteur manufacturier au Québec et en Ontario, 1960–1980." *Canadian Studies* 18 (Spring): 54–78.

Faucher, Philippe, André Blais, Robert Young, and Manuel De La Fuente. 1985. "Politique commerciale et politique industrielle du Canada." In *La nouvelle division internationale du travail et le Canada*, edited by Duncan Cameron and François Houle. Ottawa: Presses de l'Université d'Ottawa.

Fayerweather, John. 1982. "Elite Attitudes Toward Multinational Firms." In *Host National Attitudes Toward Multinational Corporations*, edited by John Fayerweather. New York: Praeger.

Finger, J.M. 1981. "The Industry-Country Incidence of Less than Fair Value Cases in U.S. Import Trade." *Quarterly Review of Economics and Business* 21 (Summer): 260–79.

Finger, J.M., H. Keith Hall, and Douglas R. Nelson. 1982. "The Political Economy of Administered Protection." *American Economic Review* 72 (3): 452–66.

Finlayson, Jock A. 1985. "Canadian International Economic Policy: Context, Issues and a Review of Some Recent Literature." In *Canada and the International Political Economic Environment*, volume 28 of the research studies prepared for the Royal Commission on the Economic Union and Development Prospects for Canada. Toronto: University of Toronto Press.

Finlayson, Jock A., and Mark W. Zacher. 1983. "The GATT and the Regulation of Trade Barriers: Regime Dynamics and Functions." In *International Regimes*, edited by Stephen Krasner. Ithaca, N.Y.: Cornell University Press.

Flanagan, Scott C., and Russell J. Dalton. 1984. "Parties Under Stress: Realignment and Dealignment in Advanced Industrialized Societies." *West European Politics* 7 (January): 7–23.

Flora, Peter, and Jens Alber. 1981. "Modernization, Democratization and the Development of Welfare States in Western Europe." In *The Development of Welfare States in Europe and America*, edited by Peter Flora and Arnold J. Heidenheimer. New Brunswick: Transaction Books.

Forster, Bruce A., and Ray Rees. 1983. "The Optimal Rate of Decline of an Inefficient Industry." *Journal of Public Economics* 25 (November): 227–43.

Fortin, Pierre. 1984. "Le chômage des jeunes au Québec : aggravation et concentration (1966–1980)." *Relations industrielles* 39: 419–48.

Frey, Bruno S. 1978. "Politico-Economic Models and Cycles." *Journal of Public Economics* 9: 203–20.

Frey, Bruno S., and Friedrich Schneider. 1981. "Recent Research in Empirical Politico-Economic Models." In *Contemporary Political Economy: Studies in the Interdependence of Politics and Economics*, edited by Douglas A. Hibbs and Heino Fassbender. Amsterdam: North-Holland.

Gagnon, Jean-Marie, and Benoît Papillon. 1984. *Risque financier, taux de rendement des entreprises canadiennes et intervention de l'État*. Ottawa: Economic Council of Canada.

Galbraith, William. 1984. "When Small Is Big." *Canadian Business Review* (Summer): 36–40.

Gallarotti, Giulo M. 1985. "Toward a Business-Cycle Model of Tariffs." *International Organization* 39 (Winter): 155–89.

George, Roy. 1983. *Targeting High Growth Industry*. Montreal: Institute for Research on Public Policy.

Gerschenkron, Alexander. 1962. *Economic Backwardness in Historical Perspective*. Cambridge, Mass.: Harvard University Press.

Gervais, M. et al. 1969. "Éléments de comparaison." In *Terre, paysan et politique : structures agraires, systèmes politiques et politiques agricoles*. Paris: SEDEIS.

Glassberg, Andrew. 1973. "The Linkage Between Urban Policy Outputs and Voting Behaviour: New York and London." *British Journal of Political Science* 3 (July): 341–61.

Glenday, Graham, and Glenn P. Jenkins. 1981. *Labour Adjustment: An Overview of Problems and Policies*. Ottawa: Task Force on Labour Market Development.

Glenday, Graham, Glenn P. Jenkins, and John C. Evans. 1982. *Worker Adjustment Policies: An Alternative to Protectionism*. Ottawa: North-South Institute.

Goldberg, Walter H. 1983. "Behavioural and Organizational Aspects of MNC-Host Government Relations." In *Governments and Multinationals: The Policy of Control Versus Autonomy*, edited by Walter H. Goldberg. Cambridge: Oelgeschlager, Gunn and Hain.

Gollner, Andrew. 1983. *Social Change and Corporate Strategy*. Stanford: Issue Action Publications.

Goode, William J. 1978. *The Celebration of Heroes: Prestige as a Social Control System*. Berkeley: University of California Press.

Gould, Frank. 1983. "The Development of Public Expenditures in Western Industrialized Countries: A Comparative Analysis." *Finances publiques* 38: 38–69.

Grady, Patrick, ed. 1980. *Peering Under the Inflationary Veil*. Ottawa: Economic Council of Canada.

Graham, Norman A. 1982. "Developed Countries and Multinational Corporation Threat, Perception and Policy Response in France and the United Kingdom." In *Host National Attitudes Toward Multinational Corporations*, edited by John Fayerweather. New York: Praeger.

Granatstein, J.L. 1985. "Free Trade Between Canada and the United States: The Issue that Will Not Go Away." In *The Politics of Canada's Economic Relationship with the United States*, volume 29 of the research studies prepared for the Royal Commission on the Economic Union and Development Prospects for Canada. Toronto: University of Toronto Press.

Grant, R.M. 1983. "Appraising Selective Financial Assistance to Industry: A Review of Institutions and Methodologies in the United Kingdom, Sweden and West Germany." *Journal of Public Policy* 3 (October): 369–97.

Grant, Wyn. 1980. "Business Interest and the British Conservative Party." *Government and Opposition* 15 (Spring): 143–61.

______. 1982a. "The Government Relations Functions in Large Firms Based in the United Kingdom." *British Journal of Political Science* 12 (October): 513–16.

______. 1982b. *The Political Economy of Industrial Policy*. London: Butterworth.

Green, Christopher. 1984. *Industrial Policy: The Fixities Hypothesis*. Toronto: Ontario Economic Council.

Green, Diana. 1983. "Strategic Management and the State: France." In *Industrial Crisis: A Comparative Study of the State and Industry*, edited by Kenneth Dyson and Stephen Wilks. Oxford: Martin Robertson.

Grey, Rodney de C. 1981. *Trade Policy in the 1980's: An Agenda for Canada/U.S. Relations*. Montreal: C.D. Howe Research Institute.

Haas, Ernest B. 1968. *The Uniting of Europe: Political, Social and Economic Forces, 1950–1957*. Stanford: Stanford University Press.

Hager, Wolfgang. 1982. "Industrial Policy, Trade Policy and European Social Democracy." In *National Industrial Strategies and the World Economy*, edited by John Pinder. London: Croom Helm.

Hall, Robert E., and Alvin Rabushka. 1983. *Low Tax, Simple Tax, Flat Tax*. New York: McGraw-Hill.

Hamilton, Carl. 1983. *Public Subsidies to Industry: The Case of Sweden and Its Shipbuilding Industry*. Washington, D.C.: World Bank.

Harris, Richard G. 1985. *Trade, Industrial Policy and International Competition*. Volume 13 of the research studies prepared for the Royal Commission on the Economic Union and Development Prospects for Canada. Toronto: University of Toronto Press.

Harris, Richard G., and David Cox. 1984. *Trade, Industrial Policy and Canadian Manufacturing*. Toronto: Ontario Economic Council.

Hatch, James, Larry Wynant, and Mary Jane Grant. 1982. "Bank Loans to Small Business." *Canadian Banker and ICB Review* 89 (February): 6–14.

______. 1983. "Federal Lending Programs for Small Business: No Longer Needed?" *Canadian Public Policy* 9 (September): 362–73.

Hawkins, Robert G. 1972. "Tariffs and Tariff Structure: An International Comparison." In *The United States and International Markets*, edited by Robert G. Hawkins and Ingo Walter. Lexington, Mass.: D.C. Heath.

Helleiner, G.K. 1977. "The Political Economy of Canada's Tariff Structure: An Alternative Model." *Canadian Journal of Economics* 10 (May): 318–26.

Henry, R., B. Koffman, and M. Charette. 1984. "The Evolution of the Canadian Industrial Structure." Ottawa: Department of Regional Industrial Expansion. Mimeographed.

Herander, Mark G., and J. Brad Schwartz. 1984. "An Empirical Test of the Impact of the Threat of U.S. Trade Policy: The Case of Antidumping Duties." *Southern Economic Journal* 51 (July): 59–79.

Hibbs, Douglas A. 1982. "On the Demand for Economic Outcomes: Macro-economics Performance and Mass Political Support in the U.S., Great Britain and Germany." *Journal of Politics* 44 (May): 426–62.

Hicks, Alexander, and Diane Swank. 1984. "On the Political Economy of Welfare Expansion: A Comparative Analysis of 18 Advanced Capitalist Democracies, 1960–1971." *Comparative Political Studies* 17 (April): 81–121.

Hiemenz, Ulrich, and Kurt V. Rabenau. 1976. "Effective Protection of German Industry." In *Public Assistance to Industry*, edited by W.M. Corden and G. Fels. Boulder, Col.: Westview Press.

Hindley, Brian. 1980. "Voluntary Export Restraints and the GATT's Main Escape Clause." *World Economy* 3 (November): 313–41.

Hirszowicz, Maria. 1981. *Industrial Sociology: An Introduction*. Oxford: Martin Robertson.

Hodge, Robert W., Paul M. Siegel, and Peter H. Rossi. 1966. "Occupational Prestige in the United States: 1925–1963." In *Class, Status and Power: Social Stratification in Comparative Perspective*, edited by Reinhard Bendix and Seymour Martin Lipset. New York: Free Press.

Hodges, Michael. 1974. *Multinational Corporation and National Government: A Case Study of the United Kingdom's Experience, 1964–1970*. Westmend: Saxon.

Holland, Daniel M. 1980. "The Situation in Other Countries." In *Peering Under the Inflationary Veil*, edited by Patrick Grady. Ottawa: Economic Council of Canada.

Hood, Neil, and Stephen Young. 1979. *The Economics of Multinational Enterprise*. London: Longman.

Hulten, Charles R., and James W. Robertson. 1984. "The Taxation of High Technology Industries." *National Tax Journal* 37 (September): 327–47.

Ilgen, Thomas L. 1983. "Better Living Through Chemistry: The Chemical Industry in the World Economy." *International Organization* 37 (August): 647–81.

Ippolito, Dennis S., Thomas G. Walker, and Kenneth L. Kolson. 1976. *Public Opinion and Responsible Democracy*. Englewood Cliffs, N.J.: Prentice Hall.

Jackson, John H. 1969. *World Trade and the Law of GATT*. New York: Bobbs-Merrill.

Jacobson, Gary C., and Samuel Kernell. 1981. *Strategy and Choice in Congressional Elections*. New Haven: Yale University Press.

Jenkin, Michael. 1983. *The Challenge of Diversity: Industrial Policy in the Canadian Federation*. Ottawa: Science Council of Canada.

Jenkins, Glenn P. 1980. *Costs and Consequences of the New Protectionism: The Case of Canada's Clothing Sector*. Ottawa: North-South Institute.

Jenson, Jane. 1975. "Party Loyalty in Canada: The Question of Party Identification." *Canadian Journal of Political Science* 8 (December): 543–53.

______. 1976. "Party Strategy and Party Identification: Some Patterns of Partisan Allegiance." *Canadian Journal of Political Science* 9 (March): 27–49.

Jéquier, Nicolas. 1974. "Computers." In *Big Business and the State: Changing Relations in Western Europe*, edited by Raymond Vernon. Cambridge, Mass.: Harvard University Press.

Johnston, Richard. 1985. *Public Opinion and Public Policy in Canada*. Volume 35 of the research studies prepared for the Royal Commission on the Economic Union and Development Prospects for Canada. Toronto: University of Toronto Press.

Jones, J.C.H., and L. Caudadio. 1984. "Organized Labour, Regional Political Bias, and the Canadian Tariff Structure." *Relations industrielles* 39: 695–709.

Jouanneau, Daniel. 1980. *Le GATT*. Paris: Presses universitaires de France.

Kamien, M.I., and N.L. Schwartz. 1982. *Market Structure and Innovation*. Cambridge: Cambridge University Press.

Katzenstein, Peter. 1978. "Conclusion." In *Between Power and Plenty*, edited by Peter Katzenstein. Madison: University of Wisconsin Press.

______. 1980. "Capitalism in One Country? Switzerland in the International Economy." *International Organization* 34: 507–37.

______. 1983. "The Small European States in the International Economy: Economic Dependence and Corporatist Politics." In *The Antinomies of Interdependence*, edited by John Ruggie. New York: Columbia University Press.

Kaufman Percell, Susan. 1981. "Business-Government Relations in Mexico: The Case of the Sugar Industry." *Comparative Politics* 13 (January): 211–35.

Kellough, Howard J., and Peter F. McQuillan. 1983. *Taxation of Private Corporations and Their Shareholders*. Toronto: Canadian Tax Foundation.

Keman, Hans. 1984. "Politics, Policies and Consequences: A Cross National Analysis of Public Policy-Formation in Advanced Capitalist Democracies (1967–1981)." *European Journal of Political Research* 12 (July): 147–70.

Kiesl, Peter Karl. 1981. "Canadian and American Approaches to Foreign Direct Investment and International Trade Policies." *Comparative Social Research* 4: 135–61.

Kiewitt, D. Roderick. 1983. *Macroeconomics and Micropolitics: The Electoral Effects of Economic Issues*. Chicago: University of Chicago Press.

King, Anthony. 1973. "Ideas, Institution and the Policies of Governments: A Comparative Analysis." *British Journal of Political Science* 3 (July): 291–313.

King, Meryns, and Don Fullerton, eds. 1984. *The Taxation of Income from Capital: A Comparative Study of the United States, the United Kingdom, Sweden and West Germany*. Chicago: University of Chicago Press.

Kingdon, John W. 1984. *Agendas, Alternatives and Public Policies*. Boston: Little, Brown.

Kirk Laux, Jeanne. 1978. "Global Interdependence and State Intervention." In *Canada's Foreign Policy: Analysis and Trends*, edited by Brian W. Tomlin. Toronto: Methuen.

Kock, K. 1969. *International Trade Policy and the GATT, 1947–1967*. Stockholm: Alqvist and Wiksell.

Krasner, Stephen D. 1976. "State Power and the Structure of International Trade." *World Politics* 28 (April): 317–47.

______. 1978. *Defending the National Interest: Raw Material Investments and U.S. Foreign Policy*. Princeton: Princeton University Press.

Krasner, Stephen D., ed. 1983. *International Regimes*. Ithaca, N.Y.: Cornell University Press.

Krauss, Melvyn B. 1978. *The New Protectionism: The Welfare State and International Trade*. New York: New York University Press.

Kravis, I., Alan Heston, and Robert Summers. 1980. "International Comparison of Real Product and Its Composition." *Review of Income and Wealth* 26: 19–67.

Kreile, Michael. 1983. "Public Enterprise and the Pursuit of Strategic Management:

Italy." In *Industrial Crisis: A Comparative Study of the State and Industry*, edited by Kenneth Dyson and Stephen Wilks. Oxford: Martin Robertson.

Kreinin, Mordechai E. 1980. "U.S. Foreign Economic Policy: An Overview." *Journal of Economic Issues* 14 (September): 703–34.

Krugman, Paul R. 1984. "The U.S. Response to Foreign Industrial Targeting." *Brookings Papers on Economic Activity* 1: 77–132.

Küster, George H. 1974. "Germany." In *Big Business and the State: Changing Relations in Western Europe*, edited by Raymond Vernon. Cambridge, Mass.: Harvard University Press.

Lal, Deepak. 1980. "Politicians, Economists and Protection — the Deaf Meet the Blind." *World Economy* 3 (September): 151–61.

Latouche, Daniel. 1985. *Canada and Quebec, Past and Future: An Essay*. Volume 70 of the research studies prepared for the Royal Commission on the Economic Union and Development Prospects for Canada. Toronto: University of Toronto Press.

Lavergne, Réal P. 1983. *The Political Economy of U.S. Tariffs: An Empirical Analysis*. Toronto: Academic Press.

Lawrence, Robert Z. 1983. "The Myth of U.S. Deindustrialization." *Challenge* 26 (November/December): 22–29.

Lawson, Fred. 1983. "Hegemony and the Structure of International Trade Reassessed: A View from Arabia." *International Organization* 37 (Spring): 317–39.

Lazar, Fred. 1981. *The New Protectionism: Non-Tariff Barriers and Their Effects on Canada*. Toronto: James Lorimer.

Leanos, Theodore P. 1984. "Concentration and Centralization of Capital in Agriculture." *Studies in Political Economy* 13 (Spring): 99–117.

Lemieux, Vincent. 1979. *Les cheminements de l'influence : systèmes, stratégies et structures du politique*. Quebec: Presses de l'Université Laval.

Le Pors, Anicet. 1977. *Les béquilles du capital : transferts état-industrie, critère de nationalisation*. Paris: Seuil.

Le Pors, Anicet, S. Denis, H. Gresh, and J.C. Paté. 1971–1972. "Transferts État-industrie." *Statistiques et études financières*, série orange.

Lewis, James R. 1984. "Regional Policy and Planning: Convergence and Contradiction." In *The State in Capitalist Europe*, edited by Stephen Bornstein et al. London: Allen and Unwin.

Lilla, Mark. 1984. "Why the 'Income Distribution' Is so Misleading." *Public Interest* 77 (Fall): 62–77.

Lipset, Seymour M., and William Schneider. 1983. *The Confidence Gap: Business, Labor, and Government in the Public Mind*. New York: Free Press.

Lipson, Charles. 1983. "The Transformation of Trade: The Sources and Effects of Regime Change." In *International Regimes*, edited by Stephen D. Krasner. Ithaca, N.Y.: Cornell University Press.

Litvak, I.A., and C.J. Maule. 1974. *Climate for Entrepreneurship: A Comparative Study*. Ottawa: Department of Industry, Trade and Commerce.

MacDonald, L. Ian. 1984. *Mulroney : De Baie Comeau à Sussex Drive*. Montreal: Éditions de l'Homme.

Mackuen, Michael B. 1983. "Political Drama, Economic Conditions, and the Dynamics of Presidential Popularity." *American Journal of Political Science* 27 (May): 165–93.

Mahon, Rianne, and Lynn Krieger Mytelka. 1983. "Industry, the State and the New Protectionism: Textiles in Canada and France." *International Organization* 37 (Fall): 551–81.

Malinvaud, E. 1982. "Wages and Unemployment." *Economic Journal* 92 (March): 1–13.

Mansfield, Edwin. 1985. "Technological Change and the International Diffusion of Technology: A Survey." In *Technological Change in Canadian Industry*, volume 3 of the research studies prepared for the Royal Commission on the Economic Union and Development Prospects for Canada. Toronto: University of Toronto Pres.

Markusen, James R. 1985. "Canadian Gains from Trade in the Presence of Scale Economies and Imperfect Competition." In *Canada–United States Free Trade*, volume 11 of the research studies prepared for the Royal Commission on the Economic Union and Development Prospects for Canada. Toronto: University of Toronto Press.

Marsh, David. 1985. "The Politics of Private Investment." In *Canadian Industrial Policy*, volume 44 of the research studies prepared for the Royal Commission on the Economic Union and Development Prospects for Canada. Toronto: University of Toronto Press.

Maskus, Keith E. 1984. "Rising Protectionism and U.S. International Trade Policy." *Economic Review* (July/August): 3–18.

Matthews, R.A. 1980. *Canadian Industry and the Challenge of Low-Cost Imports*. Ottawa: Economic Council of Canada.

McAllister, Ian. 1982. *Regional Development and the European Community: A Canadian Perspective*. Montreal: Institute for Research on Public Policy.

McCallum, John. 1983. "Inflation and Social Consensus in the Seventies." *Economic Journal* (December): 784–805.

McCallum, John, and André Blais. 1985. "Government, Special Interest Groups and Economic Growth." In *Responses to Economic Change*, volume 27 of the research studies prepared for the Royal Commission on the Economic Union and Development Prospects for Canada. Toronto: University of Toronto Press.

McFetridge, Donald G. 1977. *Government Support of Scientific Research and Development: An Economic Analysis*. Toronto: University of Toronto Press.

______. 1982a. *A Framework for the Analysis of the Effect of Small Business Subsidies*. Ottawa: Carleton University, Department of Economics.

______. 1982b. "Tax Measures and Small Business Financing." *Small Business Financing Review* (Ottawa).

______. 1984. "The Federal Business Development Bank." Ottawa. Mimeographed.

McFetridge, Donald G., and Jack P. Warda. 1983. *Canadian R&D Incentives: Their Adequacy and Impact*. Toronto: Canadian Tax Foundation.

McKay, David, and Win Grant. 1983. "Industrial Policies in OECD Countries: An Overview." *Journal of Public Policy* 3 (February): 1–12.

McKeown, Timothy J. 1983. "Hegemonic Stability and 19th Century Tariff Levels in Europe." *International Organization* 37 (Winter): 73–91.

______. 1984. "Firms and Tariff Regime Change: Explaining the Demand for Protection." *World Politics* 36: 215–33.

McKerrie, Robert B., and Werner Sengen Berger. 1983. *Job Losses in Major Industries: Manpower Strategy Responses*. Paris: OECD.

Melvin, James R., and Bruce W. Wilkinson. 1968. *Effective Protection in the Canadian Economy*. Ottawa: Economic Council of Canada.

Merciai, Patrizio. 1981. "Safeguard Measures in GATT." *Journal of World Trade Law* 15 (January/February): 41–65.

Messerlin, Patrick A. 1983. *Bureaucracies and the Political Economy of Protection: Reflections of a Continental European*. Washington, D.C.: World Bank.

Migué, Jean-Luc. 1979. *Les nationalismes au Canada : perspective économique*. Montreal: C.D. Howe Research Institute.

Mikdashi, Zuhayr. 1974. "Aluminum." In *Big Business and the State: Changing Relations in Western Europe*, edited by Raymond Vernon. Cambridge, Mass.: Harvard University Press.

Miles, Caroline. 1976. "Protection of British Textile Industry." In *Public Assistance to Industry*, edited by W.M. Corden et G. Fels. Boulder, Col.: Westview Press.

Montmarquette, Claude. 1981. "Politique budgétaire de stabilisation et taille relative des gouvernements." *Public Finance* 26(2): 244–66.

Morici, Peter, and Laura L. Megna. 1983. *U.S. Economic Policies Affecting Industrial Trade: A Quantitative Assessment*. Washington, D.C.: National Planning Association.

Mosley, P. 1976. "Towards a 'Satisfying' Theory of Economic Policy." *Economic Journal* 86 (March): 59–72.

———. 1984. "Popularity Functions and the Role of the Media: A Pilot Study of the Popular Press." *British Journal of Political Science* (January): 117–33.

Murray, J. Alex, and Lawrence LeDuc. 1982. "Changing Attitudes Towards Foreign Investment in Canada." In *Host National Attitudes Toward Multinational Corporations*, edited by John Fayerweather. New York: Praeger.

Musgrave, Richard A., and Peggy B. Musgrave. 1980. *Public Finance in Theory and Practice*. New York: McGraw-Hill.

Mutti, J. 1982. *Taxes, Subsidies and Competitiveness Internationally*. Washington, D.C.: National Planning Association.

Norris, Keith, and John Vaizey. 1973. *The Economics of Research and Technology*. London: Allen and Unwin.

Ohlin, Gorau. 1978. "Subsidies and Other Industrial Aids." In *International Trade and Industrial Policies*, edited by Steven S. Warnecke. New York: Holmes and Meier.

Olson, Mancur. 1965. *The Logic of Collective Action*. Cambridge, Mass.: Harvard University Press.

———. 1982. *The Rise and Decline of Nations: Economic Growth, Stagflation, and Social Rigidities*. New Haven: Yale University Press.

Organisation for Economic Co-operation and Development. 1975. *Objectifs et instruments des politiques industrielles : une étude comparative*. Paris: OECD.

———. 1976. *Government Purchasing: Rules and Procedures in OECD Member Countries*. Paris: OECD.

———. 1978. *Policies for the Stimulation of Industrial Innovation: Analytical Report*. Paris: OECD.

———. 1982. *Innovation Policy: Trends and Perspectives*. Paris: OECD.

———. 1983a. *Textile and Clothing Industry*. Paris: OECD.

———. 1983b. *Positive Adjustment Policies: Managing Structural Change*. Paris: OECD.

———. 1983c. *Investment Incentives and Disincentives and the International Investment Process*. Paris, OECD.

———. 1983d. *Historical Statistics, 1960–1981*. Paris: OECD.

———. 1983e. *Transparency for Positive Adjustment: Identifying and Evaluating Government Intervention*. Paris: OECD.

———. 1984a. *Tax Expenditures: Review of the Issues and Country Practices*. Paris: OECD.

———. 1984b. *Mergers, Policies and Recent Trends in Mergers*. Paris: OECD.

———. 1984c. *Revenue Statistics of OECD Member Countries, 1965–1983*. Paris: OECD.

———. 1984d. *Historical Statistics, 1960–1982*. Paris: OECD.

———. *National Accounts of OECD Countries*. Paris: OECD, annual publication.

Oulton, Nicholas. 1976. "Effective Protection of British Industry." In *Public Assistance to Industry*, edited by W.M. Corden and G. Fels. Boulder, Col.: Westview Press.

Paloheimo, Heikki. 1984. "Distribution Struggle and Economic Development in the 1970s in Developed Capitalist Countries." *European Journal of Political Research* 12 (July): 171–91.

Pearson, Charles, and Gerry Salembier. 1983. *Trade, Employment, and Adjustment*. Montreal: Institute for Research on Public Policy.

Peat, Marwick and Associates. 1981. *Federal Policies to Stimulate Private Sector Employment*. Ottawa: Task Force on Labour Market Development.

Pentland, Charles. 1985. "North American Integration and the Canadian Political System." In *The Politics of Canada's Economic Relationship with the United States*, volume 29 of the research studies prepared for the Royal Commission on the Economic Union and Development Prospects for Canada. Toronto: University of Toronto Press.

Perry, David B. 1976. "Corporate Tax Expenditures." *Canadian Tax Journal* 24 (September/October): 528–34.

Pestieau, Caroline. 1972. "NTBs and the Need for Manufactured-Goods Exports from Developing Countries." In *Non-Tariff Trade Barriers as a Problem in International*

Development, edited by Caroline Pestieau and Jacques Henry. Montreal: Economic Policy Committee/Private Planning Association of Canada.

Peterson, Rein. 1977. *Small Business: Building a Balanced Economy*. Erin, Ontario: Porcépic.

Pinchin, H.M. 1979. *The Regional Impact of the Canadian Tariff*. Study prepared for the Economic Council of Canada. Ottawa: Minister of Supply and Services Canada.

Pinder, John. 1982. "Industrial Policy and the International Economy." In *National Industrial Strategies and the World Economy*, edited by John Pinder. London: Croom Helm.

Ponssard, Jean-Pierre, and Gérard de Pouvourville. 1982. *Marchés publics et politique industrielle*. Paris: Economica.

Postner, Harry H. 1976. *Factor Content of Canadian International Trade: An Input-Output Analysis*. Ottawa: Economic Council of Canada.

Poulantzas, Nicos. 1974. *Les classes sociales dans le capitalisme aujourd'hui*. Paris: Seuil.

Protheroe, David R. 1980. *Imports and Politics: Trade Decision-Making in Canada, 1968–1979*. Montreal: Institute for Research on Public Policy.

Przeworski, Adam, and Henry Teune. 1970. *The Logic of Comparative Social Inquiry*. New York: Wiley.

Ray, Edward John. 1981a. "The Determinants of Tariff and Non-tariff Trade Restrictions in the United States." *Journal of Political Economy* 89: 105–21.

______. 1981b. "Tariff and Non-tariff Barriers to Trade in the United States and Abroad." *Review of Economics and Statistics* 63 (May): 161–68.

Raynauld, André, and François Vaillancourt. 1984. *L'appartenance des entreprises, le cas du Québec en 1978*. Quebec: Conseil de la langue française du Québec.

Ritchie, Gordon. 1983. "Government Aid to Industry: A Public Sector Perspective." *Canadian Public Administration* 26 (Spring): 36–47.

Robertson, David. 1977. *Fail Safe for Trade Liberalization*. London: Trade Policy Research Centre.

Rothwell, Roy, and Walter Zegveld. 1981. *Industrial Innovation and Public Policy*. Westport: Greenwood Press.

______. 1984. "Designing and Implementing Innovation Policy." *Policy Studies Review* 3 (May): 436–45.

Rousseau, H.P., and F. Taurand. 1984. "Financement de la sécurité du revenu et taxes sur la masse salariale." *Canadian Public Policy* 10 (December): 459–68.

Ruggie, John Gerard. 1983. "International Regimes, Transactions, and Change Embedded Liberalism in the Postwar Economic Order." In *International Regimes*, edited by Stephen D. Krasner. Ithaca, N.Y.: Cornell University Press.

Rugman, A.M. 1981. "Research and Development by Multinational and Domestic Firms in Canada." *Canadian Public Policy* 7: 604–16.

Salamon, Lester M., and John J. Siegfried. 1977. "Economic Power and Political Influence: The Impact of Industry Structure on Public Policy." *American Political Science Review* 71: 1026–44.

Sales, Arnaud. 1983. "Intervention de l'État et positions idéologiques des dirigeants des bureaucraties publiques et privées." *Sociologie et sociétés* 15 (April): 13–42.

Saunders, Ronald S. 1980. "The Political Economy of Effective Tariff Protection in Canada's Manufacturing Sector." *Canadian Journal of Economics* 13 (May): 340–48.

______. 1984. *Aid to Workers in Declining Industries*. Toronto: Ontario Economic Council.

Schmidt, Manfred G. 1982. "The Role of Parties in Shaping Macroeconomic Policy." In *The Impact of Parties: Politics and Policies in Democratic Capitalist States*, edited by Francis G. Castles. Beverly Hills: Sage.

______. 1983. "The Welfare State and the Economy in Periods of Economic Crisis: A Comparative Study of Twenty-Three Nations." *European Journal of Political Research* 11 (March): 1–27.

______. 1984. "The Politics of Unemployment: Rates of Unemployment and Labour Market Policy." *West European Politics* 7 (July): 5–25.

Schonfield, Andrew. 1965. *Modern Capitalism*. London: Oxford University Press.

Schwartz, Mildred A. 1967. *Public Opinion and Canadian Identity*. Berkeley: University of California Press.

Science Council of Canada. 1984. *Industrial Development in Canada*. Ottawa: The Council.

Scitovsky, Tibor. 1976. *The Joyless Economy: An Inquiry into Human Satisfaction and Consumer Dissatisfaction*. New York: Oxford University Press.

Shapiro, Daniel M. 1983. "Entry, Exit and the Theory of the Multinational Firm." In *The Multinational Corporation in the 1980s*, edited by Charles P. Kindleberger and David B. Audretsch. Cambridge, Mass.: MIT Press.

Shepherd, Geoffrey. 1983. "Textiles: New Ways of Surviving in an Old Industry." In *Europe's Industries: Public and Private Strategies for Change*, edited by Geoffrey Shepherd, François Duchêne and Christopher Saunders. Ithaca, N.Y.: Cornell University Press.

Siegfried, John J. 1974. "Effective Average U.S. Corporation Income Tax Rates." *National Tax Journal* 24 (June): 245–59.

Sigler, John H., and Dennis Goresky. 1974. "Public Opinion in United States–Canadian Relations." *International Organization* 28 (Fall): 637–71.

Simeon, Richard. 1976. "Studying Public Policy." *Canadian Journal of Political Science* 9 (December): 548–81.

Smith, Roger S. 1979. *Tax Expenditures: An Examination of Tax Incentives and Tax Preferences in the Canadian Federal Income Tax System*. Toronto: Canadian Tax Foundation.

Stegemann, Klaus. 1973. *Canadian Non-Tariff Barriers to Trade*. Montreal: Economic Policy Committee/Private Planning Association of Canada.

———. 1982. "Special Import Measures Legislation: Deterring Dumping of Capital Goods." *Canadian Public Policy* 8 (Fall): 573–86.

Stern, Arthur A. 1984. "The Hegemon's Dilemma: Great Britain, the United States, and the International Economic Order." *International Organization* 38 (Spring): 355–87.

Stoffaës, Christian. 1978. *La grande menace industrielle*. Paris: Calmann-Lévy.

Stokes, Donald E. 1967. "Parties and the Nationalization of Electoral Forces." In *The American Party System: Stages of Political Development*, edited by Walter Dean Burour and William Nisbet Chambers. New York: Oxford University Press.

Summers, R., and A. Heston. 1984. "Improved International Comparisons of Real Product and Its Composition, 1950–80." *Review of Income and Wealth* 30 (June): 207–62.

Surrey, Stanley S. 1973. *Pathways to Tax Reform: The Concept of Tax Expenditures*. Cambridge, Mass.: Harvard University Press.

Takacs, Wendy E. 1981. "Pressures for Protectionism: An Empirical Analysis." *Economic Inquiry* 19 (October): 687–93.

Tarasofsky, A., T.G. Roseman, and H.E. Waslander. 1981. *Ex Post Aggregate Real Rates of Return in Canada: 1947–76*. Ottawa: Economic Council of Canada.

Thirsk, Wayne R. 1983. "Fiscal Harmonization in the United States, Australia, West Germany, Switzerland, and the EEC." In *Federalism and the Canadian Economic Union*, edited by M.J. Trebilcock, J.R.S. Prichard, T.J. Courchene and J. Whalley. Toronto: University of Toronto Press.

Thorne Riddell, Thorne, Stevenson and Kellogg. 1981. *Small Business Venture of Capital Supply and Demand Analysis*. Ottawa: Department of Industry, Trade and Commerce.

Trebilcock, Michael. 1985. *The Political Economy of Economic Adjustment*. Volume 8 of the research studies prepared for the Royal Commission on the Economic Union and Development Prospects for Canada. Toronto: University of Toronto Press.

Trebilcock, Michael J., Douglas G. Hartle, J.R.S. Prichard, and Donald N. Dewees. 1982. *The Choice of Governing Instruments*. Study prepared for the Economic Council of Canada. Ottawa: Minister of Supply and Services Canada.

Treiman, Donald J. 1977. *Occupational Prestige in Comparative Perspective*. New York: Academic Press.

Tupper, Allan. 1982. *Public Money in the Private Sector*. Kingston: Queen's University, Institute for Intergovernmental Relations.

Tyson, Laura, and John Zysman. 1983. "American Industry in International Competition." In *American Industry in International Competition*, edited by John Zysman and Laura Tyson. Ithaca, N.Y.: Cornell University Press.

United Nations. Annual. *Annual Statistics of International Trade*, Vol. 1, *Trade by Country*. New York: United Nations.

United States. Joint Committee on Taxation. 1983. *Taxation of Banks and Thrift Institutions*. Washington, D.C.: Government Printing Office.

Urich, René. 1983. *Pour une nouvelle politique de développement régional en Europe*. Paris: Economica.

Urspring, Heinrich W. 1984. "Macroeconomic Performance and Government Popularity in New Zealand." *Comparative Political Studies* 16 (January): 457–77.

Usher, Dan. 1983. *The Benefits and Cost of Firm Specific Investment Grants: A Study of Five Federal Programs*. Kingston: Queen's University, Institute for Economic Research.

Vernon, Raymond. 1974 "Enterprise and Government in Europe." In *Big Business and the State: Changing Relations in Western Europe*, edited by Raymond Vernon. Cambridge, Mass.: Harvard University Press.

______. 1985. "Le contrôle des entreprises multinationales : le cas des États-Unis." *Études internationales* 16 (June): 303–23.

Vogel, David. 1983. "The Power of Business in America: A Reappraisal." *British Journal of Political Science* 13 (January): 19–47.

Walter, Ingo. 1972a. "Barriers to International Competition: The Application and Liberalization of Non-Tariff Distortions." In *The United States and International Markets*, edited by Robert G. Hawkins, and Ingo Walter. Lexington, Mass.: D.C. Heath.

______. 1972b. "Barriers to International Competition: The Nature of Non-tariff Distortions." In *The United States and International Markets*, edited by Robert G. Hawkins and Ingo Walter. Lexington, Mass.: D.C. Heath.

Walters, Robert S. 1982. "The U.S. Steel Industry: National Policies and International Trade." In *The Emerging International Economic Order: Dynamic Processes, Constraints, and Opportunities*, edited by Harold K. Jacobson and Dusan Sidjanski. Beverly Hills: Sage.

Warnecke, Steven J. 1975. "Introduction." In *Industrial Policies in Western Europe*, edited by Steven J. Warnecke and Ezra Suleiman. New York: Praeger.

Watson, William G.S. 1983. *Primer on the Economics of Industrial Policy*. Toronto: Ontario Economic Council.

Wescott, Robert F. 1983. "U.S. Approaches to Industrial Policy." In *Industrial Policies for Growth and Competitiveness: An Economic Perspective*, edited by F. Gerard Adams and Lawrence R. Klein. Lexington, Mass.: D.C. Heath.

Whalley, John. 1983. "Induced Distortions of Interprovincial Activity: An Overview of Issues." In *Federalism and the Canadian Economic Union*, edited by M.J. Trebilcock, J.R.S., Prichard, T.J. Courchene and J. Whalley. Toronto: University of Toronto Press.

Wilkinson, Bruce W., and Ken Norrie. 1975. *Effective Protection and the Return to Capital*. Ottawa: Economic Council of Canada.

Wilks, Stephen. 1983. "Liberal State and Party Competition: Britain." In *Industrial Crisis: A Comparative Study of the State and Industry*, edited by Kenneth Dyson and Stephen Wilks. Oxford: Martin Robertson.

Wilks, Stephen, and Kenneth Dyson. 1983. "The Character and Economic Context of Industrial Crisis." In *Industrial Crisis: A Comparative Study of the State and Industry*, edited by Kenneth Dyson and Stephen Wilks. Oxford: Martin Robertson.

Wilson, Bryan R. 1970. *Rationality*. New York: Harper.

Wilson, Jeremy R. 1980. "The Impact of Communications Developments on British Columbia Electoral Patterns 1903–1975." *Canadian Journal of Political Science* 13 (September): 509–35.

Winham, Gilbert R. 1978. "Bureaucratic Politics and Canadian Trade Negotiation." *International Journal* 34 (Winter): 64–90.

Winn, Conrad. 1985. "Ministerial Roles in Policy Making: Vote Seeker, Shaman and Other Incarnations." In *Canadian Industrial Policy*, volume 44 of the research studies prepared for the Royal Commission on the Economic Union and Development Prospects for Canada. Toronto: University of Toronto Press.

Wonnacott, Paul, and Ronald J. Wonnacott. 1982. "Free Trade Between the United States and Canada: Fifteen Years Later." *Canadian Public Policy* 8 (October): 412–28.

Woodside, Ken. 1979. "Tax Incentives Versus Subsidies: Political Considerations in Government Choice." *Canadian Public Policy* 5 (Spring): 248–56.

______. 1983. "The Political Economy of Policy Instruments: Tax Expenditures and Subsidies in Canada." In *The Politics of Canadian Public Policy*, edited by Michael M. Atkinson and Marsha A. Chandler. Toronto: University of Toronto Press.

Woodward, R.S. 1974. "The Capital Bias of DREE Incentives." *Canadian Journal of Economics* 7 (May): 161–74.

______. 1979. "The Effectiveness of DREE's New Location Subsidies." *Canadian Public Policy* 5 (Spring): 248–52.

Yoffie, David B. 1983a. "Adjustment in the Footwear Industry: The Consequences of Orderly Marketing Agreements." In *American Industry in International Competition: Government Policies and Corporate Strategies*, edited by John Zysman. Ithaca, N.Y.: Cornell University Press.

______. 1983b. *Power and Protectionism: Strategies of the Newly Industrializing Countries*. New York: Columbia University Press.

Young, Stephen, and A.V. Lowe. 1975. *Intervention in the Mixed Economy: The Evolution of British Industrial Policy, 1964–1972*. London: Croom Helm.

Yuill, Douglas, Kevin Allen, and Chris Hull. 1980. *Regional Policy in the European Community: The Role of Regional Incentives*. London: Croom Helm.

Zysman, John. 1977. *Political Strategies for Industrial Order: State, Market and Industry in France*. Berkeley: University of California Press.

______. 1983. *Governments, Markets and Growth: Financial Systems and the Politics of Industrial Change*. Ithaca, N.Y.: Cornell University Press.

The Collected Research Studies

Royal Commission on the Economic Union and Development Prospects for Canada

Economics

Income Distribution and Economic Security in Canada (Vol.1), *François Vaillancourt, Research Coordinator*

Vol. 1 Income Distribution and Economic Security in Canada, *F. Vaillancourt* (C)*

Industrial Structure (Vols. 2-8), *Donald G. McFetridge, Research Coordinator*

Vol. 2 Canadian Industry in Transition, *D.G. McFetridge* (C)
Vol. 3 Technological Change in Canadian Industry, *D.G. McFetridge* (C)
Vol. 4 Canadian Industrial Policy in Action, *D.G. McFetridge* (C)
Vol. 5 Economics of Industrial Policy and Strategy, *D.G. McFetridge* (C)
Vol. 6 The Role of Scale in Canada–US Productivity Differences, *J.R. Baldwin and P.K. Gorecki* (M)
Vol. 7 Competition Policy and Vertical Exchange, *F. Mathewson and R. Winter* (M)
Vol. 8 The Political Economy of Economic Adjustment, *M. Trebilcock* (M)

International Trade (Vols. 9-14), *John Whalley, Research Coordinator*

Vol. 9 Canadian Trade Policies and the World Economy, *J. Whalley with C. Hamilton and R. Hill* (M)
Vol. 10 Canada and the Multilateral Trading System, *J. Whalley* (M)
Vol. 11 Canada–United States Free Trade, *J. Whalley* (C)
Vol. 12 Domestic Policies and the International Economic Environment, *J. Whalley* (C)
Vol. 13 Trade, Industrial Policy and International Competition, *R. Harris* (M)
Vol. 14 Canada's Resource Industries and Water Export Policy, *J. Whalley* (C)

Labour Markets and Labour Relations (Vols. 15-18), *Craig Riddell, Research Coordinator*

Vol. 15 Labour-Management Cooperation in Canada, *C. Riddell* (C)
Vol. 16 Canadian Labour Relations, *C. Riddell* (C)
Vol. 17 Work and Pay: The Canadian Labour Market, *C. Riddell* (C)
Vol. 18 Adapting to Change: Labour Market Adjustment in Canada, *C. Riddell* (C)

Macroeconomics (Vols. 19-25), *John Sargent, Research Coordinator*

Vol. 19 Macroeconomic Performance and Policy Issues: Overviews, *J. Sargent* (M)
Vol. 20 Post-War Macroeconomic Developments, *J. Sargent* (C)
Vol. 21 Fiscal and Monetary Policy, *J. Sargent* (C)
Vol. 22 Economic Growth: Prospects and Determinants, *J. Sargent* (C)
Vol. 23 Long-Term Economic Prospects for Canada: A Symposium, *J. Sargent* (C)
Vol. 24 Foreign Macroeconomic Experience: A Symposium, *J. Sargent* (C)
Vol. 25 Dealing with Inflation and Unemployment in Canada, *C. Riddell* (M)

Economic Ideas and Social Issues (Vols. 26 and 27), *David Laidler, Research Coordinator*

Vol. 26 Approaches to Economic Well-Being, *D. Laidler* (C)
Vol. 27 Responses to Economic Change, *D. Laidler* (C)

* (C) denotes a Collection of studies by various authors coordinated by the person named. (M) denotes a Monograph.

POLITICS AND INSTITUTIONS OF GOVERNMENT

Canada and the International Political Economy (Vols. 28-30), *Denis Stairs and Gilbert R. Winham, Research Coordinators*

Vol. 28 Canada and the International Political/Economic Environment, *D. Stairs and G.R. Winham* (C)
Vol. 29 The Politics of Canada's Economic Relationship with the United States, *D. Stairs and G.R. Winham* (C)
Vol. 30 Selected Problems in Formulating Foreign Economic Policy, *D. Stairs and G.R. Winham* (C)

State and Society in the Modern Era (Vols. 31 and 32), *Keith Banting, Research Coordinator*

Vol. 31 State and Society: Canada in Comparative Perspective, *K. Banting* (C)
Vol. 32 The State and Economic Interests, *K. Banting* (C)

Constitutionalism, Citizenship and Society (Vols. 33-35), *Alan Cairns and Cynthia Williams, Research Coordinators*

Vol. 33 Constitutionalism, Citizenship and Society in Canada, *A. Cairns and C. Williams* (C)
Vol. 34 The Politics of Gender, Ethnicity and Language in Canada, *A. Cairns and C. Williams* (C)
Vol. 35 Public Opinion and Public Policy in Canada, *R. Johnston* (M)

Representative Institutions (Vols. 36-39), *Peter Aucoin, Research Coordinator*

Vol. 36 Party Government and Regional Representation in Canada, *P. Aucoin* (C)
Vol. 37 Regional Responsiveness and the National Administrative State, *P. Aucoin* (C)
Vol. 38 Institutional Reforms for Representative Government, *P. Aucoin* (C)
Vol. 39 Intrastate Federalism in Canada, *D.V. Smiley and R.L. Watts* (M)

The Politics of Economic Policy (Vols. 40-43), *G. Bruce Doern, Research Coordinator*

Vol. 40 The Politics of Economic Policy, *G.B. Doern* (C)
Vol. 41 Federal and Provincial Budgeting, *A.M. Maslove, M.J. Prince and G.B. Doern* (M)
Vol. 42 Economic Regulation and the Federal System, *R. Schultz and A. Alexandroff* (M)
Vol. 43 Bureaucracy in Canada: Control and Reform, *S.L. Sutherland and G.B. Doern* (M)

Industrial Policy (Vols. 44 and 45), *André Blais, Research Coordinator*

Vol. 44 Industrial Policy, *A. Blais* (C)
Vol. 45 The Political Sociology of Industrial Policy, *A. Blais* (M)

LAW AND CONSTITUTIONAL ISSUES

Law, Society and the Economy (Vols. 46-51), *Ivan Bernier and Andrée Lajoie, Research Coordinators*

Vol. 46 Law, Society and the Economy, *I. Bernier and A. Lajoie* (C)
Vol. 47 The Supreme Court of Canada as an Instrument of Political Change, *I. Bernier and A. Lajoie* (C)
Vol. 48 Regulations, Crown Corporations and Administrative Tribunals, *I. Bernier and A. Lajoie* (C)
Vol. 49 Family Law and Social Welfare Legislation in Canada, *I. Bernier and A. Lajoie* (C)
Vol. 50 Consumer Protection, Environmental Law and Corporate Power, *I. Bernier and A. Lajoie* (C)
Vol. 51 Labour Law and Urban Law in Canada, *I. Bernier and A. Lajoie* (C)

The International Legal Environment (Vols. 52-54), *John Quinn, Research Coordinator*

Vol. 52 The International Legal Environment, *J. Quinn* (C)
Vol. 53 Canadian Economic Development and the International Trading System, *M.M. Hart* (M)
Vol. 54 Canada and the New International Law of the Sea, *D.M. Johnston* (M)

Harmonization of Laws in Canada (Vols. 55 and 56), *Ronald C.C. Cuming, Research Coordinator*

Vol. 55 Perspectives on the Harmonization of Law in Canada, *R. Cuming* (C)
Vol. 56 Harmonization of Business Law in Canada, *R. Cuming* (C)

Institutional and Constitutional Arrangements (Vols. 57 and 58), *Clare F. Beckton and A. Wayne MacKay, Research Coordinators*

Vol. 57 Recurring Issues in Canadian Federalism, *C.F. Beckton and A.W. MacKay* (C)
Vol. 58 The Courts and The Charter, *C.F. Beckton and A.W. MacKay* (C)

FEDERALISM AND THE ECONOMIC UNION

Federalism and The Economic Union (Vols. 58-72), *Mark Krasnick, Kenneth Norrie and Richard Simeon, Research Coordinators*

Vol. 59 Federalism and Economic Union in Canada, *K. Norrie, R. Simeon and M. Krasnick* (M)
Vol. 60 Perspectives on the Canadian Economic Union, *M. Krasnick* (C)
Vol. 61 Division of Powers and Public Policy, *R. Simeon* (C)
Vol. 62 Case Studies in the Division of Powers, *M. Krasnick* (C)
Vol. 63 Intergovernmental Relations, *R. Simeon* (C)
Vol. 64 Disparities and Interregional Adjustment, *K. Norrie* (C)
Vol. 65 Fiscal Federalism, *M. Krasnick* (C)
Vol. 66 Mobility of Capital in the Canadian Economic Union, *N. Roy* (M)
Vol. 67 Economic Management and the Division of Powers, *T.J. Courchene* (M)
Vol. 68 Regional Aspects of Confederation, *J. Whalley* (M)
Vol. 69 Interest Groups in the Canadian Federal System, *H.G. Thorburn* (M)
Vol. 70 Canada and Quebec, Past and Future: An Essay, *D. Latouche* (M)
Vol. 71 The Political Economy of Canadian Federalism: 1940–1984, *R. Simeon and I. Robinson* (M)

THE NORTH

Vol. 72 The North, *Michael S. Whittington, Coordinator* (C)

Commission Organization

Chairman

Donald S. Macdonald

Commissioners

Clarence L. Barber
Albert Breton
M. Angela Cantwell Peters
E. Gérard Docquier
William M. Hamilton
John R. Messer
Laurent Picard
Michel Robert
Daryl K. Seaman
Thomas K. Shoyama
Jean Casselman-Wadds
Catherine T. Wallace

Senior Officers

Executive Director
J. Gerald Godsoe

Director of Policy
Alan Nymark

Secretary
Michel Rochon

Director of Administration
Sheila-Marie Cook

Senior Advisors
David Ablett
Victor Clarke
Carl Goldenberg
Harry Stewart

Director of Publishing
Ed Matheson

Directors of Research
Ivan Bernier
Alan Cairns
David C. Smith

Co-Directors of Research
Kenneth Norrie
John Sargent

Research Program Organization

Economics

Research Director
David C. Smith

Executive Assistant & Assistant Director (Research Services)
I. Lilla Connidis

Coordinators
David Laidler
Donald G. McFetridge
Kenneth Norrie*
Craig Riddell
John Sargent*
François Vaillancourt
John Whalley

Research Analysts
Caroline Digby
Mireille Ethier
Judith Gold
Douglas S. Green
Colleen Hamilton
Roderick Hill
Joyce Martin

Politics and the Institutions of Government

Research Director
Alan Cairns

Executive Assistant
Karen Jackson

Coordinators
Peter Aucoin
Keith Banting
André Blais
Bruce Doern
Richard Simeon
Denis Stairs
Cynthia Williams
Gilbert R. Winham

Research Analysts
Claude Desranleau
Ian Robinson

Office Administration
Donna Stebbing

Law and Constitutional Issues

Research Director
Ivan Bernier

Executive Assistant & Research Program Administrator
Jacques J.M. Shore

Coordinators
Clare F. Beckton
Ronald C.C. Cuming
Mark Krasnick
Andrée Lajoie
A. Wayne MacKay
John J. Quinn

Administrative and Research Assistant
Nicolas Roy

Research Analyst
Nola Silzer

*Kenneth Norrie and John Sargent co-directed the final phase of Economics Research with David Smith